A SPORTSMAN'S
LIBRARY

100 ESSENTIAL, ENGAGING, OFFBEAT, AND OCCASIONALLY ODD FISHING AND HUNTING BOOKS FOR THE ADVENTUROUS READER

STEPHEN J. BODIO

LYONS PRESS
Guilford, Connecticut

An imprint of Globe Pequot Press

TO THE UNACKNOWLEDGED CREATORS:
THE EDITORS PAT RYAN, ED GRAY, NICK LYONS,
AND THE LATE LES LINE.

Copyright © 2013 by Stephen J. Bodio

Lyons Press is an imprint of Globe Pequot Press.

Project editor: Meredith Dias
Text design: Maggie Peterson
Layout: Casey Shain

ISBN 978-0-7627-8025-9

Library of Congress Cataloging-in-Publication Data
    Bodio, Stephen.
    A sportsman's library : 100 essential, engaging, off-beat, and
occasionally odd fishing and hunting books for the adventurous reader /
Stephen J. Bodio.
      p. cm.
    Includes bibliographical references and index.
    ISBN 978-0-7627-8025-9 (alk. paper)
    1. Hunting—Bibliography. 2. Fishing—Bibliography. I. Title.
Z7514.H9 B63
[SK33]
016.799—dc23
                                                    2012044955

Printed in the United States of America

10 9 8 7 6 5 4 3 2 1

CONTENTS

PART 2: WINGSHOOTING

PART 3: GENERAL HUNTING, GUNS, TRAVEL, MIXED, AND MISCELLANEOUS

ACKNOWLEDGMENTS

Booksellers:
Jim Adams, K. C., Jerry Lane, Nicholas Potter.

Editors:
The dedicatees, plus Jim Babb, Silvio Calabi, Daniel Cote, Allen Jones, Ralph Stewart.

Writers, living and dead, here and absent; friends and even foes.

Special:
Libby, once more.

Extra efforts:
Laurie Gregg at The Village Press in Magdalena,
Yvonne Magener at the Magdalena Public Library, and
Gerry Cox, the perfect first reader and sharp-eyed critic.

There can be only one law about hunting. Unless a part of the beauty one destroys passes into the spirit of the destroyer in adding to his skill, style and delicacy, it is a mere waste of life. There is a very strong bond in nature between the slayer and his victim.

—Roy Campbell

Digressions, incontestably, are the sunshine—they are the life, the soul of reading; take them out of this book for instance—you might as well take the book along with them.

—Lawrence Sterne

APOLOGIA

I was delighted when my friend and editor Allen Jones suggested that I write a book about the best one hundred sporting books. But I soon realized that I had taken on an impossible task, by definition. If I chose one hundred books by that standard, it felt like an insufficient number; two hundred books would not be a definitive set of the "best." But worse, a volume restricted to only the *best* sporting literature would risk being boring. Most of the choices would be so familiar that they will have appeared a hundred times before and already be in many readers' libraries. An entertaining and informative selection of one hundred significant or essential hunting and fishing books must include ones chosen for other reasons, especially to—I am trying to avoid the word "merely"—amuse. How could I not include George Leonard Herter's *Bull Cook and Authentic Historical Recipes and Practices?* You would not only lose "Doves Wyatt Earp," but you would also miss reading about Beethoven's Spam and the Virgin Mary's spinach. So forget "best." Substitute "essential" and, at least as important, "entertaining." The number is arbitrary, but a good one—big enough for diversity, small enough to manage, clear enough not to tempt the writer to squeeze in nine more favorites. I here present you with exactly one hundred genuinely fascinating books, with some necessary wiggle room provided by "Also Reads" at the end of each chapter.

Given an arbitrary number, choosing becomes a form of pleasant discipline, demanding only decent memory, some balance in subject, a fan's eagerness to share, and, inevitably, just a bit of arrogance; what else, really, is strong opinion? I won't deny subconscious coin-flipping. I started in a breathless afternoon's rush and wrote down from memory about 130 titles on a yellow legal pad. This became my basis. But it took another several months, including an all-nighter to make my last big cut, before I was as satisfied with my list as deadlines would allow; I spent more time arranging and choosing than I did writing the book. Sometimes I had to take a particular book where any one of three might have done, or, with less angst, pass over something considered "important" because I liked something else better. If there were two good books on a single subject, I often dropped one so that I could have space for something different. And I broke every self-made "rule" at least once.

So what are my credentials; who am I to choose? First, my work includes a sideline in reviewing books that dates back to the 1970s and sometimes threatens to overwhelm my "real" writing, starting with the "Bodio's Review" column in *Gray's* in those years. But what really shapes this book is that, to quote a youthful statement by novelist-sportsman Thomas McGuane, "I read like a son-of-a-bitch." I have amassed, cut, sold, and rebuilt three whole libraries, driven not just by intermittent dire finances but by my obsessions and even whims. The English mystery writer Dorothy L. Sayers made "As my whimsy takes me" the motto of her fictional hero's family; it has always seemed like good advice to me. If you prefer real rather than fictional advisers, how about the critic Randall Jarrell's motto: "Read at will!" I learned more about what books are essential, or in some way "necessary," every time I rebuilt.

Next, I have lived the kind of life chronicled in my sporting library. By profession, though educated mostly as a biologist, I am a writer, unhyphenated; a writer of sporting, travel, and nature books who has also published some fiction and even a poem or two, a bird hunter, a shotgun aficionado, a lifelong fisherman, and a falconer. I am a New England Yankee who has lived over half of his sixty-some years in a remote New Mexico cattle town, a wanderer who has ridden with Kazakh eaglers in Mongolia and caught malaria in a jungle camp in Zimbabwe, but who has put in a lot more hours chasing jackrabbits with houndsmen on the high plains. I am an enthusiastic game cook whose paternal Swiss-border Italian family were hunters and poachers who knew more about growing and preparing good food than I ever will. My other side numbers generations of piscivorous Scot gallowglasses and other maritimers on both sides of the Western Ocean; beneath a cheerfully arrogant motto, the McCabe coat of arms sports three horizontal salmon. I have no idea why. . . .

I started this project with five conscious principles and discovered two more. The stated ones were these:

Many classics are boring. "Influential" is a non-starter. Many books have a temporary or even long-term influence, for practical or faddish reasons, and are still unreadable. Collector versus reader's copies: Which do you want? To a high-end dealer, "reader's copy" means something the dog ate, but both possess the all-important *words*. I have some nice books in this list, but I would generally advise cheaper equivalents, some collectible themselves.

In 1993, reviewing books for *Fly Rod & Reel,* I was accused of writing something nice about someone I knew. I had, and will. My argument goes like this: First, the world of outdoor writers, even the larger world of letters, is a small one. Sometimes I think we all know each other. So, I will not give a good review to a bad book by a friend. I will bend over backwards to be fair to those with whom I have had disagreements. I will *not* give a bad review to someone I do not like.

Most hatch-matching/how-to books do not make the cut. That I have been saying "Fish the Adams and the Hare's Ear and ignore the hatch" since I was about eighteen has nothing to do with this, of course. Nevertheless, "shoptalk is lyrical" (Thomas McGuane). I will make exceptions.

At this point it may be worth adding a quote from my old *FRR* credo as to why I won't ignore books by friends, nor ones not Shakespeare-level masterpieces. A reader complained that I praised "a lot of books. *A River Runs Through It* is one of four or five books worth touting." I replied, "Under a regimen of noticing only books as good as Maclean's I might do one review every two years, or even fewer." But also see my Honor Roll of "perfect" works at the end. . . .

Other principles emerged as I wrote. At first glance the numbers seemed weighted toward hunting rather than fishing books, and I was not sure why. (My first sporting quarry was a fish, a tiny native brook trout that I caught at the age of six, on a worm, in a stream now lost in a culvert under Interstate 95 in Massachusetts. I ate it.) It would be facile to say that I am more hunter than fisherman because I live in a dry environment where it takes some effort to fish, but it's a little more subtle than that. I believe that the term hunting *encompasses* fishing. Both are about killing, eating, the taking of energy to live. Hunting in the broadest sense is serious and elemental; without a possibility of "capture, kill, eat," the purest form of catch-and-release can seem a little decadent. C&R is a good management tool, but people who fish and never eat fish make me nervous. The English philosopher A. A. Luce argues that fishing without eating fish is ethically suspect. A member of a ruder generation, I once called it "politically correct fish torture" and "playing with your food," in print.

A more surprising "bias" also emerged: I realized I made little distinction between sport and subsistence hunting. If you think the line is clean, you have never read the rich literature of English poaching or hunted with those who were until recently condescended to as "primitives." Arseniev's tribal companion Dersu and Richard Nelson's native hunters remind me of my late Mongolian Kazakh friend Manai, master of golden eagles, who when asked why he hunted did not speak of the value of pelts or the necessity of controlling the wolves that preyed on his stock, but said, "because it is the most interesting thing that I know."

You may well be surprised (but I hope entertained) to see how wide a net I cast. My choices include a comic book, a medieval falconry book by an emperor, an art book on exotic fly materials, a book about a failed commercial shark fishing operation, a novel about 1950s gun writers, and a couple of terrifying narratives about man-eating beasts. You will find still-useful shooting advice (in verse) in a modern edition of a seventeenth century tutorial, timeless advice on how to catch rats, the latest theories on Paleolithic cave painting, and a postmodern collection of dead elephant photographs first hung in a gallery in Manhattan. Fishing poetry by a former poet laureate of England now shares covers with the oddest allegedly true statement I know: "Being eaten by a hyena is less painful than you think." Characters and storytellers include aristocrats and ivory poachers, cowboys and a nun; the quarry can be as refined as a chalkstream trout, as ambiguous as the fox in its different guises, as humble as a flathead cat on a trotline.

A library that contains every book suggested in this one will afford the dedicated reader a lifetime of reading pleasure. If you read them all, you'll encounter great novelists and poets, walk in fear in dark forests, learn how a Best gun is made, and add several good recipes to your collection. I hope I have arranged a feast.

FOREWORD
Jameson Parker

Do you remember a very silly movie back in the '60s called *Our Man Flint?* It was a parody of the James Bond movies and starred the late James Coburn as Derek Flint, the world's greatest . . . Well, the world's greatest just about everything: master spy, heavyweight boxing champion of the world, judo champion, occasional *premier danseur* with the Bolshoi, winner of five Olympic gold medals in five different sports, fluent in fifteen languages, expert in the use of . . . and on, and on. You get the idea.

Stephen Bodio is the literary equivalent of Derek Flint. The difference is he's the real McCoy and not a parody of anything, unless it's one of those eccentric Victorian polymaths who casually dashed off tomes about various obscure topics that intrigued them, tomes that are now considered *the* definitive work on that particular subject. Bodio's range of interests, and the depth with which he has pursued those interests, puts him in that rather intimidating league. Have a question about fine guns? Bodio's written a book about them. The book is called *Good Guns,* and I frequently use it as a reference, stealing shamelessly from it. Falconry? He's written a book about that. Eagles? Ditto. Hunting in the steppes of central Asia with eagles and the nomadic tribesmen who love them? Ditto. Dogs? Check out his blog, *Stephen Bodio's Querencia*. Rare breeds of dogs? Check out his blog. Coursing? Blog. Coursing with rare breeds of dogs? Blog. Paleo-art, paleo-history, obscure corners of history, entomology, good food, birds and wildlife of all kinds in all parts of the world, great books and great writing, poetry, mundane hunting and fishing of the kind more familiar to most of us? *Stephen Bodio's Querencia* has it all. Do you doubt it? Consider this quote, from this volume, of vintage Bodio:

"Much as I love dinosaur hunting, it is beyond the scope of this book."

Who else could legitimately write that line?

Which brings me to the epigraph in this book from Lawrence Sterne about digressions. I am going to digress.

The name of his blog is taken from another of his books, *Querencia,* an extraordinarily graceful and moving study of life and love and loss and the lessons we learn from those things. I read it out loud to my wife back when it first came out in the early '90s, and parts of it made us roar with laughter and delight, while other parts . . . as Charles Dickens put it in *Great Expectations:*

"Heaven knows we need never be ashamed of our tears, for they are rain upon the blinding dust of earth overlying our hard hearts." If you have not read *Querencia,* do so.

A book about the top echelon of "sporting literature" demands a literary Derek Flint. Who else but Steve Bodio could have compiled a list that ranges from Emperor Frederick II's thirteenth-century Latin treatise on falconry, *De Arte Venandi cum Avibus,* to Brian Plummer's dark and wickedly funny late twentieth century *Tales of a Rat-Hunting Man?* If the function of literature is to both open a window onto what it means to be a human in a certain time and a certain place, and to inspire ways of being and living within one's own time and place, the canon of "sporting literature" is as long and distinguished as it is neglected by mainstream readers. (I have put "sporting literature" in quotes because, while it may be customary to apply labels to every damn thing in the world, I don't believe it is productive to do so to works of art. Duke Ellington's comment about music applies to literature: "There are two kinds of music. Good music, and the other kind.")

Nabokov said a writer may "be considered as a storyteller, as a teacher, and as an enchanter. A major writer combines these three—storyteller, teacher, enchanter—but it is the enchanter in him that predominates and makes him a major writer." All the writers covered in these books are enchanters. Most of them open a window onto the real world as it is or was in their lives, a world they knew intimately in ways very few people ever did and even fewer people do today. Even those who open windows onto worlds of their own imagining create fairytales from which we can learn almost as much as we do from the real world, perhaps—sometimes—even more. But it is the extraordinary range of this selection that makes it so remarkable, a range that makes you realize how wonderfully vast and rich our world still is, if only we approach it with T. H. White's sensible advice in mind: "Learn why the world wags and what wags it. That is the only thing the mind can never exhaust, never alienate, never be tortured by, never fear or distrust, and never dream of regretting. Learning is the thing for you. Look at what a lot of things there are to learn . . ."

More than anything else, this book will make you hunger for reading. We all live in a world where the hands of the clock spin faster and faster, and where so much—too much—information rushes at us willy-nilly from the television, truck radio, and Internet, so that the idea of sitting down and reading for the sheer joy of reading becomes a guilty pleasure, a pleasurable sin, and if someone catches you at it, you react much as you might if your mother-in-law rang the doorbell while you were making love to her daughter in the afternoon. Apart from inspiring us to read so many books, Bodio becomes the voice of the priest in Reconciliation, telling us it's all right; there is nothing to feel guilty about. Just curl up and read.

And more: Bodio's writing about each of his choices opens his own windows. He talks about the difficulty he had in narrowing his choice of "essentials" down to a mere one hundred (plus "necessary wiggle room") when so many wonderful and deserving volumes presented themselves. I know precisely what he means: I started to select examples of his, Bodio's, writing to illustrate his skill and ability to enchant, and found myself with so many chosen quotes that narrowing them down was comparable to choosing which child you should throw off the troika to lighten the load and distract the pursuing wolves.

On his own childhood:

I attended a peculiar private Catholic grammar school in the pre-Vatican II years, run by a French order of teaching nuns who still wore the traditional habit. One nun fashioned welded abstract sculpture wearing welder's goggles over her wimple. Another, from Ireland, taught us altar boys to rappel 50 feet down a rope in the on-site quarry, by example. The principal once asked me (I was ten) to bring my .22 to reduce the population of crows swarming around the gables of the former mansion, and there was an equestrian statue of an armed Joan of Arc in every room.

How could you not learn at such a school? How could you not be inspired by—and perhaps fall a little in love with—a rappelling nun?

On Russell Chatham:

Once, we were enjoying a hangover breakfast in a trendy Santa Fe restaurant, where the rather camp waiter seemed mildly offended by the sheer size of my order of chorizo, tortillas, eggs, potatoes, and chili. He turned to Russ, who without batting an eye said: "I'll have two of everything that he's getting, plus an extra side of sausage."

I have always longed to own a painting by Russell Chatham; that thumbnail would make me choose him to stand at my back in a fight.

On hunting:

Of course anyone who is single-minded about his passions in a terminally ironic society runs the risk of looking a bit comic. One of the multiple beauties of this work is that [he] knows that hunting is, in Ortega's sense, a serious business; it doesn't matter what fools think of you. A hunter's perception teaches you about life and death and makes you intimate with the land you love; what you learn out there will provide endless delight and solace despite meager worldly rewards, or tragedy.

Who hasn't taken dog and gun—or rod and reel—and gone out to forget his troubles?

On lost times:

Victorian "progress" and the spread of vices like respectability and driven pheasant shooting changed the culture, making the old anachronisms into still-splendid dinosaurs who wrote down tales of braver days.

And yet today we look back on the Victorians as happy dinosaurs in braver days.

Bodio is himself a still-splendid dinosaur, rightly unapologetic for his passions. Literature, guns, birds of prey, birds for the table, food of all kinds (two—or possibly more, depending on your definitions of both food and cooking—of the selections in here are cookbooks), fishing, the magic and ambiguities of the hunter's world that can never be explained or even conveyed to today's urbanized shopping mall children, art, dogs, and literature again, all are celebrated here. This may be the most expensive book you will ever buy, for it will inspire you to go out and buy more. I can't think of a better way for anyone to spend his or her money.

Jameson Parker was a working actor for over a quarter century, best known for his starring role as A. J. in the long-running 1980s series *Simon & Simon.* He now makes his living as a writer for a variety of hard-copy and online magazines, and is the author of the critically acclaimed memoir, *An Accidental Cowboy.* He is also the author of three novels available through his website, www.readjamesonparker.com.

Part 1

FISHING

"In our family, there was no clear line between religion and flyfishing."

—NORMAN MACLEAN

CHAPTER 1

The Curtis Creek Manifesto
by Sheridan Anderson
1978

My first choice, its precedence determined by the alphabet, stands out from all the rest; it is both a comic book ("graphic work," today's preferred term, seems pretentious and out of synch with the book's spirit) and a how-to. Although it is published by a mainstream fishing publisher, Frank Amato, it is what I might call a hippie book, a product of the old semi-lost nature-literate Northern California bohemia that produced John Steinbeck's Cannery Row novels, the poet Gary Snyder, and Stewart Brand's *Whole Earth Catalog*. I would advise the nervous to read before they reject it; *The Curtis Creek Manifesto* is the best beginner's fly-fishing manual ever written; or rather, drawn.

Those drawings are whimsical but utterly clear in their intent. You never have any doubt what his hairy, gnome-like protagonist is doing or how to imitate it yourself. Anderson's advice and priorities are subtly different than that in most primers. Perhaps because he grew up fishing on little Sierra creeks, not unlike the small New England brooks of my youth, he puts more emphasis on stalking—"the sneaky art of approach"—than any other novice's adviser I know. His simplification of nymph fishing technique is all anyone needs to start.

His treatment of flies mirrors my credo ("fish the Adams and the Hare's Ear, ignore the hatch!"). Although he gives a couple of pages of fly types, he does not make detailed recommendations. This emphasis focuses the beginner's attention where it should be, on observation and technique and reading the water, rather than on equipment. His final pronouncement is even more specific than mine: "the hot-shot angler can probably do pretty well anywhere in the country armed with nothing more than a #16 gold-ribbed Hare's Ear."

Anderson defines "Angling expertise" as "a highly coordinated synthesis of skillful casting, imaginative stalking, keen vision, quick reflexes, plenty of savvy, and lots of experience." *Curtis Creek* itself is both a synthesis and a distillation, a necessary first read that you appreciate all the more when you have spent many years on the stream. The late Harmon Henkin, alleged Trotskyite and legendary tackle trader, whose book on fly-fishing equipment is still the best of its kind, said it right: "Every beginning fly fisher should be issued, along with rod, reel, line, and leader, a copy of this wonderful angling comic book."

ALSO READ:

Fly Tackle, by Harmon Henkin

California Fly Fisher magazine (a continuing exemplar of the unique cross-pollination of nature, art, and sport in Northern California)

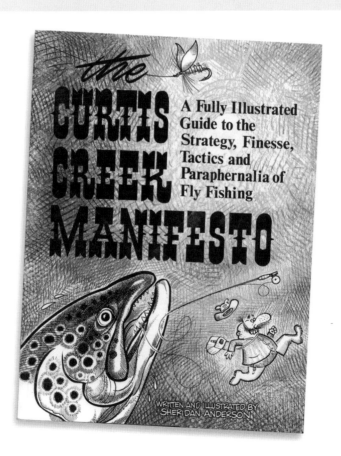

CHAPTER 2

Fly-Fishin' Fool
by James R. Babb
2005

Jim Babb embraces multitudes. A Tennessean of old heritage living the life of a Maine Yankee, he has been a marine publisher and a fiction writer, and the best editor of *Gray's Sporting Journal* since Ed Gray left. A self-described "sixties revenant," he is also a knowledgeable fan of Victorian fiction who easily quotes the likes of George Eliot.

But Babb is two things above all: a fisherman and one hell of a funny writer—no matter how serious the subject, he can never quite suppress his comic sense. He is *naturally* funny, someone who throws away perfectly good lines in e-mails; he once described his former grade-school teacher as looking like "a soft ice cream sculpture of the Buddha."

As with not a few writers here, it is hard to recommend a single book; often what we buy in an author is their "sense and sensibility." I chose *Fly-Fishin' Fool* for the wisdom of its title. Babb rings changes on the nature of foolery, but what emerges after reading all the essays—silly, serious, even profound—is that Babb's fool is a wise one, more like a crazy mountain poet in old Japan than a court jester playing to his audience.

Philosophers say many subtle things when they say one simple one. A few quotes from *FFF* say volumes about the nature of fly fishing, sport, and writing. First, its subject: "it's about that minor subspecies of foolishness called fly fishing, where intelligent men and women spend thousands of dollars and thousands of hours in an often vain effort to catch fish they'll mostly let go."

From a George Eliot–inspired defense of worm fishing against purists, a free-associating sequence in the course of which he compares fly fishing to bouillabaisse, bouillabaisse to a hotchpotch, and a hotchpotch to "unserious" worm fishing: "Somehow over the years this simple peasant dish became rigidly dogmatic haute cuisine, with extremists defining burn-at-the-stake heresy as whether you do or do not add mussels or white wine . . . it's possible

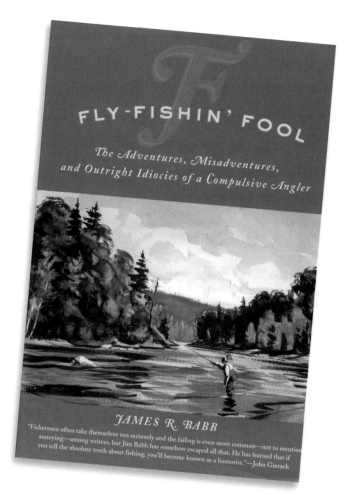

to spend so much time seriously fishing that you forget why you go fishing in the first place."

Finally: "there's no one right way to write about fly fishing. I write about it the only way I can, as a natural born damn fool who finds almost everything at least a little funny and likes sharing this with his friends."

ALSO READ:

His peers: John Gierach, Ed Gray, Harry Middleton, Seth Norman; and *The Curtis Creek Manifesto,* by Sheridan Anderson

CHAPTER 3

The Book of St. Albans (The Art of Fishing with An Angle)
by Dame Juliana Berners
1486

"Walton was a miserable old plagiarist who owed what he knew about fishing to a lady, to Dame Juliana . . ."

—G. E. M. Skues, in a letter to the poet Patrick Chalmers

"Print the legend."

—The Man Who Shot Liberty Valance

The Book of St. Albans, of which "The Art of Angling" became a part, was the first English sporting book, published in 1486 in another world. It was the first English book to use color printing. The fishing portion was added in 1496 by the printer Wynkyn the Worde. It reached its final form in 1810 when Joseph Haselwood published 150 copies of a facsimile edition complete with a 104-page "modern" introduction and investigation.

Neither of these versions is affordable by mortal humans. But in 1966 Abercrombie and Fitch (the venerable New York sporting emporium and purveyor of fine sporting goods and bespoke guns where Hemingway jousted with Lillian Ross, not the contemporary exploiter of youthful bodies that so horrified the late William F. Buckley) published a facsimile edition of the facsimile.

The A and F edition is not too hard to find and is still affordable for almost anyone. It is a bibliophile's wet dream, with fine paper, reproductions of both the 1810 and the 1496 fonts complete with color when needed, and a texture that looks like letterpress, although it isn't. The text pages alone are pretty enough to frame.

The authorship is . . . something else. Haselwood quotes a handwritten note in the fly leaf of the copy he used as the original:

"This Booke was made by the Lady Julian Berners, daughter of Sr. James Berners, of Berners-Roding, in Essex, Knight, and Sister, to Richard Lord Berners. She was Lady Prioress of Sopwell . . ." He adds, "The above appears to be the only biographical incidence which now can be traced to the life of this lady." In an unpublished manuscript, T. H. White calls her "a rather mythical abbess." Did she exist?

The importance of the work to history is beyond argument. In *Origins of Angling* John McDonald says, "it is the first, and no better essay on fishing has been written." This particular edition is also worth buying as a Book-Shaped Object. That term is usually an insult describing best-selling non-books and worse, but in this instance I mean it is so beautiful that you might frame every page.

The Haselwood text alone would be worth buying as a book. Falconers should love it but won't because Haselwood published his study in the sport's long decline, between the almost unbelievable Colonel Thornton (ca. 1800) and its modern revival. He quotes a contemporary: "The diversion of hawking by reason of the trouble and expence [sic] in keeping and breeding the hawk, and the difficulty of management of her in the field, is in a great measure disused: especially since sportsmen arrived to such a perfection in shooting . . . I therefore shall take no notice of it." As I said in another book once, "the rise of such vices as respectability and driven pheasant shooting."

Buy *St. Albans* for the typography, the history, and to put on the shelf with the delightful John McDonald. Buy it because there will never be an affordable edition again. Was she real? When the scholar Helen Macdonald put the question to me, my answer was an instinctive "yes"; the author gained no credibility by claiming to be a woman, but did it anyway. Make up your own mind; meanwhile, I'm printing the legend.

ALSO READ:
The Origins of Angling, by John McDonald
The Compleat Angler, by Izaak Walton
De Arte Venandi cum Avibus, by Frederick II
A Northern Tour, by Col. Thomas Thornton. Thornton was incredibly accomplished and rich enough to follow his whimsies. Then he exaggerated! The mountains of Scotland are not quite of Himalayan height. . . .
The English Country Squire and His Sport, by Roger Longrigg

CHAPTER 4

Noodling for Flatheads: Moonshine, Monster Catfish, and Other Southern Comforts
by Burkhard Bilger
2000

"We chose to watch"

—St. Augustine of Hippo

Nowadays the *New Yorker* finally seems to live down to founder Harold Ross's sneers at the "little old lady from Dubuque." Despite the attitude of that old master of snark, 'twasn't always so. A surprising number of the very diverse writers collected here were profiled in, reviewed by, or even wrote for the "old" *New Yorker,* including Vance Bourjaily, Brian Plummer, gun writer Jack O'Connor, and Angus Cameron's collaborator Judith Jones.

Today's generation of writers there are unconsciously rather than "reactively" urban. There are shining exceptions. I wish Bill Buford, both the former editor of England's quarterly *Granta* and a competent hog butcher, would do more pieces like his profile of Joe Hutto, whose *Illumination in the Flatwoods* is among my choices. It is also worth looking for the byline of Burkhard Bilger. Though these days he lives in places like Cambridge and Brooklyn, he grew up in Oklahoma, and remembers. His first collection, *Noodling,* is not just a fishing and hunting book; it includes other arcane rural pursuits like chicken fighting. But as it also contains stories ranging from the title sport (catching monster catfish bare-handed, often while submerged), through squirrel hunting and the music of trail hounds, it easily earns a place here.

Like all the best *New Yorker* writers, Bilger enters odd communities and describes their inhabitants with a naturalist's fascination. He never condescends; just when you think he is a post-modern *New Yorker* snot, he comes out with this: "Some of these traditions are illegal, others merely obscure; some ancient, others are modern. But the people who practice them share an undeniable kinship. Unlike so many of us, bent on wealth, promotion, or a few seconds of prime time, they cling to dreams that force them ever deeper underground."

Nor is he afraid to consider the possible truth of his subject's knowledge against the conventional "wisdom": "To born-again fly-fishermen—some of whom write laws for state fish and wildlife departments—noodlers rank even lower than paddlefish . . . the fact is, however, that noodling poses little threat to the environment." If noodling is legal in only seven states, the reason has less to do with the environment than with ethics—and ethics of a perversely genteel sort—in the words of one ichthyologist in Missouri "It's just not the sporting thing to do."

He similarly comes to a unique insight about hounds: "Dependent, petulant, overly excitable, most dogs are easy to imagine as terminal teenagers. But these coonhounds were different: though loyal beyond reason, they had careers of their own . . . on this night, listening to the dogs howling down a trail, so nearly like a pack of wolves, I couldn't help but wonder if they hadn't managed, against all odds, to break free of their adolescence, to transcend their domesticity by returning to the hunt."

Our homogenizing Waring blender of a civilization needs more enthusiasts and interpreters of its endangered and misunderstood "Old Ways." Burkhard Bilger has enough enthusiast in him to be a first-class interpreter, a de facto defender, and conservator of the surviving remnants of "Old Weird America."

ALSO READ:
Florida Frenzy, by Harry Crews

CHAPTER 5

Dark Waters
by Russell Chatham
1988

In the 1960s, after the so-called Golden Age and before *Gray's Sporting Journal*, the market for literary writing about hunting and fishing was even more limited than it is now. Still, some of the best essays about field sports appeared then, in a magazine that no longer prints anything to do with the outdoors. I don't want to credit the organization; I salute one woman, Pat Ryan, the articles editor of *Sports Illustrated* in the late 1960s and early '70s: Her unerring eye for good work gave us some of the first stories by Thomas McGuane, Jim Harrison, Russell Chatham, and William Hjortsberg, plus some of the best works by veterans like William Humphrey, Bil Gilbert, Robert F. Jones, and more.

You can see the work of her "alumni" today—some, like McGuane, in venues like the *New Yorker,* some in *Fly Rod & Reel* and *Gray's*. Any literate sporting reader should have a shelf of books by the stars of Ryan's old stable. Here I would like to commend a modern classic: fisherman-painter (writer, publisher, restaurateur) Russell Chatham's collection, *Dark Waters*.

Dark Waters is as bright with nuance and color as his paintings, and full of fury against assorted stupidities—aesthetic, culinary ("Eating well-done steak is not unlike eating an alarm clock"), sporting. Chatham is a man of appetites and raging, sometimes raving, enthusiasms, for rivers, fish, good company, good food, and less socially acceptable excesses. In this hypocritical era it's fine to see someone three-dimensional and un-chic, with the courage to defend his obsessions. He relates a conversation with climber Yvon Chouinard: "We agreed that to be anything less than passionate about these very personal enterprises is unacceptable."

Dark Waters is divided into three parts: "The Field," mostly on hunting; "Home," a mix of essays, delectations, and opinions; and "Dark Waters," twelve fishing pieces. "The Field" begins with a version of his notorious 1976 *Gray's* tale, "The Great Duck Misunderstanding," which prompted a few

angry letters and many whoops
of joy. About ducks, and eating, and excess, it contains the
famous "naked woman with
a parrot" scene. The outraged
letters prompted Chatham to
write a reply, in which he stated
what I have taken as my credo
in "outdoor writing": "Fishing
and hunting, in my under-
standing of those activities, are
not properly considered vehicles for escape from the other,
often less interesting parts of
life. They are an addition."

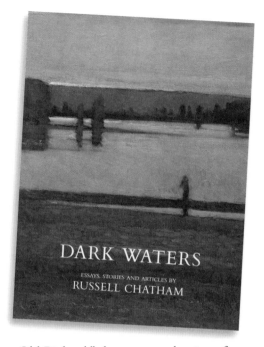

"The Field" also contains
a haunting memoir of Cha-
tham's friend Richard Brauti-
gan, still recalled in Montana as "Poor Old Richard," the tormented writer of
that strange, lyrical object *Trout Fishing in America.* "Home" features essays on
his hero Roderick Haig-Brown, Edward Curtis's photograph "Kutenai Duck
Hunter," and a couple of rowdier pieces. "Into the Country, Out of Your
Head," in which he cheerfully confesses to all manner of indulgence, may still
draw fire. But he insists that these are things to be indulged in only *after* fishing; *during* fishing "I never even drink beer when I'm fishing . . . fishing is not
that kind of fun . . . Fishing and hunting, painting and writing are a mixture
of childlike enthusiasm—fun if you will—and sharply focused energy. The
successful combination of excited wonder and fierce effort produces a new
sensation: satisfaction, perhaps the greatest thrill and most important goal in
our lives."

In "Eating Around" the subject is obvious, though glorious food pervades the book. I have eaten and even cooked with Chatham, and all the
stories are true. Once, we were enjoying a hangover breakfast in a trendy
Santa Fe restaurant, where the rather camp waiter seemed mildly offended by
the sheer size of my order of chorizo, tortillas, eggs, potatoes, and chile. He
turned to Russ, who without batting an eye said, "I'll have two of everything
that he's getting, plus an extra side of sausage." (See also his PBS interview
with Jim Harrison: "It was only a *small* deer . . .")

A taste?

> . . . *the woodcock will have been hung, undrawn and unplucked, for at least several days to develop and heighten their unique, wild flavor. Roasting of the birds is done in a very hot oven for perhaps seven or eight minutes so that the meat remains rare.*

> *The sauce, which is enormously important, is . . . strained over the pieces of bird as they rest on the croutons fried in butter and spread with intestines and foie gras. The heads are used as garnish, the tiny brain considered a delicacy. When we are in line for this princely meal, the part of the cellar we look hardest at contains the old Margaux, Rothschilds, or Echezeaus.*

As I stagger away from the table, let me remind you that the rest of the book is full of fishing essays, many lyrical, all informative, and not a few angry, particularly about the abuse and decline of the fisheries in Chatham's native California.

Recently Chatham has returned to his roots in the Bay Area. He has not published a California fishing book since *The Angler's Coast* in the 1980s. Dare we hope to see more fishing writing in his future?

ALSO READ:
Trout Fishing in America, by Richard Brautigan
The Raw and the Cooked, by Jim Harrison

CHAPTER 6

The River Why
by David James Duncan
1983

When *The River Why* by David James Duncan came out in 1983, I approached it with trepidation. It was the first, much-ballyhooed piece of fiction published by the Sierra Club, and it seemed on first perusal to be sort of Tom Robbins-ish whimsical, sporting what looked like a pretentious number of quotes at chapter headings, from every possible source—Tolstoy, Meister

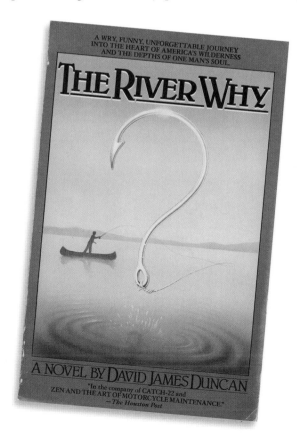

Eckhart, Jim Harrison, Homer, Eugen Herrigel, and many, many more. It was a first novel, and I don't generally like to be too hard on first novels, so I put it aside.

Later I picked it up, and couldn't put it down. It was long, word-drunk, digressive, silly, honest, rambling, ingenious, good-hearted, and laughing-out-loud funny. *River* purports to be the autobiography of Augustine Orviston, better known as "Gus the Fish," a fishing prodigy, the unlikely offspring of Henning Hale-Orviston ("H2O," a pompous fly-fishing poo-bah who out-Schwieberts the late Ernest Schwiebert) and his rollicking Idaho redneck wife, Carolina Carper Orviston. The novel is, among other things, a serious quest for meaning, but considering that it's more circuitous than *Tristam Shandy,* you might not notice. It shines with satire, good environmental ethics, and a not-too-reverent love of all good fishing. It *is* whimsical, and Duncan's prose not only occasionally resembles Tom Robbins's, he also quotes him. But it's all good fun, and good writing.

For what it's worth: Though it had remained on my shelf, I still approached *TRW* warily the second time around in 2012, only to rediscover its delights. Read (or reread) this irresistible nugget: "I *have* lived the gallant fisher's life, and I learned that *not* fishing is crucial to the enjoyment of fishing: Fishing is a good thing, but too much of a good thing is a bad thing. I don't know why the chronic candy-lover so quickly becomes the toothless hypoglycemic, the athletic champ the has-been chump, the dashing Don Juan the diseased lecher, but I know they do. And so does the constant angler become a water-brained, jibbering jerk-worshipper."

ALSO READ:
Trout Fishing in America, by Richard Brautigan
For atmosphere, anything by Russell Chatham and Roderick Haig-Brown

CHAPTER 7

Going Fishing
by Negley Farson
1942

Negley Farson was a reporter who lived an impossibly adventurous life and was a public figure in his time. If Roy Chapman Andrews, the archetypical scientist/adventurer, was the real-life model for Indiana Jones, then Farson was the Platonic ideal of the Foreign Correspondent. As macho as Hemingway's image, he roamed the world with typewriter, fly rod, fedora, booze, and cigarettes. He married Bram Stoker's niece and was an eyewitness to the Russian Revolution, the rise of the Nazis, and the partition of India. He knew Bolsheviks and aristocrats, Hitler and Gandhi, Caucasian bandits and Irish revolutionaries; he was accused of being both a capitalist (for fishing with a fly) and a Communist agent.

He fished through all of it. His adventure in autobiography, *The Way of a Transgressor,* is full of fishing and even has a piece on killing a whale. In his first chapter he remembers his first experiences surf casting in New Jersey. When he was twelve, his aunt Edith thwarted such an expedition, and his reaction defined his life: "That was another incentive, to fish, fish, fish; and the further away from home it was, the better it would be."

So it's fitting that his most reprinted book is his 1942 *Going Fishing*. A seamless combination of fishing, autobiography, and travel, it roams from the Jersey shores of his youth through Scotland and British Columbia, to lesser-known places like the Caucasus and Yugoslavia. He was one of the first outsiders to discover Chile's fishing; as early as 1937 he said of its trout that though "they might not reach the size of those prodigious rainbows of New Zealand . . . for fitness and fighting quality they may have their equal. I doubt if finer rainbows can be found anywhere else in the world."

Going Fishing is also a perfect example of why I dislike genre divisions in writing. It *is* a fishing book, full of good details for the obsessed angler. For instance, Farson likes his tools as we all do, and can say why: "I love rods, I suppose, with the same passion that a carpenter, a violinist, or a Monaco pigeon shot love their implements. I love using them. But if I can't, I can get a lot of fun by just taking them out of their cases and looking at them."

But then he adds something original and strange: "I've used them for politics." At the risk of committing deconstruction, I think he intends more. Farson's "politics" include choosing patterns with an Irish rebel, who loosens up and tells his secrets, and teaching xenophobic Caucasian tribesmen how to catch a trout on a fly. Fishing bridges gaps between snooty chefs and revolutionaries. Sharing a passion can be a writer's door into another culture; fishing did for Farson what falconry has done for me, all through the world.

Nor was Farson a single-subject obsessive who couldn't see the inhabitants of the banks because he was staring so hard at his tippet. I laughed when he said, in his chapter on the Caucasus: "This is a fishing book. I cannot go into the joys of those days in the high Caucasus." Because he *does;* I have read entire volumes that give less flavor of the country. In the next paragraph he describes the multiple cultures in those mountains, their feuds, horse relays, and how he nearly fell off a precipice because his rod was so long it caught on overhanging ledges; not to mention local food and what the correct spices are! (His preceding paragraph was about cannibalism in Russia.) It is hard to believe that anyone will ever write a better traveling-while-fishing book.

A bonus: *Going Fishing* is profusely illustrated with wood engravings by Charles F. Tunnicliffe, the last master of that technique and one of the finest illustrators of the twentieth century. Any reasonable printing with good reproductions of the Tunnicliffe illustrations is worth whatever you pay for it, and it won't be much.

ALSO READ:
Negley Farson's *The Way of a Transgressor*

CHAPTER 8

Trout Bum
by John Gierach
1986

I don't know how he does it, but he does; as much as it pains the snobs, America's best-selling trout writer is still among its best. *Trout Bum* was his first collection. In it he invented, or at least formalized, the term "trout bum," just as Robert F. Jones did with "hippie" (for *Time* in the 1960s—you can look it up). Gierach is still an exemplar of his own concept.

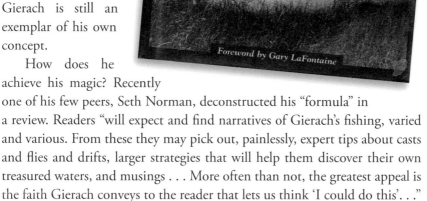

How does he achieve his magic? Recently one of his few peers, Seth Norman, deconstructed his "formula" in a review. Readers "will expect and find narratives of Gierach's fishing, varied and various. From these they may pick out, painlessly, expert tips about casts and flies and drifts, larger strategies that will help them discover their own treasured waters, and musings . . . More often than not, the greatest appeal is the faith Gierach conveys to the reader that lets us think 'I could do this'. . ."

"I could do this." Probably you couldn't, nor write about it as well if you tried. It can be a subtle effect. Anyone knows what a trout is, right? Gierach isn't so sure. "Exactly what a trout is, not to mention its considerable significance, is difficult to convey to someone who doesn't fish for them with a fly rod . . . What the non-angler is incapable of grasping is that, although individual fish clearly exist, *The Trout* remains a legendary creature." (And then he adds: "The *big* trout—another concept the non-fisherman thinks he understands, but doesn't.") Gierach is the existential philosopher-as-trout bum, fishing and writing his way to understanding.

In addition to questions of meaning, presented lightly, he understands the material world push and pull of *things*. My favorite Gierach quote, one that I use constantly, addresses more than the fly rods in my life. "A friend once asked, 'How come a guy who dresses in rags and drives a smoky old pickup can afford such snazzy tackle?' 'It should be obvious.'" Well, yes.

This first collection covers Gierach's eternal "snazzy" bamboo rod habit, plus such universal trout bums' obsessions as small streams, fly choice, night fishing, and road trips. (By the way, some snobbish anglers apparently deplore the term "Trout Bum"; I prefer it to, say, ace climber and Patagonia founder Yvon Chouinard's "Dirtbag," an honorific worn with pride by a richer sporting demographic.)

John Gierach is still rolling out his columns and collections, and I can find something nice to say about every one. But why not start here, with the birth of the legend? Amazingly, quality first editions are still cheap.

ALSO READ:
All of Gierach's books

CHAPTER 9

The Well-Tempered Angler
by Arnold Gingrich
1965

Arnold Gingrich, founder and editor of *Esquire,* was a connoisseur, with the virtues and vices of the breed. He fished obsessively, often on private waters, with little, bitty rods (he didn't enjoy or particularly approve of his one experience with Ernest Hemingway's saltwater behemoths), and collected things; among them were fishing tackle, violins, writers, books, and wives.

Despite his clubman's unshakable air of privilege, he accumulated a vast amount of knowledge, as well as things. He learned how to cast a long line with a tiny rod from the likes of Lee Wulff, about the making of flies from all the stars of the time, and he had an encyclopedic knowledge of everything written about fish and fishermen, one that is unlikely to be equaled today. He was shrewd about the psychology of fishing, and, of course, collecting.

Gingrich is the only person included here to have written his own Book on Books, the excellent *The Fishing in Print* (I made a conscious effort not to look at it while compiling this one, for better or for worse). Even good books on books can be a little dusty; I prefer *Well-Tempered.* In the realm of "things," it includes some of the best material on tackle written, despite being a little dated, and to my tastes a bit warped by his obsession with six-foot rods, although he makes the best case for them anyone could. If you grew up reading about dry flies, bamboo, Hardy, and Scotch whiskey, you are meant for this book. It is also rich in material only he could have written on places and personalities.

He includes a modest book section, the better for being trimmed down to his personal basic canon, which he numbers at an odd thirty-two. His picks seem wise but inexplicably over-classified, by two systems no less—asterisks for literary value and crosses for technical value; at least he didn't plot them on a graph. It may amuse the reader or confirm my folly to know we share only four choices, although I considered several more; his list leans toward ancient history on the one side and how-to on the other.

His company of friends comprised the high end of Manhattan's sporting literati at the time (the 1930s through the 1960s), when New York dominated the scene in a way that it never can again. Magazines may still have their roots in Manhattan, but now all the writers don't live there; despite the fact that Hemingway and Faulkner never did, in those days you practically had to move there for your voice to be heard in our field.

Insular? Yes, but. In his chapter "The Boys Upstairs at Manny Wolf's," about the real "Mid-town Rod, Gun, Bloody Mary and Labrador Retriever Society," he describes a hole-in-the-wall above a nondescript bar where the regulars included Gingrich, Lee Wulff, Ernest Schwiebert, Ed Zern, Dick Wolters, Jim Rikhoff, Ralf Coykendall, Peter Barrett, Clare Connelly, Gene Hill, John McDonald, sporting artist John Groth, and at least in those days half the reporting staff of the *New York Times* and the *Herald Tribune*. Yeah, the utter absence of women now looks embarrassingly anachronistic (where for instance was Joan Salvato Wulff, who could outcast them all?), but still, what student of sporting literature would not want to be a fly on the wall for all that lyrical shoptalk?

And the stories: of Hemingway and the Gulf Stream, of salmon on big rivers and trout on chalk streams, of fishing with Maclean and Wulff. Gingrich's memories chronicle a past just remote enough to be exotic, but close enough in time to be formative for every reader of this book, whether he or she knows it or not.

Bonus: Nice drawings by John Groth, ubiquitous in his time, who appears elsewhere in this book; they include an amusing portrait of Gingrich on the rear cover, reminding you once again how much he looks like the Monopoly Man or Mr. Peanut.

ALSO READ:

The Fishing in Print, by Arnold Gingrich

Byline: Ernest Hemingway, by Ernest Hemingway, which contains much of his *Esquire* sporting journalism

Gene Hill

Ed Zern

CHAPTER 10

A River Never Sleeps
by Roderick L. Haig-Brown
1946

A River Never Sleeps is every fly fisher's favorite literary fly-fishing book after *A River Runs Through It*. Among serious fly fishers it may well edge out McLean's book—in reaction against its popularity, or because it is more of an actual *fishing* book.

I found myself wondering why it was so beloved. It was on my long list, but I hadn't read it in years. People I respected, like the Berkeley book dealer Jim Adams, singled it out, but I resisted for months out of sheer orneriness. Finally I relented, read, and yielded, because . . . *damn* but it's good!

Roderick Haig-Brown came from a comfortable county English background (Sussex; his parents knew Thomas Hardy), raised in the last glow of Edward's Indian summer, before the Great War destroyed Europe's traditions. He learned ones like the ways of upper-class fishing on private water; for a time he was a self-described "very arrogant" Halfordian dry-fly snob.

But as a young man he emigrated to wild Vancouver Island, where for a time he supported himself by subsistence fishing, hunting, and trapping, and blew up his inherited Jeffrey game gun setting off fireworks (a late fruit of those feral years might be his eerie cougar novel, *Panther,* whose protagonist is eaten by wolves in the last sentence). The backwoodsman became a magistrate, an outspoken conservationist, a wilderness advocate, and a proto-Green—not unlike a damper northern version of Aldo Leopold. (Leopold's philosophy was forged in the high-desert Gila country; Haig-Brown's standing waist-deep in the Campbell River.)

His aristocratic piscatorial traditions and rituals were transmuted rather than lost. Now he fished and celebrated public waters. "The North American is probably the luckiest fisherman in the world. He can range a whole continent of lakes and streams and up and down the shores of two oceans; he can catch salmon and trout and char, bass and pike and muskie, sailfish and

"Not since Walton has there been a writer who can describe the joys of fishing as does Roderick Haig-Brown."

—*The Boston Post*

A
Roderick L. Haig-Brown
River Never Sleeps

tarpon and tuna, and seldom enough run up against man or sign that seeks to bar his way."

I am bemused by the idea that writers from a region share a certain poetic sensibility. The Englishman became a westerner; did he also become a "Pacific Rim" poet as well? He writes beautifully of the state of mind the Japanese call *mono no aware,* the melancholy at the heart of existence. On the pleasant gloom at the winding-down of the year, he says, "September has a touch of the year's death in it. One notices it a little more sadly and fearful as one grows older . . . now I shrink a little from the implications of the first cool nights, remembering the dark days of last winter, the cold that cut back the laurels, the snow that buried the pastures, and the long slow waiting for spring whose coming seemed delayed on into months that really should be summer . . . September is one of the loveliest months of the year." Or: "If one has to die, I should think that November would be the best month for it." Of course, like most who accept finitude (e.g., his Zen hermit counterparts in Japan), he is a cheerful man; one who drinks with Indian spearfishermen, trolls for salmon on the sea, and celebrates pike.

Yes, pike: "There is so much about a pike for the imagination to work on . . . the love of dark, deep places, the flat head and long jaws still with sharp teeth, the cold upward staring eyes, even the mottled green and olive brown of his sides and back which allow him to melt into invisibility against an underwater background of reeds and rushes. A pike lurks . . . this is the very stuff of good pike legend: crocodile, serpent, dragon; lurking, lying in wait, dangerous, mysterious; of the swampy marges in the blackest depths; seen only in breath-taking terrorizing glimpses." It pleases this contrarian that a man celebrated as a "salmonoidiac" still loves the dragon!

Haig-Brown wrote more good books than most people read. Why pick *A River Never Sleeps* over, say, *Return to the River* or the two-volume *Western Angler?* They're all good, as is the cougar novel. But I choose *RNS* because it has it all—nature, history, practical fishing advice, the digressive thoughts of an artist of angling who kept his good traditions and began new ones. And because he concluded his wonderful book with these words: "I still don't know why I fish, or why other men fish, except that we like it and it makes us think and feel."

ALSO READ:
Haig-Brown's *Return to the River, Western Angler, Panther,* the four season books

CHAPTER 11

Collected Poems
by Ted Hughes
2003

Ted Hughes was one of the two or three best twentieth-century postwar poets writing in English, and has always written well about animals. But this enormous posthumous collection is not just (just?) about nature (animals and birds, otters and hawks and crows and swifts, jaguars and a vivid dead pig, rivers, fish, kingfishers, damselflies, cormorants), life, death, love, awe, dread, and mystery—it's also about *fishing.* A few of his piscatorial titles include "Salmon-taking Times," "Go Fishing," "An August Salmon," "Night Arrival of Sea-Trout," "The Live-Bait" (his empathy for which may make you quit using bait), "Eighty, and Still Fishing for Salmon," and above all, perhaps, "Be a Dry-Fly Purist." Don't go to it for an easy read—Hughes writes serious, sometimes startling, modern poetry. But this is one of those rare books that they'll be reading a century from now.

Hughes explicitly loves fish, and fishing, perhaps more than any other poet. I put "The Pike," maybe the best poem about fish in the English language, in the "Honor Roll." For another kind of enthusiasm, try this from "Dry-Fly Purist":

> *(And she said:*
> *'When I hooked*
>
> *My first salmon, that salmon*
> *In the Ferry Pool, it was I never*
> *Expected nobody ever told I had never*
> *Known anything not*
> *Riding over jumps all I could think it*
> *Was like having my first baby – ')*

Salmon were perhaps his favorite fish (and quarry); a salmon, "with the clock of love and death in his body," pervades the book. The poems are as fierce as Hughes's cormorant's "fossil-chip eye." If you love rivers, poetry, and the original use of language, get this one.

ALSO READ:
Selected Poems, by James Dickey (not quite as oriented to hunting and fishing as Hughes, but "The Heaven of Animals," "In the Shark's Parlor," and "Extinction" alone are worth the price of the book)

CHAPTER 12

My Moby Dick
by William Humphrey
1978

William Humphrey straddled two or three worlds. Born in 1924 in East Texas, where he was known as Billy Joe, he rapidly transformed himself through talent and ambition into a New York Bohemian, and eventually an upstate squire with European airs and graces. He wrote three unforgettable big books, three volumes of short stories, and an endless stream of sporting essays. He disdained any pretense; he loved the best guns and rods, but to the end of his days, he retained his East Texas twang, at least in English. I still grin at memories of his unmistakable voice on the telephone, talking in a rapid, redneck drawl about literary and sporting matters, then teasing me by bursting into long passages of Parisian French or classical Italian. As I would protest, I could just about follow the first.

I'll deal with Bill's "biggest" novel and his other big books in the third section. For now I might note that it's a young man's bold book, a country epic, bursting with mythical monsters of many kinds—his father, a wild boar, a 10-gauge magnum Purdey shotgun—and that it takes place in the dark swampy woods of East Texas. *My Moby Dick,* written in his autumnal years, is a master work of a different kind—an elegant old man's fable, ostensibly about the narrator's efforts to capture a battle-scarred old trout he calls "Old One-Eye" in a minuscule Massachusetts stream. I suppose it is a quest; though only the length of a novella, it deliberately apes our culture's quintessential monster hunt, *Moby Dick.* In its own way, of course—its rueful wit and tongue-in-cheek modesty are a long way from Melville's weighty prose (and though it is set in Massachusetts, from Thoreau's, who nevertheless provides its perfect epigraph: "Time is but the stream I go a-fishing in."). That air of bittersweet melancholy is what lies beneath the surface of Humphrey's mock-epic.

Which doesn't mean it's not funny. He begins, of course, with "Call me Bill." Bill soon informs us how he doesn't roam, though the real Humphrey

most certainly did. Bill's fastidious; not only does he want to fish only in a
beautiful, difficult, nearby stream—he wants to fish for trout, with a devotion he labels "monotheistic" and soon likens to that of a fanatic Moslem, in
a passage where he compares a trashed trout stream to a pig farm in Mecca.

His fanaticism soon narrows his focus to not just trout, but *a* trout,
Old One-Eye. After a semi-scientific explanation of trout metabolism, he
describes his quarry and grail with two consecutive phrases as paradoxical as

a Zen koan: "a fish that big cannot be caught," and "a fish that big is too big not to be fished for."

Bill opens his campaign, pretending utter ignorance of fishing's conventions. He reads, ponders, devises a strategy, invents a fly; he argues with a skeptical "Chorus," personified in one small local boy: "Still using them artificial flies, I see."

On closing day he still hasn't caught the fish. "Closing day!" reminds his relentless young Chorus; Bill ripostes with a Shakespeare quote: "Has come. Aye, Caesar. But not gone," to which Chorus replies, "Huh?" But on his fifth cast, Bill hooks the fish. And irony yields to the joy of battle.

> *Straight up from the water he rose again. Higher than before he rose. It was not desperation that drove him. There was exuberance in his leap, joy of battle, complete self-confidence, glory in his own singularity. Polished silver encrusted with jewels of all colors he was, and of a size not to be believed even by one who had studied him for weeks.*

Of course, One-Eye breaks off, with "a final toss of his head"; of course, Chorus calls Bill a "Dummy." But wise old Bill soon knows better: "I was sure I would never get over it . . . but now I wonder, would I really rather have that fish, or a plaster replica of him, hanging on my wall, than to see him as I do in my memory, flaunting his might and his majesty against that rainbow of his own making? . . . He is the one fish of my life that has not grown bigger in my recollection, the one that needs no assistance from me."

A small thing, but perfect. In the third section the real William Humphrey will return, with Something Completely Different.

ALSO READ:
William Hunphrey's *The Spawning Run,* and his collected sporting works, *Open Season*

CHAPTER 13

Blood Knots
by Luke Jennings
2010

On the cover of the new American edition of *Blood Knots,* I am quoted as saying that it is the best book with fishing in it since *A River Runs Through It.* Absolutely true, but *Blood Knots,* an English memoir of fishing high and low, falconry, prep schools, mentors, and fathers and sons, is set on a different planet than Maclean's. They have one fascinating thing in common: They make no compromise about their fly-fishing lore, but they make all its arcana comprehensible and even fascinating to non-sporting readers. *Blood Knots* opens with a mysterious scene set in an urban canal full of trash that runs behind a London warehouse yard. The narrator is fishing for monster pike in the dark. Despite the squalor, it evokes a haunted, poetic atmosphere, almost Gothic in its ambience; as Jennings says later, "the near-Gothic air of neglect that makes the fisherman's heart race." And one more thing: If you are as attuned to nuance as any English angler, you will notice it is a scene of coarse, not salmonid "game," fishing.

From this striking setting, Jennings goes back and advances from his youth to the present on many parallel tracks; his tale, and his father's; a fisherman's life from his first attempts with a worm through fly fishing and falconry. The narrative trains also run through boarding school (which he neither hates nor idealizes); religion, honor, heroism, esthetics; the dead-serious debate between dry-fly purists and nymph fishers; mentors and their disciples; and something else, something that we Americans find alien or deny. Even in modern England, his modest background and intense but unsnobbish attention to standards brings in a question of class.

Jennings's naturalist's taxonomy should amuse (and inform) everyone and comfort no one. A boorish aristocratic officer who attempts to insult his heroic middle-class father during the Second World War is sent to the front for his presumption. His mentor, Robert Nairac, high priest of sporting standards, teaches his pupil the mysteries of the dry fly but is also a master of pike fishing. At first he seems the perfect gentleman, but his more perceptive pupils came to realize "He wasn't teaching us how to be gentlemen, rather how to act the part if we needed to." Nairac was a subversive and a traditionalist, a believer and an esthete, and finally a secret agent, a martyr to one of the filthy little wars of our time.

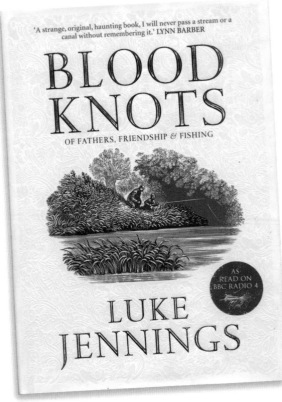

What does this have to do with sport's arbitrary self-limiting rules, and fishing? Everything, actually. Let me digress one more time through a metaphor, about life and esthetic standards: Jennings's explanation of how even the most liberal Catholic who remembers the old rituals feels about the new ones: "the Catholicism of my childhood was crumbling before my eyes, the Latin Mass giving way to a series of cringe-makingly inept translations as a thousand years of tradition bowed to the liberal orthodoxies of the Second Vatican Council launched by Pope Paul VI."

Still puzzled? Skip to chapter 13, the discussion of the dry-fly purism of Halford versus the cheery pragmaticism of G. E. M. Skues, written so zestfully that my wife, Libby, mercifully innocent of the debate, volunteered to me that it was the most interesting chapter of the book. In 1910 Skues, "a lawyer and life-long free-thinker," dared advance the heresy that fishing a nymph below the surface was not only effective but sporting. If fly fishers had armies, he would have started a war; the traditionalists reacted with a fury more typical of religious wars. Skues remained cheerfully adamant; "an authority who lays down a law and dogmatizes it is a narcotic, a soporific, a stupefier, an opiate." Only the Second World War temporarily quieted the debate.

Now, I have no difficulty preferring Skues's style. But my fellow iconoclast Jennings reminds me of the pull of the Dark(?) Side: "Upstream nymph fishing is a demanding art and it took me many years and many missed fish to even begin to get the hang of it. But it hadn't the poetry and airy lightness of the dry-fly. It doesn't, for the duration of a stolen afternoon or evening, bring back the age of gold."

Are we there yet? With a born storyteller's sneakiness, Jennings has woven greater meaning out of layers of narrative, tragedy, reflection, and elegant description. Nature is the source of beauty and terror, but knows no morals; "the swooping hawk, the belling stag and the rising trout connect me with nature whose rhythms and laws are unchanging. There is no pity there, and no sentimental narrative, only the knowledge that you are part of a continuum." Sport and art add something; it is no accident that the pupil became a critic, a novelist, and a near-Halfordian; an artist and a sportsman.

> . . . the rules we impose on ourselves are everything—especially in the face of nature, which, for all its outward poetry, is a slaughterhouse. It's not a question of willfully making things harder, but of a purity of approach without which success has no meaning . . . the fiercest joy is to be a spectator of your own conduct and find no cause for complaint.

Skues is in this book, as is White's *The Goshawk*, two of the sacred volumes mentioned in *Blood Knots*. Halford is not, but neither are many other canonic texts.

ALSO READ:
The short story "The Black Rabbit" in T. H. White's *Gone to Ground*

CHAPTER 14

Full Creel:
A Nick Lyons Reader
by Nick Lyons
2000

This compilation of mine would not exist without the editors to whom it is dedicated. Pat Ryan presided over the golden years of *Sports Illustrated,* kept several of the writers represented here in groceries during their crucial years, and gave them their first magazine assignments. Ed Gray wrote perfect short essays, but his historical accomplishment was to invent *Gray's Sporting Journal* on a vividly imagined nineteenth-century-style template, earning immortality in our little corner of the multiverse. He hired Ryan's alumni and discovered many new writers.

The third, Nick Lyons, didn't preside over a magazine, but his passions made him the most important editor and publisher of twentieth-century outdoor literature. The various iterations of his presses published editions of many books included here. But he also *wrote;* wrote well, fished, wrote, sold cheaply to magazines; taught literature for years while writing for dollars like the rest of us, while keeping high standards; edited for a big house or two and eventually founded his own first version. Gradually he evolved his unique and indispensable niche, discovering, reviving, reeling in, and encouraging more good writers than any other sporting editor in history.

Meanwhile he kept writing, constantly, prolifically, not succumbing to hook-and-bullet clichés, writing better stuff than most ever achieved—the dust jacket of this volume claims 400 articles and eighteen books. All the while living a busy modern life, being a husband to an artist who, though patient, was not all that enamored of fishing, raising a family in New York City, vacationing, always too briefly, in his beloved Montana, taking innocents like me out to dinner in Manhattan restaurants and giving them advice they understood only decades later, *and . . .*

(Now, if my machine only allowed, I would put in an infinity sign.)

On the front of this collection, compiled from decades of Nick Lyons's occasional prose and any number of those eighteen books, the excellent Vermont novelist Howard Frank Mosher says that Nick writes better about fishing than anyone since Hemingway and Norman Maclean. With respect . . . naah. Maclean was sui generis, a once in a lifetime superannuated prodigy, and Hemingway a sacred monster from another generation. Both grew up rural in a less frenetic time, fishing almost genetically. Nick is a different kind of angler, thoroughly modern, analytical and intellectual, self-doubting, bourgeois, urban: The Fisherman.*

If you are a collector, you would be better off getting a bunch of his old books in good condition, but if you are primarily a reader and a fisher, this huge omnibus, also available in paperback, is not just the best of Nick, it's as good a window as you can get into the soul of the modern fly fisher. I'm going to add one quote, which might give you material for years of contemplation.

The object of all fishing is to gull a fish. Some anglers find pleasure in doing this by any legal means. I like a prescribed court, a code of reasonable limits. My object, by choice, is to gull the fish with a single fly . . . ultimately I do not fish for the trout's pleasure or convenience, but for mine. I do not think the trout has a sense of fairness—or a sense of very much at all.

Need more convincing? Listen to Tom McGuane define the unique virtues of an old friend: "the ruminations of an unpretentious and intelligent angler, discovering such treasure in the richness of the natural world that there is no need whatsoever to claim it as art of religion. Like all the best angling writers, the biggest part of his job is the expression of gratitude."

Read 'em all.

ALSO READ:
I have a sentimental fondness for Lyons's very first, *The Seasonable Angler,* and two uncommon later books: *My Secret Fish-Book Life* and *My Secret Fishing Life.*

---

*"The Fisherman: who looks like you and me." Russell Chatham has an original cartoon by the late Gus Kliban that shows F-man seated next to a king on the end of a dock, drowning worms, with thought balloons above their heads. The fisherman's says: "Fuckin' king." The king's says: "Fuckin' *fisherman.*"

CHAPTER 15

A River Runs Through It
by Norman Maclean
1976

I don't know how they do it today, but during my Cambridge years, the Harvard Coop put out its new books on a waist-high table. They must have had a good buyer. I picked up *Ninety-Two in the Shade* there, several William Humphrey novels, and *In Patagonia,* which led me to obtain every Bruce Chatwin first edition when it was still new.

In 1976 I picked up a pretty blue book with a mountain scene on the cover, opened it, and read: "In our family, there was no clear division between religion and fly-fishing," then skipped to the end of the story to read: "I am haunted by waters." Though I had never heard of Norman Maclean, I sensed a new world opening between those phrases.

(Have you ever heard of a "Jane Chord"? I thought I had, though I have apparently been using a flawed concept for three or four decades. I defined it thus: The first and last sentences of a work, ideally, combine to reveal its deepest meaning. I would explain to anyone who cared that the chord was first written down by the late modernist critic Hugh Kenner, who got the concept from either his friend the avant-garde filmmaker Stan Brakhage or from Stan's wife, Jane, and named it after her. I passed this contagious meme to everyone I knew. But for this book I checked Google, which, though it credits Kenner and Brakhage, claims you use only the first and last *words*. On Maclean this yields "I waters." Hmmm. Print the legend?)

A River Runs Through It is one of those rare works that would be literature whether it were about trout or garbage trucks, and transcends banal games. Nor should the fact that it became a popular movie blind one to the fact that it is an immortal book, one of the few such about fishing.

If *River* is not the best first book ever, it is certainly the best first book by a wise, reflective old man, whose writing and, I suspect, speech were steeped like Cormac McCarthy's in Shakespeare and the classics since childhood— a continuing advertisement for them all. Before it became a book, it was

honored in a perverse way, rejected eighty times by post-literate or anti-nature English majors and B-school graduates before it found its niche and made the press rich. One immortal, if luckily anonymous, clone complained, "This has trees in it!"—a spontaneous utterance that now defines a genre so broad it includes every title here. You can read it aloud, every word; if you read it to your kids, you will entertain them and give them a better education than they can get in ten years in school.

If you bought the book you are reading now, you have already read *A River Runs Through It*. Read it again.

CHAPTER 16

Mattanza
by Theresa Maggio
2000

Naturally most of the books here are about "sport" in the narrow sense, but great writing on hunting and fishing resists such boundaries. Is the traditional Mediterranean bluefin tuna harvest fishing, big game hunting, a late Paleolithic survival, a roundup, a ritual akin to bullfighting, or all of the above? Theresa Maggio's haunting memoir of the last Sicilian tuna hunters does not try to answer that question, but makes you wonder.

She begins with a quote from mythologist Joseph Campbell: "The essence of life is that it lives by killing and eating." Titled *Mattanza* (the Italian word for killing), her book vividly details the practical aspects of diverting, netting, and killing tuna, and reveals its mythic place in Mediterranean culture from the prehistoric to the present. Maggio's good luck was that, as both a reporter and an American with a local background, she could enter into the society of the *tonnerati* and come back with a story illustrating our old, unbreakable ties to nature.

Every spring, as the remnants of the once-great Atlantic bluefin tuna schools return to the Sea of Sicily, they are met by barrier nets that divert them through an intricate series of traps to a chamber of death. There the hunters raise them to the surface and hook them into surrounding boats in a frenzy of violence and beauty. Maggio brings readers to the scene: "I saw the tuna as the men saw them, face on, flesh ringing in the gaffs, each one a muscled weight out of water," she writes. "One after the other the tuna gasped and thrashed, then, stunned and defeated, slid into the hold. Thrashing, they bled and died at my feet."

For centuries, a series of head fishermen, still known by the Arabic title of *rais,* have held authority on Favignana, an island off the Sicilian coast. Now, with tuna numbers depleted by longliner's nets and Japanese factory ships, when the ultimate destination of the bluefin's flesh is a Tokyo salaryman's

business lunch or an upscale Manhattan sushi bar rather than a Sicilian fisherman's plate, only a few are left.

Maggio first visited Favignana with a lover who was a fisherman. She came back after they had split, to record a disappearing ritual of great meaning. She became more a participant than an observer; as one *rais* said to her, "you are a *tonnorata,* a member of the crew." Although she never romanticizes the difficulty of the *tonnarato*'s way of life and faithfully records both the intermittent boredom of provincial life and her occasional sparring with her all-male crew, she also sees its subtle virtues. She seems as cheerful, fatalistic, practical, and romantic as her fishermen, and as happily free of psychobabble. No whining allowed; "Sicilians," she says, "understand that one cannot defy one's nature."

She finds majesty and meaning in the old cycles of life and death. Her writing can be reportorial and lyrical in the same sentence: "The bluefin were to ancient Mediterranean people what the buffalo was to the American Plains Indian: a yearly miracle, a reliable source of protein from a giant animal they revered, one that passed in such numbers that the cooperation of the entire tribe was needed to kill them and preserve their meat." The irony of the shared fate of the buffalo and the tribes needs not be explicit.

As everywhere these days, the Old Way—"the humble skills of men who have to work with lackadaisical unpredictable nature," as Luigi Barzini says— is giving way to consumerism. "The island is being gentrified to death," says Leonardo, an old fisherman. "It will be an uninhabited island with summer houses here for the rich from Palermo." The fisherman's situation is not hopeless—their co-op has bought the lease to the trap—but now they stage the *mattanza* more as a tourist event than for needed protein. Maggio strikes an optimistic note, speculating that tourists who "came not knowing they would witness an ancient rite that connected them to their own past, and to their common destiny . . . might look at the bluefin and see themselves swimming again where they were born, struggling, begetting, and dying in the same room."

It would be pretty to think so, as a more famous writer said. We can only hope she is right, and thank her for her story.

ALSO READ:
Mens' Lives, by Peter Matthiessen

CHAPTER 17

Harpoon Venture
by Gavin Maxwell
1952

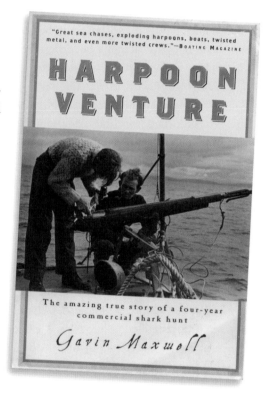

"Great sea chases, exploding harpoons, boats, twisted metal, and even more twisted crews."—BOATING MAGAZINE

HARPOON VENTURE

The amazing true story of a four-year commercial shark hunt

Gavin Maxwell

If you say the name "Gavin Maxwell" to any literate reader, they will likely think of *Ring of Bright Water.* His 1961 love letter to the wild west of Scotland and the otters who lived with him there became an unlikely bestseller, making its author famous overnight. *Ring* is a wonderful book and, like most of Maxwell's, hard to classify. They are usually considered "travel writing," but I'll suggest a better idea below.

Maxwell was born in 1914 to an aristocratic family of unusual intellectual achievement. In his youth he was interested in natural history and not much else. He studied estate management at Oxford, painted, and made an ornithological expedition to Finland. In the war he became a major in Special Forces, though was plagued by ill health. Afterwards, fascination drew him to the Western Isles; he was thirty-one, looking for a purpose.

He soon invented a scheme amazing in its crazed impracticality: He would outfit a harpoon boat, build a commercial basking-shark fishery on the Isle of Soay (which he bought), and invent a new industry for the depressed local economy. The plan was typically Maxwellian, combining romance, adventure, and danger with nature and an impulse to do good. It was also typical in that it cost an enormous amount of money and he leaped into it without looking. He later admitted "when, in November, I found myself a civilian, I had finally made up my mind to experiment in commercial shark fishing. I had gone further than that: I had taken the first false step and bought a worthless and entirely unsuitable boat." As Mark Cocker would write in *Loneliness and Time,* its record "was inevitably a book about failure."

But what a failure! All Maxwell's books are adventurous participatory essays in autobiography, despite their nominal subjects—the vanished Marsh Arab culture of Iraq, otters, the brigand-lords of the Atlas Mountains, basking sharks; he wrote most of them before the explicit fad of New Journalism gave such books a category. Superficially he was an unlikely action hero, suffering from "synovitis of the right ankle, a duodenal ulcer and enlarged heart." He had trouble with his circulation and would die of lung cancer at fifty-five, perhaps because he smoked eighty cigarettes a day.

Contradictory? He was also utterly intrepid, a crack shot, stoic, and even funny about pain and disaster. The bookshelf on the *Sea Leopard* reveals more: "Eliot's *East Coker* was, I remember, stained by the damp green kiss of its green-covered neighbor, *Le Tannage des Peaux des Animaux Marins* [Marine Animal Skin-Tanning]; *Adamastor* rubbed shoulders with its avowed enemies, *The Condemned Playground* and *Enemies of Promise,* and next to them came Hogben's *Principles of Animal Biology,* Empson's *Seven Types of Ambiguity,* Huxley's *Evolution,* and *A History of the Whale Fisheries.* Technical works on ballistics and navigation alternated with tattered novels, of which Evelyn Waugh claimed seven out of twenty . . ." Is the librarian an Oxford esthete, a man of action, a biologist? Maxwell shed tears for an otter but hated the then-unsanctified killer whale. He had an affair with the poet Kathleen Raine and used a line from one of her poems as the title of his most popular book, but believed her curse had caused the death of its otter hero.

He and his merry crew hunted sharks for three years. The chase was exciting, but the shoreside part refused to go smoothly. They never achieved a reliable harpoon, partly because Maxwell had an idea he could not drop (he was still fiddling with it when the company went bankrupt). His formula for pickling shark flesh went awry; they didn't use enough salt and ended up with *sixteen tons* of rotting flesh.

They were not much better at catching "dragons."

I bounded back from the gun as the flat of the tail slammed wetly on to the boat's side a foot below the gunwale. Then the shark was down under the water and the rope streaking out from the fair-lead at tremendous speed . . . I stared, incredulously, watching a thin trickle of smoke rising from the rope where it passed over the metal—the first time I had ever seen a rope running out fast enough to be practically catching fire. I was aware of Dan behind me, trying hopelessly to slow the rope enough to catch a half-turn on the winch, but the speed was too great for him to do anything. It was a matter of seconds before the heavy thump of the rope snapping off short at the iron ring to which it was tied—a three-inch yacht manila rope with a breaking strain of about two tons.

Money dwindled, problems multiplied. *Sea Leopard* was riddled with dry rot; its replacement boat ran aground. By 1950 the Soay Island Shark Fishery, a venture of "almost unlimited derring-do," had collapsed. But Maxwell had observed well, and in 1952 he published the history of his most stirring failure.

Today almost no one knows it. Are today's readers too sophisticated for sea tales or bloody adventures? The deserved success of Patrick O'Brian would seem to argue against both points. *Harpoon Venture* has an appeal as complex as Maxwell's character. First, it is one of the few great modern sea tales. He offers science for the biologically minded naturalist and reflections on harpoons for the engineer or weapons buff; Maxwell always admired precision machines, expensive cars, and fine guns. Finally, you have his powers of observation. He will turn from his problems to observe passing beauty with the delicacy of a Buddhist poet: "A single gannet was fishing the Sound of Soay; he rose in a spiral, snow-white against the dark sea cliffs, and descended arrow-like, vertically, to strike a small splash from the surface of royal-blue glass."

Maxwell spent his life in ceaseless motion, living beyond his means, writing down his experiences as fast as he lived them in order to stay afloat. Just once he complained: "I work for increasingly long hours every day, working simultaneously on *The House of Elrig* and *Lords of the Atlas,* but with an ever growing sense of frustration . . . like an aphis, immobile and solicitously kept alive in a cell by ants who tended me assiduously for my daily excretion of written words." It's a feeling most writers know, but despite all his serious and comic disasters he seemed a happy man, amused and delighted by the world and people around him. He had the trick of looking at things sidelong; "Everything askance, and it all shines on," as Thomas McGuane said in *Ninety-Two in the Shade.* Any Maxwell is worth reading, but this one has it all: the smell and heave of the sea, magical animals, Hemingway's "weather." If you read it, you will realize that Gavin Maxwell never really failed.

CHAPTER 18

The Origins of Angling
by John McDonald
1963

In 1963, John McDonald, a New York businessman, decided to make Dame Juliana's *The Treatise of Fishing with an Angle* accessible to the modern reader. The result, completed with the assistance of *Sports Illustrated* magazine, is this lucid companion to the ancient, alien black-letter weirdness of *The Book of St. Albans.* It is less a narrative than a compendium: an intelligent, uncranky commentary; a photographic facsimile of the *Treatise,* using a Yale manuscript that is more than five hundred years old; another facsimile of the first printed text, with a modern transcript on facing pages; and a color insert showing McDonald's reconstructions of the Berners' flies, with suggestions for materials. You can still find one for less than a new coffee-table book.

McDonald had no doubt of the importance or the goodness of this work. In his introduction he says that "no better essay on fishing has been written." As to its importance, he shows us how the book made the first argument for the importance of angling as a sport. "Sport fishing was not recognized in writing until the fishing *Treatise* suddenly appeared, very like a hunting treatise, but gently mocking the heroic sports. The hunter's lips blister from the horn . . . the hawk ignores the hawker's shouting and whistling and is often sick from the diseases of birds. The fowler returns from his snares, cold, wet, and empty-handed. But fishing with an angle rod brings good spirits and a fair old age."

McDonald is the first close reader to catch another important innovation in the *Treatise;* despite its date, it was not written for the aristocracy. The angler, he says, "was like to have been a merchant; very likely not a noble and not a landowner, since fishing had none of the dignity, ceremony, and hierarchal associations of medieval hunting. If he read the *Treatise on Fishing* it would have been for practical instruction and not to learn the language and manners of an aristocrat."

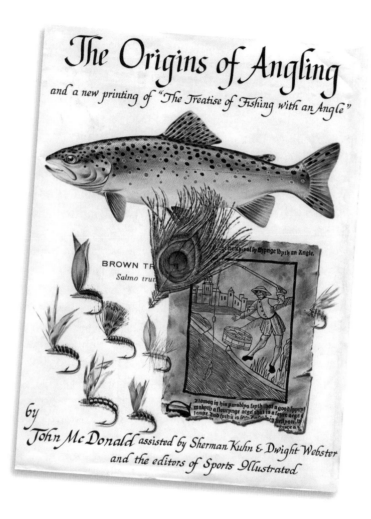

The funniest and most original part of *Origins* other than the flies, is McDonald's wry, intelligent overview of earlier thoughts on Dame Juliana. He begins in 1748 with William Oldys, a stuffy old London antiquarian driven to verbose incoherence by the mere notion that a nun could do such *things*. Oldys begins, "one cannot reconcile the notions those subjects inspire, of their authors being so expert and familiarly practiced and those robust and masculine exercises, with the character of such a sedate, grave, pious, matron-like Lady, as the Prioress of a Nunnery is imagined to be . . ."

He then works himself up into a sputtering froth: "Indeed, we have, and so we may have had, your romping, roaring hoydens that will be for horsing and hunting after the wildest game, in the most giddy company; but to join so much of these rough and impetuous diversions, as is required to obtain the proficiency of aforesaid, with the most serene and solemn profession of a mortified and spiritual life in herself, and the charge or care of training it in others, must make an unaccountable mixture."

He then, in the vernacular, loses it, babbling about "motley masquerades" and "an indistinction of petticoat and breeches" and "concorporation of sexes," finally rising to a furious crescendo. "The images that arise out of several representations of this religious Sportswoman or Virago, though one can scarcely consider it without thinking Sir Tristram, the old Monkish Forester, and Juliana, the Matron of the Nuns, had united to confirm John Cleveland's *Canonical Hermaphrodites.*"

McDonald finds Oldys's hysterical misogyny as funny as any modern reader must, and after reviewing other relevant antiquarians and historians, makes the reasonable suggestion that Berners may have retired to the nunnery after a more vigorous and secular youth. (He also makes a fair case for the fact that she was the author of the other parts of the "Boke," but perhaps not of the *Treatise.*) He brings up the old speculation that she retired to her cloister after an unhappy love affair and suggests that perhaps her lover was Edward, the second Duke of York and author of *Master of Game.* It would make a hell of a novel.

I'd like to offer a mild dissent and a whimsical defense of the at least remote possibility that a sporting nun might exist. I attended a peculiar private Catholic grammar school in the pre-Vatican II years, run by a French order of teaching nuns who still wore the traditional habit. One nun fashioned welded, abstract sculpture wearing welder's goggles over her wimple. Another, from Ireland, taught us altar boys to rappel fifty feet down a rope in the on-site quarry, *by example.* The principal once asked me (I was ten) to bring my .22 to reduce the population of crows swarming around the gables of the former mansion, and there was an equestrian statue of an armed Joan of Arc in every room.

I have digressed far enough, or maybe just enough, to demonstrate *The Origins of Angling's* diverse virtues, combining as it does a scholarly inquiry into the origins of angling, an intriguing historical mystery, an illustrated manual for tying Renaissance-era flies, and a key to reading a manuscript so old that its language and thought can be as alien as that of another world. The combination is irresistible.

CHAPTER 19

Ninety-Two in the Shade
by Thomas McGuane
1973

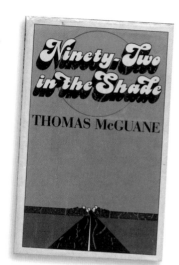

In the early 1970s, Thomas McGuane gave me and many other young writers the keys to the highway. It's not just a blues song. Writing about Jack Kerouac, McGuane used the same words, adding, "I won't have a thing said against him."

It is hard to see today what an effect McGuane, Harrison, and a few other original writers of the late 1960s and early 1970s had on the coming generation of literary males. (Not just Pat Ryan's Americans, either; in England, journalistic hybrids of Waugh and Hemingway, like the tragically short-lived Bruce Chatwin, were springing up like mushrooms.) Instead of being a chronicler of suburban angst, suddenly you might cast a line, shoot a rifle, train dogs, read European novelists, journey to strange places, and be unabashedly, even arrogantly, literate. As I wrote in recollection: ". . . it seemed there might be a place for me in the West, where you could be young and wild but also a gentleman of literature, where you could appreciate a Parker and an Adams, a .270 or a Leonard rod, not to mention both Turgenev and Edward Abbey." Later, Jay McInerney would write that "Thomas McGuane extended Hemingway's literary tradition into the Rock 'n' Roll era and convinced me I wasn't the only person who wanted to be Hemingway and Keith Richards at the same time."

But the work must hold up, and continue. McGuane's work does, in venues ranging from the *New Yorker* to fishing magazines (see his recent novel *The Cadence of Grass*). *Ninety-Two*, his fiercest and most provocative early novel, holds up almost scarily well. The tale of a deadly but never humorless territorial duel between rival flats-fishing guides in the Keys, it seamlessly melds language, nature, sport, black comedy, and poignant suspense as perfectly as any book of the twentieth century. I could fill the next three pages with lapidary quotes, but one may suffice.

Two spotted rays shot out in front of the boat and coursed away on spot-
ted rings, their white ventrals showing in their hurry; then vanished
in the glare. The water was still and glassy, green over the turtle grass
bottom. There were birds everywhere now, soaring out before them—the
cormorants that rested on stakes and mangroves to dry out their wings,
the anhingas, gulls, frigate birds, and pelicans, the waiting herons and
cranes in every variation of slate, whites upon whites, emblematic black
chevrons or stripes, wings finished in a taper or left rough-ended. They
threaded the Keys amidst this aerial display over uncounted fish cours-
ing the tidal basin, over a bottom itself home to over a million kinds of
animal, that walked, stalked, and scuttled by every tropism from heat
to light and lived in intermeshing layers, layer upon layer, that passed
through each other like light and never touched.

McGuane also hunts and has written fine hunting fiction; his best short
stories, in the collection *To Skin a Cat,* can stand with the sporting tales of
Caroline Gordon and Turgenev. If you like *Ninety-Two* you should look at
this one too. The heart and precision of great pointing dogs are at the center
of his most explicitly sporting tales. The best one in the book, one of two
about pointers and mortality, is "Flight." Here McGuane assumes Turgenev's
role, narrating a fiction as himself on his beloved Montana plains. He tells a
wonderful story, evoking a west of almost painful beauty.

We shot another brace in a ravine. The dogs pointed shoulder to shoul-
der and the birds towered. We retrieved those, walked up a single, and
headed for a hillside spring with a bar of bright buckbrush, where we
nooned up with the dogs. The pretty bitches put their noses in the cold
water and lifted their heads to smile when they got out of breath drink-
ing . . . We stretched out on one elbow, ate with a free hand, and looked
off over the prairie, to me the most beautiful thing in the world. I wish I
could see all the grasslands, while we still have them.

No one has said it better.

ALSO READ:
Thomas McGuane's *To Skin a Cat;* for sporting nonfiction, see chapter
78, *An Outside Chance*

CHAPTER 20

Small in the Eye of a River
by Frank Mele
1996

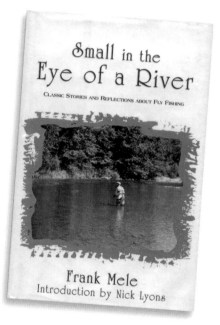

A mystery inherent in both sport (whatever that is) and capital-A Art is the relation of tools and materials to action and spirit. Those who aspire to mastery must always be conscious of their tools and materials on some level, though an over-emphasis on objects can be a detriment. Lousy tools can make it hard to learn a skill; bad brushes don't help the painter, soft old rods will never dry a fly, and the miserable single-shot .410 I started out with could well have turned me away from bird hunting forever. The other book on materials here, Paul Schmookler's lavish treasury of exotic feathers, is unself-consciously about "stuff." Frank Mele's book, which grew from the meditative essay "Once in a Blue Dun Moon," is more subtle and more ambiguous.

Mele was an artist in words and music, a violinist with the Rochester Philharmonic and a violist with the Pittsburgh Symphony and Modern Art String Quartet. He was also, variously, a novelist, a sometime drunk, and an utterly fanatic trout fisher of the most rarefied kind. He was wryly self-aware, unlike, say, George Bird Evans, perhaps because he knew he was nuts and it amused him.

Mele pursued fish, technique, master anglers (all of them somehow warped, obsessive; somehow broken), tackle, and tools. But above all he pursued a mysterious grail: a cape of feathers, neck hackle from a game rooster of a particular color: Blue Dun. He is started on this endless road by a drunken wannabe "mentor," who tells him that he cannot tie his favorite fly without the real article. Pounding the table, his friend insists it is "mandatory that this fly be tied with a Blue Dun hackle! Else it is not a Quill Gordon fly!"

These words, says Mele, plunged him into both a "nightmare of frustration" and a lifelong quest. At first he is not even sure what the color of this Platonic ideal might be. His damnable mentor lures him on. "I don't know how to describe it. One simply has to see the natural Blue Dun for himself, with his own eyes. Only then can he understand. It is one of Nature's rare moods. It is color and light, making their ways out of chaos and darkness."

His pursuit never ended, despite the fact that he knew it was a little crazy; he admits as much. In his years touring the country as a freelance "symphonist," "as each music season rounded its peak and spring was faintly visible in the distant valley, the voice of obsession would begin loudening a command to action. The trail was faint, often washed out, but, like a stubborn hound, I would return to certain crossways, hoping for a cold scent that would lead to a Blue Dun cape of quality . . ." He even convinced himself his quest had a practical end: "I had long ago formulated the theory that the natural Dun-hackled fly would take trout anywhere in the world at one time or another."

He eventually acquired "a small number" of Blue Dun capes, which he describes as "nestling about each other in all the glory of their muted iridescence." He says that most were acquired "honorably," in a defensive manner that makes the reader doubt it; he will not even allow himself to count them. Or possibly not acquired so honestly—Mele constructs masks beyond masks. It seems at best an ambiguous, if poetic, resolution.

The rest of the book, though without clichés, is devoted to more conventional delights. His fishing tales include a Japanese parable and one dating from the Roman Empire, with Dun of course. He becomes so maddened by his obsessions that he nearly gives up fishing, but relents: "I was myself again, unrepentant, but whole and free."* He could never repudiate his pursuit of perfection, art, and beauty, of "Dun." Shining gamecock feathers with an unearthly blue tint remain his life's central symbol and metaphor, his expression of the eternal "why?" Why do we fishers, artists, "small-time creators" step outside of normal life to pursue such things? Maybe we can only answer with our tales and pictures, "productions of time" that strive for timelessness. Mele finishes with an almost Japanese note of melancholy, comparing the lives of mayflies—"lives mortal, fragile, and flawed"—to our own.

---

* My Explorer's Club mentor, the legendary Himalayan climber, big game hunter, and Jesuit priest Anderson Bakewell, S.J., used to say to me in jesting wonderment: "St. Francis Borgia supposedly gave up hawking, hunting, and women. I just barely managed to give up the last."

CHAPTER 21

The Earth Is Enough: Growing Up in a World of Trout and Old Men
by Harry Middleton
1991

The Earth is Enough is a memoir of a boy's teenage years spent with two ancient and eccentric uncles in the Ozarks, and it's like nothing you have ever read. The time is the mid-1960s; his uncles are a weird combination: hillbillies, "socialist bums" (Middleton's father's phrase), and above all, Orvis-level trout fly purists. One keeps three books at his bedside: novels by Hemingway and Flaubert and Horace Kephart's *Camping and Woodcraft*, quoted here:

> *Albert flicked his wrist and the rod shuddered as though it had been molded out of Jell-o; the line shot through the guides and lay on the damp grass like a strand of spun silk. Again his wrist twitched, a fluid, unbroken motion, all energy transferred in an instant from rod to line, and the line traveled almost in slow motion, moving up and behind Albert in a level, narrow loop until, at the instant it straightened out, the rod tip shot ahead and the line cut effortlessly through the air and back out across the yard gleaming in the dusk like a seam of moonlight.*

Come to think of it, "a fluid, unbroken motion" isn't a bad way to describe this unique book. It is a bitter indictment of the value contemporary society puts on the best writing that Harry Middleton, a former magazine editor brought low by bad luck and the economics of our trade, died while working on the local garbage truck to support his young family, while—insert the name of your favorite mediocre writer without so much as mentioning "celebrity"— continues to make a living. Poetic fly-fishing lyricism and grace from the tailgate of a garbage truck, sweet memories without a trace of bitterness—a minor miracle; it is somehow comforting to know that through the efforts of a few thoughtful people, this unique book remains as a token victory for the good and the quirky and a bit of posthumous revenge for Middleton.

CHAPTER 22

Meanderings of a Fly Fisherman
by Seth Norman
1996

There are two types of literary fishing. One, taking place entirely on the water, could be called fishing life, and is common. The other is unnamed; you might call it life-with-fishing.

Russ Chatham started me thinking about the issue more than thirty years ago, replying to a letter in the old *Gray's* that had complained of his introducing eating, drinking, and a naked woman with a parrot into a story ostensibly about duck hunting. Chatham insisted that to have meaning sport must be part of a life, rather than something removed from that life. Of course, "real" life and those things we call sport are always connected for anyone who thinks and feels deeply about them, but some writers choose to emphasize the sport, while others bring in life in all its mess and glory.

Seth Norman's first book, the wonderful *Meanderings of a Fly Fisherman,* is a perfect example of a "life." I began it one morning long ago, laid up by a bad back, and finished it in six hours, shouting out whole passages to Libby. In addition to fishing, you get fathers and sons, fathers and foster sons and daughters, schizophrenia, corruption in the Oakland police department, and sedition in Malaysia. Some is fiction, some perhaps fictionalized, and all of it rings true as human material. It's a moving book, delightful in its observations and details.

Even the lightest pieces in the book—"The Ugly Angler" and "A Lifetime of Drowning"—would be worth recommending. But it's the long pieces, most of them original for this collection—"6X Redemption," "Of Grace and a Caddis Case," "The Rhythm of a Woman and a Line," and "Throwing Dace"—that put this book in the absolute first rank.

I suspect many readers would pick "Throwing Dace," a moving portrait of age and grief and the necessity of leaving something behind, or "The Rhythm of a Woman and a Line," which combines a boy's sexual and fly-fishing initiations believably and—well, I don't use the word "sensitively" often, but it

might fit here—as their favorites. I like two odder pieces even better. "6X Redemption" is in part about how a hard-core fisherman who flings spoons and bait becomes a fly-fishing "purist," but it's also about commitment and purity and danger, as Norman flees his home in the Bay Area after his exposé of crooked Oakland police threatens his life. And the short story "Of Grace and a Caddis Case" is about keeping promises and struggling with madness, about love and schizophrenia and flies with fool's gold in the dubbing. It's flat-out amazing.

There's a good toughness in Norman's writing that I turn to with a kind of famished relief, in a genre whose characters sometimes all seem to be either business executives, lawyers, doctors, or guides. Norman's world has those crooked cops and honest investigators, mental patients, pit bulls who nearly kill his cat, friends who can't understand catch-and-release because they kill and eat everything. He used to fish off the Albany dump in San Francisco Bay with his housemate, a recently divorced cop, where an angler might choose to be armed against human predators. ("I needed these edges, of earth and land, city jungle and untamed world, extremes of solitude and companionship, solace and excitement. I needed the taut hope of a cast.") There is no cheap machismo or posturing here, but the sober acceptance of a hard world still shot through with flashes of beauty and redemption.

There are some totally off-track pieces that are just perfect. "Pilgrim's Pike" is a piece as ferocious as those fish, and funnier. Something about pike seems to bring out the wild in good angling writers: "About malice, predatory malice—I do not anthropomorphize—about green and gold beasts with binocular vision—'the better to ambush you with, my dear'—who accelerate to eight g's and seem utterly absent of fear. Dog eaters, a danger to pedestrians, fish that cut me bloody deep with their gills. My luggage is lighter for the flies they stole."

Finally, there's some serious fishing philosophy embedded here: for instance, on catch-and-release. Readers may well know that I eat fish. Norman, a catch-and-releaser, can be flippant and funny on the subject—to teenagers he says, again and again, that you can't play tomorrow if you eat the ball today. But at the end of "The Siamese Avenger," on predation, he says, "while I am under no illusion that any of us are generous to the animals we choose not to kill—and I'm often bewildered by the satisfaction we take both in catching and releasing—I will hesitate an instant after a fish leaves my hand, contemplating a game we have the luxury to play in a place where so many others play for keeps."

I can't think of a fishing book I enjoy—present tense, I read the whole thing and his next, again, for this collection—more than Seth Norman's *Meanderings*. It's one of those pieces of writing that, for days, makes everything else you read (and write) look second-rate. And he is still doing it.

ALSO READ:
Seth Norman's *The Fly Fisher's Guide to Crimes of Passion*

CHAPTER 23

The Last Pool and Other Stories
by Patrick O'Brian
1950

At best I am a selective fan of historical novels, but in 1993, when I discovered Patrick O'Brian's Aubrey-Maturin series, I fell headfirst into his world. These books are not mere "sea stories"; they resurrect the universe of the Napoleonic Wars, or, if you are a postmodern critic or a theoretical physicist, create one. I wrote an excited note to my curmudgeonly friend David, who himself has created an early nineteenth-century life on a Virginia ridgetop, to tell him he would enjoy the books, and received a short note that read: "Bodio, old boy, do you remember an old volume I sent you a number of years ago?"

I did; I loved it, and knew I still had it. I went to my library and pulled down a little faded light-green book, written in 1950: *The Last Pool and Other Stories,* by Patrick O'Brian. A volume of country and sporting tales, some straightforward, some with elements of the supernatural, it is at least a minor classic. But it is so different in tone from the nautical stories that I had not even connected the identically named author with them.

"Patrick O'Brian" contained and wrote multitudes. His career stretched from 1930 to 2000, during which he wrote children's books, animal tales, "serious" literary short stories and novels, and the twenty Aubrey-Maturin novels. He also translated Simon de Beauvoir and a French novel about Afghanistan, and wrote biographies of Pablo Picasso and the pioneering eighteenth-century botanist Joseph Banks. He posed as an erudite Irishman named Patrick O'Brian and lived his postwar life in a vineyard in the Pyrenees, but he was actually an Englishman of German descent, christened Richard Patrick Russ, born in the Buckinghamshire country house of a prosperous London family in 1914.

O'Brian's literary career and his subterfuges are baroque. The best account is his stepson Nikolai Tolstoy's affectionate insider's biography, *Patrick O'Brian.* But even he may never get to the bottom of O'Brian's cheerful deviousness.

Image courtesy of www.clearwaterbooks.co.uk

Sport winds through all O'Brian's works, even the sea stories, as do biology and natural history. His lighthearted "boys' own" 1954 ramble through Central Asia, *The Road to Samarcand,* features falconry and eagle-ry and a nice 16-bore shotgun employed on partridges. But *The Last Pool* stands alone as a book of sporting tales, and may also be the best of his several books of short stories.

Its subject matter is not all that unusual; even the supernatural overtones occur in some of T. H. White's 1930s tales and in Geoffrey Household's stories in the 1950s. It is O'Brian's atmosphere that is unique; his tales exist in an uncanny atmosphere I might call "Irish." I do not mean Irish in any picturesque sense, nor romantic; Ireland is neither cute nor quaint. As Shane McGowan sings, "It's dark and it's old." Rather, think Irish like Yeats's tombstone: "Cast a cold eye/on life, on death./ Horseman, pass by!" Several of these tales may make you smile, but more will leave you with a chill.

I hope you are not put off by his view, because O'Brian does some of the best fishing and hunting writing I have ever seen.

He took the draggled fly from the corner of its jaw—it had nearly worn free in the fight—and he stood above the fish, gazing at it with satisfied admiration. It was a perfect fish: he looked down on its small, well-formed head, the gleaming pools of its eyes, and the golden yellow under the delicate white of its throat, and it lay there quiet with labouring gills. He must weigh a good four pounds, he said, drawing his finger down the fine, pink-flecked line that divided its belly from its gorgeous spotted sides. The fish bounded at his touch, and lay still again. He saw its strong shoulders, the saffron of its fins and the splendid play of colours over its whole glowing body, and he could not find it in his heart to kill the fish.

There are more like this, several just as good on hunting with hounds, and a lyrical scene of shooting flighting ducks in the morning. The majority of the tales are straightforward, though some take unexpected turns. But if you really don't like a touch of terror, read something else. Here is the last line of another sporting story, a line that comes out of nowhere so perfectly that I am not giving anything away, a line I think might make the hair stand up on the back of your neck even with no context: "But in the pass he met the keeper of the hoard."

ALSO READ:

Patrick O'Brian's *Caesar, Beasts Royal,* and *The Road to Samarcand*

The Maharajah and Other Stories, by T. H. White

Sabres on the Sand, by Geoffrey Household

CHAPTER 24

What the Trout Said
by Datus Proper
1982

When *What the Trout Said* by Datus Proper came out, I wanted to give it some kind of award for "best book on a subject I won't read books about." My distaste for hatch-matching manuals is well known and often reiterated, but Proper, a retired diplomat (and wise and witty man, whom I would later know as a hunting companion), had written a book on imitation of stream insects that was a pleasure to read: literate, wide ranging, and even funny. Long before I knew the author, the book earned a place in my permanent library.

It's not that his thesis was all that original—he tries to see through the trout's eyes, and the trout "talks" to him by accepting or rejecting certain flies for certain reasons. It's not even his style, some of which can be a bit cute (one chapter, on tactics, is subtitled "A Much-Needed Classification of What the Rhythm Method is Good For"). It's just that Proper had such good sense and never fell into the trap of taking himself too seriously.

There are plenty of examples of this sense and humor in the book, but I'd almost own it just for his "rationale for thoughtful fishing" early in the book. Here it is in its entirety:

> *It (fishing) is as important as some of the other things that men think about, like nuclear physics.*
>
> *Trout live in the world's pleasant places and are sometimes sought by pleasant people. Where and with whom would you prefer to give your best?*
>
> *Light physical exercise liberates the brain and makes not thinking difficult.*
>
> *The frontier was conquered centuries ago, and the minutiae are what's left.*
>
> *All men are compulsive hunters, or at least I am.*

I scarcely know how to pursue enjoyment, but I am able to catch a lot of it along with my trout.

Datus Proper, fine sporting writer, unpretentious gentleman, and good hunting companion, died in his seventies after falling while fishing in Hyalite Creek. He left us all sadder, but it is hard to deny he had a sportsman's life, and death. I'll check his book for reference any day, and keep it long after I discard eighty more pretentious and less intelligent volumes.

ALSO READ:
Datus Proper's *Pheasants of the Mind*

CHAPTER 25

The Catfish as Metaphor
by M. H. Salmon
1997

Jeremy Wade gave a giant catfish an exotic name and made it a star on Animal Planet. It didn't help; catfish *still* get no respect. As I once complained: "the catfish, whether a hornpout the size of a bullfrog tadpole or a blue cat with the heft and docility of a Harley Davidson, is not going to make the cover of *Field and Stream,* let alone the columns of *Esquire.*"

In 1997 legendary southwest writer, publisher, and hound man M. H. "Dutch" Salmon embarked on a quest to fish and ponder Meaning. His (metaphorical) vehicle was the humble catfish: "Seek him out in his myriad watery haunts and you will come to know something of all your fish and fishermen, and your country, and perhaps yourself."

Salmon began his sporting life fishing for trout in upstate New York. A long arc of education and travel led him through western Minnesota and south Texas and opened his mind to other ways; by the time he landed in New Mexico, he preferred hounds and catfish to bird dogs and dry flies. He constructed an enviable life, even fathered a son who seemed to share his interests. But part of him stayed restless, unable to bury his own father's ghost. "Bud" senior, a skilled angler and wingshot, taught Dutch all he knew. But he was racked by bouts of depression, haunted by memories. Like many men of his generation, he persuaded himself that hunting and fishing were time-wasters rather than vital ways to stay sane.

But don't categorize! *Catfish as Metaphor* is not some conventionally sensitive weep-fest about estranged fathers and sons. It is a classic American road book, rambling, discursive, picaresque. Salmon drives, fishes, collects useful lore; remembers, eats, praises chicken-fried steak; debates everything from baits to conservation and occasionally stands up on his hind legs and editorializes. Sometimes, as though to refute the image of the catfish as redneck poster fish, he visits a literary figure, including Wendell Berry (who doesn't quite seem to get it) and John Graves (who does).

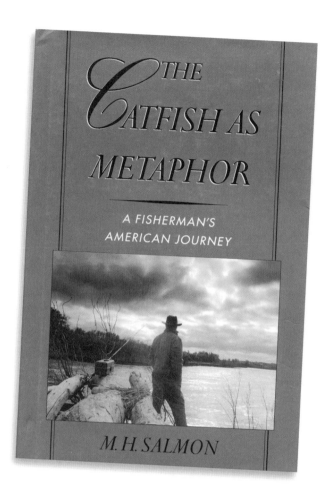

Vivid characters inhabit the passing landscape: a hunter-gatherer former clinical psychologist who poaches fox squirrels in Oklahoma roadside rest stops, using a cut-down .22; the prosperous publishers of *In-Fisherman*. (The editor of that high-tech, big-buck magazine predicts an imminent status jump for catfish because people spend so much on them. Much as I love catfish, I think not—money and social standing are mysterious, bound up with notions of "class" we do our best to ignore.)

Salmon's occasional outbursts are shrewd, and pointed. Describing a Texas friend who pays less attention to boundaries than he might, he says that if "'conservatives' succeed in privatizing public lands, or the neo-Puritans succeed in outlawing sport, poaching will become a game that many more will play."

Still, his mood is lighthearted, the narrator cheerful even when he's combative. But from time to time, something evokes memories of his mentor, his late father, and he broods on Bud's ultimate fate. Nearing home, he obliquely hints at his end in a chilling, almost casual aside: "I don't believe my father ever hunted after that. He still loved to fish though. And he had one shot left."

Like Salmon, many men of the postwar generation missed a workaholic father's guidance in the field. Some of us sought other models. Almost home, Salmon cuts through Texas to visit John Graves, as good a "trees in it" writer (chapter 60, *The Last Running*) as has ever been ignored in this country. Graves is implacably modest and self-deprecating about his great *Goodbye to a River,* telling Dutch, "It's very difficult to transcend to a larger scope when writing about hunting and fishing . . . I've never been able to do that."

I must for once disagree with Graves. Salmon elucidates: "I suspect the author meant that he never set out to write a book about hunting and fishing; he intended to write a magazine story about a river trip that took on a literary life of its own and became something more, and, as will happen when a countryman writes a book, hunting and fishing were quite naturally part of it. It seems that most of the best hunting and fishing books are written much the same way—hunting and fishing as a metaphorical place from which to view our life and times; "sport" as an access to the eternal verities of the natural world."

What he said! People ask what "Metaphor" in Salmon's title points to. Isn't it obvious?

ALSO READ:

M. H. Salmon's *Gazehounds and Coursing, Gila Descending, Tales of the Chase,* and *Home is the River*

Goodbye to a River and *Hard Scrabble,* by John Graves

CHAPTER 26

Rare and Unusual Fly Tying Materials: A Natural History
by Paul Schmookler and Ingrid Sils
1994

If you see the Great Argus pheasant in the Harvard Museum, you won't soon forget it. It crouches like an alien peacock in full display; it is adorned with four-foot wing covert feathers, held erect past vertical and spread into a fan wider than you can span with your arms and stretching up taller than your head. Each shaft is studded with a line of half inch circles that look like embedded ball bearings, even to their countershading. It is impossible to believe they are not three-dimensional; it will exercise your mind to ponder how and why evolution would shape such a thing. The Argus seems a creature from an invented planet, a world more baroque than ours.

If your first thought upon seeing this shockingly beautiful and odd being is something on the lines of "Those feathers would make a *really* good addition to a traditional Atlantic salmon fly," you are surely in *Rare and Unusual*'s intended audience; there is even an Argus feather on the back cover. If you don't, but you love the bird, you still might well covet this astonishing book.

Any library of field sport that pretends to breadth must have some books on artificial flies. We cannot enact all the adventures covered here, but we can all admire, hold, perhaps even tie a fly. I have no interest in covering how-to-tie books, no matter how historic or important; luckily there are other kinds of fly books. Frank Mele, musician and master of the esthetics of hackle, has written a unique tribute to hackle (noted elsewhere in this book). And then we have this baroque . . . object. Schmookler's Victorian subtitle is actually a good description of its contents rather than a mere advertisement. It is also so long I will only bother to quote part of it: "treating both standard and rare materials, their sources and geography . . . displayed in photographs and in the paintings and engravings of history's greatest ornithological illustrators."

This is physically the biggest book I will cover, and may have been the most expensive at first printing. If you can find one, it's worth it, because

it is a monster, a magnificent anachronistic throwback. Schmookler harks
back to the late nineteenth century's golden age of natural history collectors, sporting innovation, and fine natural history books. During those years,
scholars of private means like Sir Walter Rothschild dispatched their collectors to the far corners of the globe to stock private museums like Rothschild's

Tring. Painters like Joseph Wolf and John Gould depicted their specimens in romantic settings. And inevitably the empire's master fly tyers incorporated the feathers of such specimens into their traditional attractor patterns for Atlantic salmon; no hatch-matching here.

Today a few obsessed naturalist-esthetes haunt auctions of such Edwardian memorabilia, notably the painters Raymond Ching and Erroll Fuller, and the artistic fly tyer and author of this book, Schmookler. In it he combines his daunting knowledge of salmon fly history, zoology, and nineteenth-century art with the ability not only to tie the gorgeous flies to his own interpretations, but also to photograph them attractively. Thus the skin of the spangled cotinga, a turquoise-and-black songbird from South America, stands across from a display of flies using its feathers and the loose feathers themselves, framed by a native turquoise necklace that mirrors its color. The full-page painting by Joseph Wolf of a western tragopan, surely a contender for the most beautiful bird in the world, faces a plate of a fly using its spotted feathers like traditional jungle-fowl "eyes," framed by glistening morpho butterflies. And, of course, the Argus is there, represented by no fewer than six proprietary flies.

Some people react in horror to this book and its paler imitators, hinting that Schmookler and his ilk probably hired narcotraficantes to kill the last imperial woodpeckers for flies, or used hackle from the legally extinct Spix's macaw because it is a nice shining blue. That's a slander; the birds whose feathers are used here mostly died more than a century ago. Better to think of creations made from rare and unusual fly-tying materials as resurrected dinosaurs, reborn in an artist's imagination, a vivid reminder of how things were not that long ago.

ALSO READ:

Schmookler and Sils's other volumes: *Rare and Unusual Fly Tying Materials: A Natural History—Volume Two, Birds and Mammals* and *The Salmon Flies of Major John Popkin Traherne*

Also see art books by Erroll Fuller and Raymond Harris Ching

CHAPTER 27

Thy Rod and Thy Creel

by Odell Shepard

1930

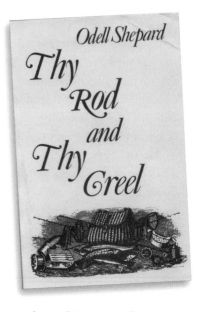

When, years ago, I first heard of this little book, it was through the praise of some serious people—Arnold Gingrich and William Humphrey, both represented here, to name two—and I wondered if such a slender, badly named essay could live up to its reputation. Shepard himself admits early on that anyone who presumed to write about such a subject as angling—in 1930!—must be "equipped either with an extraordinary knowledge of the sport, such as only a lifetime by the streamside can now give, or else with an equally phenomenal ignorance of what has been written before him." But *Thy Rod and Thy Creel,* despite its terrible title, is everything its admirers claim: perhaps the best definition and distillation of what angling (and sport and play) should always be. Whether examining the influence of childhood's memories on one's appreciation of nature or cheerfully defending fishermen against charges of laziness and "cruelty" (here what he says is even more apropos today than when he wrote it), Shepard blends scholarship, humor, and quiet wisdom. This is not a book with mere "detachable quotes" embedded in a mass of pedestrian prose; every line should be read, and it's *all* quotable. How's this for a perfect description of the angler? "Standing in one element he invades another, striving to search it thoroughly. With a fifty-foot finger of bamboo and silk and gut he probes the deeps and the shallows, feels among the riffles, glides slowly out into bays of glitter, striving toward and almost attaining a sixth sense, trying to surprise the water's innermost secret law." *Thy Rod and Thy Creel* remains an essential minor classic and an absolute must-read, eleven on a scale of ten.

CHAPTER 28

The Way of a Trout with a Fly
by G. E. M. Skues
1921

Skues's *The Way of a Trout* is a rare phenomenon: an acknowledged sporting classic that is fun to read. (I might say, "unlike X, Y, Z . . ." but I'd rather praise the good.) Suffice to say that I looked over a bunch of "classics" for every one that made the cut. In *Blood Knots,* Luke Jennings makes a slightly tongue-in cheek contrast between the caustic, aphoristic, pragmatic wit of Skues and the rigid idealism of Halford. Though as a romantic one can appreciate Halford's high standards, his perfectionism is icy, while Skues is a delight to read, and I suspect was fun to fish with.

How could you not love a book that begins with the statement, "Authority darkens council . . ." and continues, "An authority is a person engaged in the invidious business of stereotyping and disseminating information, frequently incorrect . . ."? And then goes on to elaborate in a sentence that, like the ones above, can stand alone: "An authority who lays down the law and dogmatizes is a narcotic, a soporific, a stupefier, an opiate." Skues's works are chains of epigrams, strung end to end.

His impatience with pomposity would amuse outside of trout fishing circles. Mocking a certain "learned German Professor" who wrote a fatuous

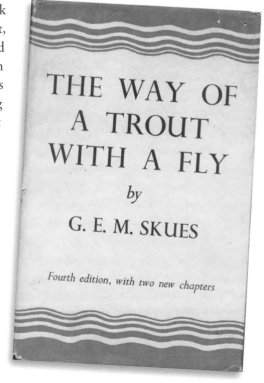

THE WAY OF
A TROUT
WITH A FLY
by
G. E. M. SKUES

Fourth edition, with two new chapters

essay on "Fish and Freewill," he paraphrases the Herr Doktor's argument: "Has a fish no option when it takes a fly? None, *when the temptation is irresistible.*" He inevitably sees the naked emperor. To those who enthuse about the discernment of fish, he opines, deadpan, that the trout is "rather a stupid person." His language even outside of these bon mots is irresistible. Listing the reasons that a trout might take a fly, he progresses through hunger and curiosity to "tyranny."

The bulk of the book is more analytical than aphoristic, though still endlessly entertaining and replete with wry, deadpan phrases. His sensible observations provide a template that could benefit any serious trout angler-fisherman anywhere. Though he wrote in a different time, his analysis of such things as what he calls "gut [i.e., leader] -shyness, which is *sheer sophistication,*" has a rueful relevance to anyone who has fished for endlessly released fish on, say, the Madison. Skues is such an entertaining and honest writer that even his most technical exegeses are entertaining. *The Way of a Trout* is a rare thing, a detailed manual for hard-core anglers that is also a delight for the dilettante or even the non-angler.

Amusing bonus point: The frontispiece is a color plate of Blue Dun flies, demonstrating that a sane man and a mad enthusiast (see Frank Mele's *Small in the Eye of a River*) can share a fascination.

CHAPTER 29

River Monsters
by Jeremy Wade
2011

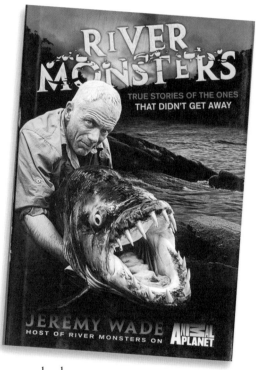

Yes, this book is loosely connected to the "reality" show of the same name on Animal Planet; it's also safe to say that Wade, a biologist and utterly obsessed fisherman as well as a writer, became a TV personality only by accident. An unlikely string of coincidences, starting with a blurry photograph on one of his self-funded shoestring expeditions to catch monster fish, caught the attention of BBC producers, and the rest is history.

Wade is of that self-selected group who has determinedly "ruined their lives for sport"; like some of us, he has made a precarious living from it. He first appeared in a wonderful self-published book, co-authored with his friend Paul Boote, called *Somewhere Down the Crazy River: Journeys in Search of Giant Fish.* Two fish bums go to India chasing the legend of the mahseer, then to the Congo in search of the even more legendary goliath tigerfish. It was a quandary which book to pick for this compilation, but *Crazy River* is hard to find and expensive, and I came down on the side of *River Monsters.*

The book seamlessly welds travel writing, good natural history, genuine sport fishing, and just a whiff of cryptozoology. Literary fishing writing tends toward fly fishing for pretty fish—a class thing? Coarse fishing for monsters often bends the other way, celebrating size and machismo. *River Monsters* avoids both clichés; neither redneck nor fashionable, it revels in the strange, the primitive, the remote, even the dangerous, enlivened by a zoologist's curiosity and a proper fisherman's respect. Wade's quarries include monstrous Indian catfish, alligator gars, freshwater sharks and stingrays, and the legendary wels of Eurasia, with side forays to examine such horrors as piranhas and the candiru. It is worth noting that he releases most of his quarry as conscientiously as a dry-fly fisherman on a spring creek. And as a proper travel writer, Wade celebrates the various people he meets on the way; he is not just some rich guy segregated in a lodge.

If, like me, you have watched the TV show and been maddened by its recapitulation of everything that has gone before at the beginning of every ten-minute segment, you might be inclined to avoid the book. Have no fear. For readers the main function of the show was to get Wade where he was going; Monsters-the-Book stands alone on its own legs, a perfectly coherent narrative with no repetition whatsoever and a hell of a lot more narrative and information than the visually entertaining but often maddening program, and has good enough descriptions that you can visualize an arapaima without ever having seen one.

Let me leave you with his apologia for not just the book but, perhaps, the fisher's life:

Casting a line into the water is like asking a question. Something could be right underneath you, but you can't see it—it's there but not there. And sometimes only a line will make it real, despite the odds against this happening being very long. After hanging limp and lifeless—maybe for hours or days or weeks or years—it will twitch and run, and the cane or carbon-fiber in your hands will bend like a divining rod. Then, if your gear and nerves are sound, you will bring something out into the light, seemingly from nowhere, from another dimension. When this happens, it has an element of magic to it, like pulling a rabbit from a hat.

ALSO READ:
Somewhere Down the Crazy River, by Paul Boote and Jeremy Wade

CHAPTER 30

The Compleat Angler
by Izaak Walton
1655

"a miserable old plagiarist . . ."

—G. E. M. Skues

"The palm of originality, and of an exquisite simplicity which cannot, perhaps, be imitated with entire success, must remain with our worthy patriarch, Izaac."

—Sir Walter Scott

"one of the most joyous pastorales even composed in any language."

—Arnold Gingrich

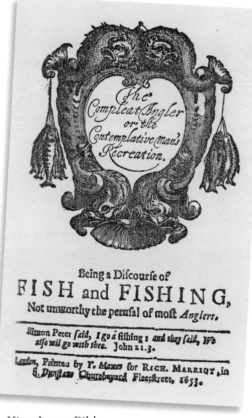

In relation to angling, Walton stands like a monolith, our slightly disreputable Shakespeare or King James Bible. He must be dealt with, but there is already enough commentary to fill a book longer than this one, and you can find it anywhere, even in English departments.

So just a few things: If you get past his archaic Cavalier's English, he's a surprisingly good read, light and wry rather than ponderous. My opinion probably lies closest to Gingrich's.

A quote? Sure, here's one on falconry, as his fisherman Piscator debates the merits of his sport with hunter Venator and falconer Auceps, who says:

> *. . . her mettle makes her careless of danger; for she then heeds nothing, but makes her nimble pinions cut the fluid air, and so makes her high way over the steepest mountains and deepest rivers, and in her glorious career looks with contempt upon those high steeples and magnificent palaces which we adore and wonder at; from which height I can make her to descend by a word from my mouth, which she both knows and obeys, to accept of meat from my hand, to own me for her master, to go home with me, and be willing the next day to afford me the like recreation.*

Walton is available in literally hundreds of editions, from cheap paperbacks to hundred-year-old facsimiles of the original that are themselves "collectible." Any sporting library must have it; do yourself a favor and get a nice one.

Part 2

WINGSHOOTING

"If a bird falls, it is like being able to bring back a token from a dream."

—VANCE BOURJAILY

CHAPTER 31

Manka the Sky Gipsy
by B. B. (Denys J. Watkins-Pitchford)
1939

As I began to write this piece, I realized that Denys Watkins-Pitchford, in his alter-ego "B. B." (as in the shot size), wrote more good books than anyone else in this book; I don't have a bibliography, but his books could well run to over fifty under both or either name. A mild confusion results from which name he was using to write or to illustrate; the later books are usually written by B. B. and illustrated by Watkins-Pitchford, but I believe some reversed the formula and some used both. Just to confuse the matter: in *Manka,* which is perhaps his quintessential book, the cover says "Written & Illustrated by Denys Watkins-Pitchford (B. B.). And of course there are all the books he illustrated for others . . . collectors beware!

B. B. was a late Edwardian who died in 1990. He was an artist (the last genius of scratchboard and woodblock print), a country gentleman, a cheerful naturalist, a breeder and collector of England's butterflies, a carp fisher, and a wildfowler. Though the last was his ruling sporting passion, he probably tried everything else. With such an output (and amazingly, I have never seen a bad book by him), choosing a work was even more difficult than usual. His two companion wildfowling books, *Tides Ending* (1950) and *Dark Estuary* (1953), both of which have watercolors in addition to his classic black-and-white illustrations, and his 1948 *Shooting Man's Bedside Book,* would all be contenders for this section, and his carp fishing book and his biography of a fox would fit in the other two sections. And those are just the few that I have read.

But I have settled on *Manka,* for real and arbitrary reasons. First, he was a natural storyteller whose greatest passion in life was wildfowling. He had the novelist's ability to enter the minds of both the passionate wildfowler and his elusive migratory quarry. In crowded Britain in particular, coastal wildfowling may be the last refuge of the romantic sportsman and lover of the wild; as in my native New England, the edges of the land are also the edges of the

great wilderness. The air above them is inhabited at certain times by creatures who acknowledge no boundaries, and whose migrations span the hemi-
spheres. Add to this the archaic firearms of the British fowler, where 8- and
even 4-bores, all built before World War II, are still not just allowed but cov-
eted, and you have the makings of a perfect sport for the lonely individualist.

B. B. shot an old hammer 8 until age reduced him to a 16-bore (still a
quirky choice). He shot avidly but sanely all his life, although he, like T. H.
White, probably identified more with the birds than with their predators.
This set of mixed loyalties, both passionately held, drives the stark tale of a
freak white pink-footed goose, hatched in Spitzbergen and wintering on the
East Anglia marshes, and his pursuer, the wildfowler "Foxy" Fordham. The

goose is elemental, and unlike many chroniclers of the lives of animals, B. B. does not claim to understand the workings of his mind; Foxy, a professional fowler and sometime poacher, may not be the most admirable character, but he is a skilled hunter who, like his quarry, strives to survive.

Their conflict is eternal and fated, almost mythical; B. B. tells it well even as you sense it unfolding toward a foreordained end. Along the way you will learn more about migrant wildfowl and the habits of old-time fowlers than from any other book I know. But what lifts this book into the rank of extraordinary are the best illustrations I think Watkins-Pitchford ever did, and what might be the best cover I know on any hunting book ever. If I were to compile a list of twenty-five books that delight me *as books,* with both words that please and beauty, an early edition of *Manka* with good paper and a dust jacket would make the cut (it was first published in 1939). That dust jacket shows a V of geese rising from lower left to upper right, the lower birds' black silhouettes against a towering white cloud, the white leading bird rising above it into a black sky just before it flies off into the *G* of Gipsy in the top type band. (The illustration only appears on the jacket.) Of the endless interior illustrations and plates, I would choose the one of Foxy peering over a bank with his big gun, a plate called "Heading North in the Spring," which is a sort of negative of the cover, and the remarkable dark landscape of Little Loch Niver with its black mountain and mirrored pool below. If you can find an old one like mine, get it, but even a paperback will make a good introduction to B. B.'s work. Beware some cheap editions of B. B.—I have not seen a bad one of *Manka*—with muddy contrast between the black and white. Once you have acquired one, you will want more.

ALSO READ:
B. B.'s *The Shooting Man's Bedside Book, The Carp Fisherman's Book, Tide's Ending, Dark Estuary, Wild Lone: the Story of a Pytchley Fox*
Morning Flight, by Peter Scott

CHAPTER 32

Pheasant Jungles
by William Beebe
1927

Will Beebe seems to be little-read today, though I don't know why. He was a scientist-generalist, an expert on birds and fish, and a student of everything, a popular writer who wrote twenty-one books and countless articles. He lived a life of improbable adventure in Asia, Central America, on and under the sea, and (quite socially) in New York City; fought in World War I and against poison arrow–shooting crossbowmen in Burma; descended in the "bathysphere" to deeper than anyone had yet ventured; shot flying fish from the bows of his launch with his 28-gauge Parker; and was a friend of Theodore Roosevelt's. He survived, still writing, into the 1960s, when as a youngster I read his new articles in *National Geographic*.

His most lasting accomplishment may be his *Monograph of the Pheasants*. Its genesis sounds more like something out of a movie's idea of a scientific expedition than a real one. Just after World War I, the Museum of Natural History in New York and Anthony Kuser, a wealthy patron, gave Beebe seventeen months leave of absence to study all the known species of pheasants in the field. He visited twenty countries, from Ceylon (now Sri Lanka) to China, and roamed through habitats from the low river jungles of Borneo to the freezing ridges of the Himalayas. If any naturalist has ever been given a better assignment, its existence escapes me!

His epic journey produced two books: the scientific monograph, later reprinted in abridged editions as *Pheasants, Their Lives and Homes,* and the amazing *Pheasant Jungles,* a journalistic account (portions were published in *Harper's* and *The Atlantic*).

Jungles is Indiana Jones meets ornithology. *Pheasants,* not quite as wild, is one of the last monographs written as though a general reader might care to see through the traveler's eyes. (I am too hard on the modern zoologist. It's a sad fact of life that rare species disappear behind impenetrable political walls. The contemporary ornithologist who did a recent survey of the pheasants

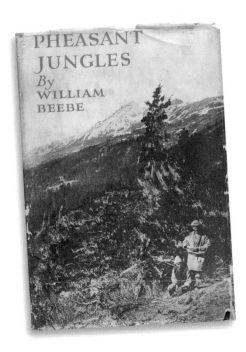

didn't have millionaire patrons and couldn't get into northern Burma or the troubled northeastern states of India, to name two places that Beebe could easily go; others have lost their wildlife.) Still, the gradual divergence of travel writing and science—we won't even talk about sporting writing!—happened only partly because of such causes. The real problem is that we've lost such generalists as Beebe.

The style is wonderful. Beebe is a more leisurely writer than most today, but not a fussy Edwardian one. Here's a short scene from the Himalayas on a cold April morning:

> *I started again on my laborious upward climb, but scarcely had I ascended a hundred feet when the cold, clammy hand of the blue mist was laid upon me, the birds swirled away, the sun blotted from view, and I shivered in the bitter dampness. I rested, panting from my exertions in the rarefied air. A black, shapeless shadow lay among the stunted bamboo above me, and when I reached it I found a cock Impeyan Pheasant, lying breast upward, dead, among the fire and rhododendron slopes which had been his home. The dreariness of the surroundings seemed enhanced; the great mountains seemed cruel; the cold winds more biting than before.*

I examined the bird and found several great talon marks where some great bird of prey had struck and then, for unknown reasons, relinquished its victim. I slung the bird over my shoulder—a cuirass of burnished metallic hues. The next surprise waited for the scene to be shifted over a ridge, five minutes later, when the sun had broken through again, and far below me a spotted dove was cooing out its soul for the very joy of life. Between two titanic halves of split rock came a sudden rustle of great wings, and swiftly there flapped away on laboring pinions a golden eagle, and vanished beyond the sky's lacery of fir needles. I went directly to the spot from which he had risen, and there found another tragedy—a cat-bear, whose fur of richest foxy red was blowing thistle-like over the moss. The great bird of prey had made two kills in quick succession. Of one I robbed him, but the other I left as I found it. In the bewildering turns of the wheel of life, one's sympathy knows not where to abide; should I be sorry for the splendid cock pheasant cut down in the full spring time, or for the harmless little cat-bear, upon which death swooped so suddenly while it was innocently grubbing for roots? Or why not be glad for the appeased hunger of the helpless eaglets in their distant eyrie.

All this and much more: glimpses of places and birds nearly vanished, of societies now altered or hidden behind impenetrable walls; the definitive collection of pheasants, all shot with a gentleman's double guns. And where else might you find such a caption as this deadpan classic? "The shooter of poisoned arrows—from the hillside just behind, he shot at us for three nights. The evening following this photograph I shot and killed him." *Autre temps . . .*

ALSO READ:
The Far Ridges by J. K. Stanford, an account of the Vernay-Cutting scientific expedition to northern Burma. Suydam Cutting was a friend of Beebe's and Theodore Roosevelt's, and a big game hunter and writer about it (*The Fire Ox*); J. K. Stanford was a well-known English ornithologist, novelist, sporting writer, and bird shooter (*No Sportsman at All, Mixed Bagmen, Bledgrave Hall, A Bewilderment of Birds*).

CHAPTER 33

The Unnatural Enemy
by Vance Bourjaily
1963

It is important that you know that *The Unnatural Enemy* first came out in 1963, because although its essence is timeless, it might not exist in the form that it does were it not for a fortuitous convergence of disparate forces. Which is to say: It is a book about bird hunting, a large part of which appeared in the *New Yorker,* which is illustrated by the impeccably urban David Levine and haunted by Hemingway's brand-new ghost, and the publishers seem to think the reader will find all of this perfectly normal.

Vance Bourjaily, who died in 2010, was one of the best of the post–World War II literary novelists. His star is in eclipse, I hope temporarily. Although he spent the requisite time in New York, his long residence in Iowa and his embrace of hunting and "Country Matters" (a rude Shakespearean pun and a phrase that is also the title of another of his good books), along with his unself-conscious masculinity, make him a little unfashionable at the moment.

Bourjaily ran the Iowa Writer's Workshop in its formative years and contributed regularly to the *New Yorker* and *Esquire.* The heyday of his nonfiction writing coincided with the rise of New Journalism. In the early and mid-1960s, Tom Wolfe and Jimmy Breslin and Gay Talese were in the ascendant, followed by Hunter S. Thompson and, a little later, at Pat Ryan's *Sports Illustrated,* Bob Jones and Harrison and McGuane and all the other sporting esthetes with rods and guns. Whether the adjective "New" implied anything not done before by Hemingway or even Ruark, I will leave to more intellectual critics than I aspire to be. But there was a hell of a lot of good writing going on.

In those years Bourjaily was in the thick of things. He was not just running the best-known writer's workshop and contributing to all the glossy magazines out of New York; he was writing good novels with Iowa and sports as settings and themes. See his baggy, ambitious, overstuffed *Now Playing at*

Canterbury, which is ostensibly about the staging of a new opera at an Iowa university told through the viewpoints of its multiple characters, but contains not only a canny understanding of music and stage but also hunting tales, a lame attempt at a graphic novel without graphics, a playlet about insurance fraud and a hidden Purdey, and a genuinely terrifying horror story about man-eating house cats. Or try *Brill Among the Ruins,* which opens with the titular hero, a liberal country lawyer, nearly drowning while shooting ducks from a boat with a 28-gauge Model 21 (how I found out that Winchester made a 28-gauge) and veers into extramarital affairs and the Biafran War.

The Unnatural Enemy is both one of the best literary bird-shooting books in English and the last time such a book was produced by the literary establishment. The recent discovery of hunting by California and New York foodies and a startling rise of interest in hunting by the latest generation of adults of both sexes give me some hope for the distant future, but I don't think the time is yet ripe for a fortyish well-known writer of any sex who writes for the *New Yorker* and, say, *The Atlantic* (we won't even mention the current men's fashion rags) to produce a book about hunting illustrated by Walton Ford—which would be the nearest equivalent.

Given the difference that fifty years makes, you may be relieved to know that *The Unnatural Enemy* reads like a contemporary work. Bourjaily's first essay is on literary influences, hunting and non-hunting; veers through a falconry scene (a good one, difficult to pull off); touches on Haig-Brown, Thoreau, *The Master of Game;* deals uneasily with Hemingway's grumpy attitudes in *Green Hills;* admires Turgenev; and nods to non-hunter Nathaniel West. It is a writer's chapter. The rest are hunters' chapters and deal with problematical and unappealing hunters on the one hand and the best of bird hunting on the other. No need for quotes on the first kind here, but it is worthwhile to note that kindly Bourjaily understands the humanity of even the worst oafs and does not indulge in the lazy common practice of building his image at their expense.

And the good stuff is wonderful.

If one of the people who object to hunting were to accuse me of relishing death, I would have to admit that the most deeply felt moment in wing shooting comes not with the flight of the bird nor with its fall. The moment comes for me when, after missed shots and missed opportunities, I hold at last the extraordinary beauty, still almost alive, of a bird I have just killed. I wonder if the whole wild patterning and color of Oriental ornament wasn't learned from the red, white, lavender, and rose of a cock pheasant, this exotically barred and whorled cousin of the peacock now improbably at home in our cornfields. The forthright green head of the mallard drake, the softly mottled breast of the duck, the formal delicacy of a bobwhite quail—when my dog has offered such a prize to my hand, one of the things that makes me a hunter is intensely satisfied.

Bourjaily rents a goose pit and hunts at home and in an odd moment goes to Uruguay to shoot tinamou. He spends an entire chapter dealing with the mildly uncomfortable matter of crow shooting, the essay from which he derives the book's title. (Even this is not a solemn, guilty essay; there is an amusing aside about his kids using crow decoys for toys.)

In the end, this best of modern bird-hunting books embodies an odd autumnal mood I sometimes associate with the years of its genesis. It is a celebration but a melancholy, thoughtful, brooding one. Bourjaily, though a countryman, is finally an exemplary modern intellectual. He hunts every-thing edible and some things that are not, and worries about it. He is puz-zled by Turgenev's innocent blood lust, tries to blame Hemingway for being callous but is finally too honest, loves to eat squirrels but finds them even harder to shoot than birds. He puzzles over his emotions, wondering why he continues to shoot birds while his "feeling towards the same bird or animal, seen while I am not hunting it, is an almost perfect love"; adding, "We grow up with more sensitivity than we can possibly use, and must, but the time we finish growing, learn that you can never stop and think or it will break your heart."

As far as I know, Vance Bourjaily never stopped hunting. His work is still worthy of attention. The particulars of his ambivalent musings on rue and joy are rooted in his time, but the themes and emotions are universal, as modern and as ancient as the fading images in a classical Chinese poem.

ALSO READ:
Vance Bourjaily's *Now Playing at Canterbury, Brill Among the Ruins,* and *Country Matters*

CHAPTER 34

The Tattered Autumn Sky
by Tom Davis
2004

When we were iconoclastic young writers, John Barsness, Tom McIntyre, and I used to have fun with the conventions of our field. We made up subgenres within the sporting field; allegedly my personal specialty was "hunting with house pets." But we all agreed that there was a venerable and often abused tradition we called, "I knew an old dog that died." The magazines used to be full of them.

We were young and unfair. Years later, discussing writing in general, John said something wiser. I had been holding forth against sentimentality; John thought I was being too harsh. "You shouldn't *commit* sentimentality, but you should *dare* sentimentality. You've gotta get close to the edge, or you risk nothing . . ."

A lot of the so-called classics of upland bird writing are nakedly sentimental, going for the easy emotion. It is no accident that critics make comparisons between sentimentality and pornography. Sadly, this is even more prevalent in southern bird dog writing; sadly, because the best of the tradition also comes from the South. (See Chapter 38, Caroline Gordon.)

Tom Davis is a bird dog man of my generation, a midwesterner of southern descent, a classicist by nature and education, who knows and lives the tradition but does not imitate it, who dares sentimentality but does not fall over the edge. Dogs win, lose, and die in his fiction and essays as in life, but the emotions he evokes are more complicated than a maudlin, easy, alcoholic tear. I selected one of the stories in this book, "Blood," for an earlier anthology. It is about the death of a dog, and it may put a lump in your throat, but it is not simple. In that anthology I called its protagonist "a sort of dark genius of a dog, a hero with a flaw." No poetic license meant; sooner or later every serious dog breeder knows, loves, and mourns such a beast.

Davis celebrates the mortal beauty of our upland sport, our canine partners, and the fleeting glories of fall. He knows—and demonstrates, more sanely than George Bird Evans and his "Head of a God"—that there is something almost beyond speech embodied in the best dogs; it is why we hunt this way.

And what Emmy did on that gray afternoon, when the wind had winter on its breath, was like salvation, a return to grace, the finding of something feared lost. She hunted as if on the end of a string, as if I could communicate with her by the force of will alone. Her fire, her élan, her searing love for the hunt shone in every crack of her tail. When she busted a brace of cockbirds, hitting scent too fast to stop, I just smiled; when she danced into a point in the crackling grass below a terrace, and a rooster materialized only to fall at my unconscious shot, I felt I was being pulled by some delicious gravity I could not resist.

I have lingered on dogs, a shared obsession. Know of Davis that he also celebrates the prairies and the sand hills and the indigenous birds of the plains, prairie fires, and prairie chickens. If you love the upland shooting life, get your nose out of those musty old Derrydales and read Tom Davis. There is no one better writing about that life today.

ALSO READ:

Game Bird Shooting, by [then] Captain Charles Askins—Senior, the nice one; written in 1931, it is the last book I know of that does the plains justice before Davis and the North Dakota poet Tim Murphy

CHAPTER 35

The Upland Shooting Life
by George Bird Evans
1971

"There are a given number of days in a lifetime and here at Old Hemlock we try to see that not one of them passes unused. We live a sort of civilized eighteenth-century country life in which there are still values, none of them based on dollars, a life in which the word "spent" means shells . . . my Far Away and Long Ago is Here and Now."

George Bird Evans was an artist, a romantic, a fanatic, and a happy man. Many of us have fantasy lives; George and his wife, Kay, created a real, not virtual, private world around their home, Old Hemlock, in West Virginia, and its surrounding grouse and woodcock coverts, his dogs, and his guns— life as a work of art. At the height of his powers he wrote this book; though he wrote many more, everything came together perfectly in *The Upland Shooting Life,* a book that could inspire anyone to want a loyal companion, a little house surrounded by giant old trees, a Belton setter with a noble skull, and an heirloom Purdey.

Of course, by any conventional standard they were mad as hatters, partners in a deliriously happy *folie à deux* that lasted until they were nearly ninety. They were small gods in their tiny world; I once sat amazed in a Massachusetts restaurant watching Kay upbraid an insufficiently attentive waitress with the admonition: "Young lady, don't you know that this is *George Bird Evans?*" (The mutual deification extended further: GBE carved a sandstone bust of his most famous dog, Ruff, and called it "Head of a God.")

Actually, I envy them. Snobs of a sort they may have been, but not simple ones; Dr. Norris's cased Purdey rode in the back of a battered Pinto rather than a Land Rover, and—delightful incongruity—they had zebra-striped wallpaper in their bathroom. I got to handle the fabled Purdey, but George paid as much reverent attention to my 28-gauge AyA sidelock.

Upland Shooting Life is a sane portrait of their just slightly over-the-top life's work. I am particularly taken by his accounts of dogs and guns. On his magnificent setters he begins: "When in 1939 Kay and I moved to Old Hemlock and could keep a gun dog, I was unable to find a type of setter I wanted. The prospect of breeding one to our taste, like custom-building a gun, was a challenge." So he did, and succeeded with his line of working beauties; competitive modern trialers who find the household gods of Old Hemlock "slow" have probably never hunted eastern woodland grouse.

As for guns, "A Gun to Remember" introduced me to the cult of the perfect, sending me on the road to either enlightenment or perdition and teaching me in one inspired lesson what a Best gun could be. I was taken by his insistence that every nuance mattered. "The relation of cheek to stock is so delicate that clenching the teeth will bulge the jaw and push the face away enough to throw the pattern off . . . My stocks are fitted for me to shoot with my mouth ajar—in part, compensating for my amazement at a grouse's flight."

George was obsessed with various esthetics of beauty—those of birds, of dogs, of guns, of art—throughout his long life. He started out as a commercial artist, doing magazine and fashion illustration in New York. The cover illustrations for his pseudonymous mystery *Hawk Watch* (by "Brandon Bird"; not bad despite its villainous eagle) bear fascinating resemblance to the fashion advertisements that my mother did in the same era. His distinctive, lively ink drawings of dogs and birds, hundreds scattered through decades of pages, make you want to own his books even before you read them.

I fell out a bit with George in the end; he would not accept the fact that when my finances were destroyed by disasters beyond my control I had to sell my guns and library and start again. More practical by nature, I could never have lived up to his code, but I'm glad somebody did; his demanding standards, though hard on others, led him to create many good sporting books and one perfect one. *The Upland Shooting Life*, with Chuck Fergus's less "elevated" *A Rough-Shooting Dog* (just a little more rooted in the real world) are the first two books I would give to any aspiring bird-dogger.

CHAPTER 36

A Rough-Shooting Dog: Reflections from Thick and Uncivil Sorts of Places

by Charles Fergus

1991

There are plenty of how-to dog books, and old magazines are full of sentimental dog stories. But even in a packed field one may find a work that stands above all the rest. Charles Fergus's *A Rough-Shooting Dog: Reflections from Thick and Uncivil Sorts of Places* is the best all-around book about life with a bird dog yet from the post–World War II years. It is "the unabashed record of a fine writer's love affair with his dog." But no cheap sentimentality here: *Rough-Shooting Dog* is simply one of the best descriptions I have ever read of what it means to pick, train, work, and fall in love with a bird dog.

Fergus's insights begin with the implications of his title. In England, a rough shoot is one where one walks up and shoots at a mixed bag of game; in other words, pretty much the way you would describe the typical American's day out with a gun and dog. Fergus adds a sense of the rugged Pennsylvania uplands where he hunts, where the versatile springer spaniel fits well, even as it does in England or New Mexico, and reminds those who need reminding that first-rate upland dogs include more than the pointing breeds.*

He begins his book by choosing Jenny ("I sensed I was on the verge of a new life. But on that clear August evening I did not know how different my life would become, or how this dog would renew and repair it."). He strikes, I think, the right note here—choosing a pup is both fun and, if you are a serious bird hunter and dog man, as opposed to keeping a hunting machine in a kennel, "as serious as a heart attack" as they say out here. The choice you make irrevocably alters your life.

---

* Having spent nearly thirty years with springers and having hunted behind several good pointing dogs owned by friends like Eric Wilcox and the late Datus Proper, I refuse to take sides; I love both kinds of dogs, and books. In Maine in 1987, Eric and I would go out for a woodcock day with one of each. Besides, I now hunt quail with an Asian saluki who impersonates a bird dog whenever I pick up a gun.

He then details his early training of the pup, making the point that he didn't acquire a dog until he could give it "the attention it deserved." Fergus laces his commentary with portraits of his country and its people and speech, shows us his roots, and meditates on professional training. Jenny was apparently so good that she could have, with proper coaching, become a field trial champion, a dog that could at that time sell for at least $2,000; "too good" (in the words of a training pro) "for just a hunter." Fergus broods, and comes up with the right answer: "*Too good for a hunter?*"

"A hunter should have the best. He owes it to himself, and to the game. He owes it to the dog to let her become what her blood directs her to become; not a player in a stylized game, but a partner, a collaborator, a fellow predator in the fields and thickets, on the trembling, savage ground of the marsh."

Gradually Jenny learns her business. Like most springers and their partners, Jenny and Fergus go after everything. Says Fergus, "I would not wish to exclude any of the species that tempt me afield." Her first kill is a wood duck, though like many Eastern hunters and dogs, Fergus and Jenny spend more time chasing ruffed grouse than any other single species. She excels at everything, going ahead with the fire of the canine star, "the field trial blood, a hot unruly chant. Be fast. Be first. Get the bird."

I know these dogs, hunted with them for many years, and have never seen anyone catch the breed's inspired, obsessive, yet still playful personalities so well. Fergus knows why, more than mere utility, humans hunt with dogs: "At first, I imagine, simply to increase their effectiveness; but later to feel the natural world more completely (even as humans gradually distanced and insulated themselves from its vicissitudes). To retain the identity of a predator by collaborating with one."

He continues his wry and sometimes pointed commentary throughout. Take, for instance, the unbridgeable gap between hunting and preserve shooting: "After one shoot, walking back to the trucks, I heard a customer telling his friend, 'That was a great hunt.' I had to bite my tongue. Because shooting driven pheasants is just that—shooting. It has nothing to do with the hunt."

And so Jenny and Fergus go, through the seasons, with delights and wisdom on every page. The book ends, fittingly, not with a final kill but with the old command "gone away, girl," as a post-season woodcock disappears into the distance. But my own favorite line is much earlier, as he buys a sack of food from a setter snob. Fifteen dollars, the man tells him and "'. . . ninety cents for the Gov'nor.'

"'Tax on dog food?'

"He grinned. 'Gov'nor says dog food is a luxury'. . . he turned his head, his dark eyes glinting. 'Course if you had a setter, we'd consider it a necessity and wouldn't charge any tax.' More laughter from the customers. I grinned back. 'I'd rather have a springer,' I said, 'and pay the tax.'"

ALSO READ:
Modern Pheasant Hunting, by Steve Grooms (more springers)
Hunting from Home, by Chris Camuto

CHAPTER 37

New England Grouse Shooting
by William Harnden Foster

1942

William Harnden Foster invented a sport and wrote a book. The now-popular sport is skeet, then meant to simulate actual bird hunting rather than test the shooter with the less "realistic" challenges of trap and live-pigeon shooting. The unique book, about which I make no pretense of objectivity, is *New England Grouse Shooting*. In my . . . pretty-informed opinion, no single category within a sport has ever had such a perfect celebration.

This is an utterly arrogant statement, so let me deconstruct it a bit. *New England Grouse Shooting* is a lyrical book that attempts to explain and teach every aspect of the so-called Golden Age of "pa'tridge" hunting. Most usages of the term "Golden Age" are anathema to me, referring to some imaginary lost time when men were men (and wore ties and tweeds), guns were doubles, bags were enormous, and . . . well, you get the idea.

But the Golden Age of grouse in New England, and possibly the upper Midwest, was an ecological phenomenon, not a social construct. It refers to the time after the cutting of the pre-Columbian forest when vast tracts of landscape, even whole states, were a mix of farm and brush and second growth and old orchard, and *Bonasa umbellus* thrived in numbers no one may ever see again. I am eternally grateful that I lived in at least the tail end of this almost mythical time.

After an introductory anecdote he calls "The Little Gun," Foster gives us background, describes the present situation, then methodically examines dogs and dog work, guns and loads for hitting birds that flush unexpectedly and then disappear in an instant, how to hit such birds, a reasonable kit for this kind of hunting, and how to shoot. Unlike most of today's manuals, he did not illustrate it with a bunch of crappy photos, but brought his considerable talents as an artist to bear in a profusion of pen and ink illustrations of everything from grouse acting as grouse to recognizable guns you want to own to old Yankees of the type that still hunted the coverts when I was a young man. He achieved the perfect fusion of text and illustration.

I started hunting grouse around 1960 with my father, who demanded that I use a single-shot, tightly choked .410. I never hit a bird with it (he shot a Browning "Sweet Sixteen" humpback autoloader on upland birds and a Model 21 heavy duck double on waterfowl). Somehow he did not make me hate the sport; when I left home at seventeen, I soon acquired my first proper grouse double, an old 20-gauge L. C. Smith field grade, and never looked back. I think I got my passion for doubles from gun writer Roger Barlow, but I'm sure the fascination my friends and I had for the old Yankee guns came straight from Foster, who shot Parkers and illustrated his work with both Parkers and Purdeys. I'm sure I was shaggier than any of his sporting gentlemen, but other than that I followed his advice like holy writ, which was a very good idea. His ideas on gun design and fit, ballistics, how to shoot at creatures who are never visible for more than a few seconds, and just about everything else (and he did think of everything) are as valid today, when good places to hunt grouse are few and far between, as they were in the early 1970s, when I spent more autumn time chasing grouse and the occasional woodcock than I did doing anything else. I know people think of me as a falconer, and I am one, but the first sport I mastered was hunting grouse à la Foster.

Foster may look like an exercise in nostalgia, but his advice is good anywhere anyone hunts birds in woodland habitat and second-growth pasture, and a lot of it works even with western quail.

The book is available in several editions. The 1947 second edition by Scribners is alleged to be the most valuable, but this is a bit of collectorial arcana that need not concern you. They are all good. Beyond its practical and nostalgic virtues, it is a book you can look at and a book that will evoke memories as long as you can see and think.

ALSO READ:
Grouse Feathers, by Burton Spiller

CHAPTER 38

Aleck Maury, Sportsman
by Caroline Gordon
1934

Caroline Gordon's *Aleck Maury* was first recommended to me when I was writing "Bodio's Review" for *Gray's*, first by an ancient shooting Jesuit from the South who had known Gordon and then, before I had read it, by a woman who said, "This is one book that all *Gray's* people should read this year." They were right; a novel in the form of the memoirs of a sometimes classics professor and full-time hunter and fisherman, *Aleck Maury* reads like some inspired mashup of Turgenev and Nash Buckingham. Later, I read an essay on the book by Thomas McGuane in a collection of pieces on "lost classics" that almost gushed: "there are sections of this book which seem to me to have been written by God." Gushing or not, he was right too. *Maury* was one of the best books in that odd collection, and in a less fatuous time would be required reading for every lit major in America.

Caroline Gordon, a novelist often overlooked because neither feminists nor northerners know quite what to make of her, based Maury on her father. But Maury is more than a particular southern gentleman: He is field sport's Everyman. Gunning for quail and dove (with a 14-gauge Greener hammer gun that had been made in London for "a hundred and fifty dollars in gold") or giving up any pretense of bargaining because he has just irrationally fallen in love with a three-legged setter, he is a man in the grip of our common obsessions. Here he considers a job offer at a small college.

> *"Daddy, Mother said tell you if you weren't going fishing this afternoon you ought to answer Uncle Harry's letter. . . ."*
> *I pulled the crumpled letter out of my pocket now and smoothed it out upon my knee, then almost jumped out of my skin when I saw the postmark: "Poplar Bluff, Missouri."*

Colonel Wyndham had mentioned the Black River at Poplar Bluff
as his favorite of all the Ozark streams.
I wired Harry Morrow that afternoon: "Will come Poplar Bluff if
you can give me only morning classes."

Of course, anyone who is single-minded about his passions in a terminally ironic society runs the risk of looking a bit comic. One of the multiple
beauties of this work is that Maury knows that hunting is, in Ortega's sense, a
serious business; it doesn't matter what fools think of you. A hunter's perception teaches you about life and death and makes you intimate with the land
you love; what you learn out there will provide endless delight and solace
despite meager worldly rewards, or tragedy.

Professor Maury's "Last Day in the Field," a coda to his life in the collection *Old Red*, is a last quiet triumph.

I went back and flushed the bird. It went skimming along the buckberry
bushes that covered that side of the swale. In the falling light I could
hardly make it out and I shot too quick. It swerved over the thicket and
I let go with the second barrel. It staggered, then zoomed up. Up, up,
up, over the rim of the hill and above the tallest hickories. I saw it there
for a second, its wings black against the gold light, before, wings spread,
it came whirling down, like an autumn leaf, like the leaves that were
everywhere about us, all over the ground.

McGuane again: "At the age of seventy, exiled among the retirees of the
day, the mystery of nature is, for Maury, utter proof against despair." Hear,
hear! If you don't like this one, I'll buy it back.

ALSO READ:

Old Red and Other Stories, by Caroline Gordon. Not all sporting, but
contains the single best Maury, "Last Day in the Field."

Jaybirds Go To Hell on Friday: The Best of Babcock, by Havilah
Babcock. My favorite of the traditional or "classic" southern bird hunting
writers, with some fishing too.

CHAPTER 39

A Book on Duck Shooting
by Van Campen Heilner
1939

It is easy to pick a definitive book on shooting ruffed grouse; who but William Harnden Foster? Guy de la Valdene nailed the American version of partridge shooting in a much more recent work, and Dutch Salmon wrote the book on catfish. But say *waterfowling* and you evoke a stream with many tributaries; even if you narrow it down to American duck shooting, you are describing a universe. Originally, before I was persuaded to actually accept the idea that one hundred books meant one hundred books, I thought I would recommend three sequential American waterfowl hunting books: Grinnell's *American Duck Shooting*, this Heilner volume, and George Reiger's *Wildfowler's Quest* to bring us up through the present.

I settled (the verb implies more surrender than this good book deserves) on Heilner, not just because it overlaps the earlier and later volumes in time, but because it contains multitudes. Heilner was, like so many writers who did their work for Knopf and Derrydale, a wealthy socialite, but he appears to have known, liked, and enjoyed the company of anyone with a passion for shooting ducks. He recruited an all-star team to create his magnum opus. The handsome plates and decorative black-and-white chapter drawings are by Lynn Bogue Hunt, whose calendars and illustrations dominated the field for decades. The great ornithologist Robert Cushman Murphy contributed the introduction. Joel

Barber, the man who practically invented the study of decoys, contributes a chapter on that subject. H. L. Betten, the best-known bird shooting writer of the West Coast, takes on the subject of boats and blinds.

The geographical range, the cast of characters in the stories, are incredible for a book written in the '30s, when so much sporting writing seemed to run the gamut from Massachusetts to Maryland, adding only a few (Yankee-owned) quail plantations as a sop to the Rebels. Heilner happily visited the Baltic, California, the soon-to-be-famous swamps of Arkansas, Mexico, the fens of East Anglia, darkest Utah, Hungary, and Romania, and provided us with anecdotes and photographs of them all. He even had a photographic portfolio of punt gunning with a youthful Peter Scott. He appears as a character in his own stories and especially photos, always bearing some version of an Ithaca double, a good gun but one that a friend refers to as the "F-150 Ford of old guns."

Heilner seemed at ease everywhere. I said he knew everybody; when I first read him I discovered one passage when a story of long-ago snapped into startling focus for me, as though to prove that theory. Heilner has a chapter about hunting sea ducks in Barnstable, Massachusetts. In it, he begins to describe a youthful hunt "not far north of Duxbury Bay and the Gurnet," with two young men named Frannie and Parker. It was a delightful intrusion of reality, for I recognized those two "young men" as the late grandfather of my first editor at *Gray's Sporting Journal* and the ancient gentleman who was for a time his landlord when Reid and I hunted those same sandbars in the early 1970s.

Reading Heilner is like that: You hunt the various habitats of the United States and the world with a garrulous and knowledgeable host who seems to know everything and wants to make sure that you will too. Add the handsome embossed cover of a Knopf Borzoi, good paper, good illustrations, and good design, and I would submit you have not *A* but *The* duck hunting book.

ALSO READ:
American Duck Shooting, by George Bird Grinnell
The Wildfowler's Quest, by George Reiger
The Eye of the Wind, by Peter Scott

CHAPTER 40

Instructions to Young Sportsmen in All That Relates to Guns and Shooting
by Lt. Col. Peter Hawker
1846

George Bird Evans hated Peter Hawker. He considered him to be a cross between a game hog and a weasel, and he did not like weasels. I find Hawker amusing. Although he was certainly a creature of excess, I see no reason to blame him for his nature. I wrote about Hawker in 1988 in a preface to an excerpt from his *Diaries:* "Hawker lived before bag limits, conservation laws, or specialization. He shot puntguns, worked dogs, and engaged in semi-legal poaching. He may have been a conscienceless killer by today's standards, but his innocent cheerful blood lust reminds me more of a goshawk than of a greedy human." As my old mentor Floyd Mansell said of a mutual acquaintance, "A *good* boy, just a little *primitive.*"

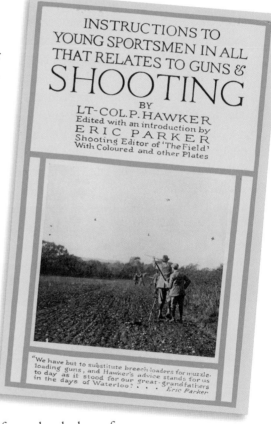

INSTRUCTIONS TO YOUNG SPORTSMEN IN ALL THAT RELATES TO GUNS & SHOOTING
BY
LT-COL.P. HAWKER
Edited with an introduction by ERIC PARKER
Shooting Editor of 'The Field'
With Coloured and other Plates

"We have but to substitute breech loaders for muzzle-loading guns, and Hawker's advice stands for us to day as it stood for our great-grandfathers in the days of Waterloo? . . . *Eric Parker*

Hawker and his contemporary, Col. Thomas Thornton, were medieval relics who lived into Victoria's reign. (Thornton was worse or at least "more." Richer, even more profligate, with a mistress who posed as his wife and his jockey, and more hawks and dogs than an Asian king, he horse-whipped enemies who objected to his betting on said mistress at the races.) Victorian "progress" and the spread of vices like respectability and driven pheasant shooting changed the culture, making the old anachronisms into still-splendid dinosaurs who wrote down tales of braver days.

Hawker was born in London in 1786, shot through fifty-one seasons, and died in 1853. He really was an excessive creature. His diaries document his bags and his joyful poaching expeditions against his neighbors, lunatic raids that could make incredibly funny movies.* But his record of one dog's service stands as an example of the astonishing numbers possible back then. "I killed during this extraordinary dog's service, and almost entirely to him, game, etc., as follows:—Up to 1812, 356; 1813, 244; 1814: 402; 1815: 320; 1816, 378; 1817, 503; 1818, 463; 1819, 253; 1820, 344; to the day of his illness. Total, 3,263 head." Hawker cut his swath on land and sea, shooting guns of all kinds, training dogs, fishing. He was the first writer to my knowledge to champion the first of the great London gun makers, Joe Manton.

Thornton was a grand if unreliable storyteller. Hawker, whose stories might have been even better, was despite his excesses a remarkable teacher. *Instructions* is one of the prime examples of "lyrical shoptalk" in sporting literature. If you read it, it will not only give you a sensory simulacrum of sport in 1814, but you will know how to judge a gun, clean a gun, shoot a period wildfowling gun ("The longer the gun the higher must be the elevation!" he yells), train a dog, prevent rust, explore a pond, run a gunning punt, stalk a curlew, make a bowl of punch ("a wine glass *nearly* full of best refined lump

---

* One of the more dubious pastimes of the shooting gentry in Hawker's time was the "sport" of raiding the preserved grounds of what were thought of as selfish or priggish landowners. If you came in by day and publicly, the only way to make you stop shooting the owner's game was to name you and cite you. Rowdy young officers and squires would organize raids on foe's plantations. From the *Diaries*, "The Raid on Parson Bond's Estate":

> *The confused rector did not know which way to run. The scene of the confusion was ridiculous beyond anything, and the invasion of an army could scarcely exceed the noise. Not a word could be heard from the cries of 'Mark!' 'Dead!' and 'Well done!', interspersed every moment with bang, bang, and the yelping of barrack curs. The parson at last mustered his whole establishment to act as patriots against the marauders. Footboys running one way, ploughmen mounted on cart horses galloping the other, and everyone from the village that could be mustered was collected to repel the mighty shock . . . The parson, having eased himself by vomit, began to speak more coherently . . . Though a large number of pheasants were destroyed, the chase did not end in such aggregate slaughter as we expected, and not more than one-third of those that were brought down were bagged, in consequence of our being afraid to turn out our best dogs; we brought away some of the parson's traps, one of which was a most terrific engine, and now hangs in the mess-room for public exhibition. Only one dog was caught the whole day, and whose should that be but Parson Bond's!*

sugar, *pounded;* twelve ditto of cold spring water; a lime and half a lemon; two wine glasses *brim full* of *old* Jamaica rum"), or a salad for a wildfowler. You will know what the best jacket for shooting is, and why you hold very differently for a shot with one of the old *fourteen-pound* duck guns than with a shorter or lighter weapon.

And more, and worse, as a friend used to say. Very few of the old sportsmen could actually describe guns or their use, or what they actually did with dogs. Hawker could.

The best edition is the one edited by Eric Parker in 1922. It has a mix of period illustrations and good photographs of tools like Hawker's fourteen-pound Manton duck gun with four-foot six-inch barrels, and has plenty of lucid explanatory notes for the modern reader.

You get a sensory grasp of history from Hawker like the one you get reading Patrick O'Brian's best novels, savoring the knowledge that they are real. For *true* illicit eighteenth-century thrills, try the *Diaries,* but read *Instructions* first. You can tell yourself this one's educational.

ALSO READ:
Peter Hawker's Diaries, by Peter Hawker
The Northern Tour, by Colonel Thomas Thornton
The English Squire and His Sport, by Roger Longrigg

CHAPTER 41

Hunter's Log
by Timothy Murphy
2011

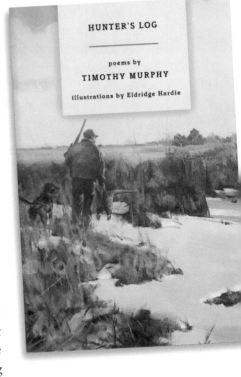

I picked this fine book of poems with some conflict. It is the right book for this collection because it is not only the work of our best poet who hunts but also because it is a book of *hunting* poems, the only contemporary one I know. But anyone who comes to enjoy this collection should look at his other books, especially my favorite, *Set the Ploughshare Deep,* a memoir in poems and prose that is the best book about the northern plains I know, and is also full of hunting.

All dedicated poets are unusual, and Timothy Murphy is unusual among poets. Perhaps the most unusual thing about him is that he is a serious working farmer in a long line of farmers, and a self-described "venture capitalist." He was also a student of Robert Penn Warren and a Scholar of the House in Poetry at Yale. That he could afford to do something else but chooses to farm in our fertile Siberia, and loves its harshness and its beauty, says something essential about his stoic character. I doubt it is an accident that his poems look to classical forms and are full of allusions to the canon. If you read widely in Murphy, you will discover the full traditional range of poetic subjects and preoccupation, which makes it all the more remarkable how many of his poems are about dogs, sport, and animals. He sings about coyotes and roadkills, trout and grouse and geese, chains of life and death, hits and misses, the Red River of the north and the Missouri Breaks. He has a funny poem about a clapped-out shotgun, and a grumpy one about posted land.

But a few themes recur: what he calls in one title "The Soul of the North," its chill and spirit and weather and how it leans and breathes chill into his country; names and themes from Ireland and the classical past; and above all the too-short lives, passionate hearts, incomprehensible skills, and sometimes simple minds of dogs. (Of course these themes can come together quite naturally. He has poems about dogs named Diktynna Thea—"Dee"—and Maud Gonne!)

He writes about dogs as only a dog man can: with love, exasperation, and triumph running neck and neck on a given hunt. He has a whole series of poems on a dog named "Feeney" (for Fenian), starting with training and ranging into old age. Here is a bit of training:

> He won his ribbon. Last night as it grew dark
> I fired the launcher dummy into stubble.
> He strained and barked but made a perfect mark,
> Taking his flawless line. Then ran a double.

Then in his prime:

> Grimly, I ran a quarter mile this morning
> with Feeney grinning ear to ear beside me,
> loping beside the slow man he was scorning,
> Ingrate, had he the stature to deride me?

But Feeney is essence of dog. Of a pheasant he manages to corral:

> Under those drifts out harder hunt began.
> Eluding every cast.
> It burrowed, bolted, ran.
> Until at least Fenian pinned it fast.
> I floundered to a roadside willow stand,
> Collapsing on a log
> Where Feeney licked my hand.
> Unworthy man, behold thy dog.

Poetry is song and its creators sing; excerpts sound lighthearted despite the mortality that surrounds us all. Let me give you a sample of a more serious-*sounding* lyric, in the voice of an owl, with just a little echo of Wallace Stevens:

> *Downward to darkness on my muffled wings*
> *I hunt the wintry silence of a dream*
> *Whose spell is shredded by a rabbit's scream,*
> *The coldest, purest note creation sings.*

I fear that too few hunting readers today pay attention to poetry, words they might come to love. Would it help you to know that Jim Babb, a man of no pretension whatsoever who is also represented in this book, wrote the introduction, calling it *Hunter's Log*. "An invitation into a world far removed from the halls of academia, a permanent hall pass into the corn rows and the sun and the rain and the heat and the cold, forever enlivened by the war of rings, the wet noses of dogs, and the shotgun's delicious blast. . ."? Would it help that the great Eldridge Hardie did the illustrations? Murphy has his farm and his dogs and his poetry, and a whole life, a life like some citizen-farmer in the late Roman Empire. I expect he doesn't need new readers as much as readers need him.

ALSO READ:
Timothy Murphy's *Set the Ploughshare Deep* and *The Deed of Gift*

CHAPTER 42

Pteryplegia: Or, The Art of Shooting Flying
by "Mr." (George) Markland
1931

Pteryplegia, an instructional poem, is the first work about shooting flying birds with a shotgun in English. (The English often prefer to forget that the practice actually started in France.) The edition I recommend holds, so to speak, two places in a sporting library: as a historical and still-sound work of advice on how to shoot, and as an exemplar of the small-press quality book. My copy, and the edition I would recommend, is the Derrydale Press limited edition of 1931.

A little loop here before we go back to its interesting text. While fine-press editions exist of a few of the books I write about here, their only values are monetary and esthetic

(and you had best know something about which ones are good if you want beauty; some of the modern ones achieve both ugliness and low value). I am not in any way a member of the cult of fine books; I am a reader.

But a few presses are worth it if you have the money. Derrydale, established by old Princetonian Eugene V. Connett III in 1927, is one. It was an all-sporting press, and many of the good hunting and fishing writers of the time published there. He recycled many of the fine Penn Press and Knopf titles. By all accounts Connett was an arrant social snob, and Derrydale also published a daunting amount of horsey trivia by his friends, but his best books are often handsome editions of books worth reading.

Currently *Pteryplegia* is only available as a Derrydale or a cheap print-on-demand. I am no Luddite and believe POD can be a good technology, but the cheap, smeared-print editions of post-copyright older works are barely worth the paper. Whereas the Derrydale is a slender, handsome volume with beautiful paper, theoretically limited to only "Five hundred copies, two hundred of which have been coloured by hand."* (Yeah, Connett used the English "coloured" on Park Avenue.) Still, honesty compels me to say that he made a very handsome book, the only Derrydale I currently own.

The poem is only twenty-nine pages long, and if you allow for the slowness of flintlock ignition, it is as relevant today as when Markland wrote it, both for shooting advice and for the habits of birds. A single example will give you the flavor. Of course, you're not buying this book to make you a better shot; they've got CD-ROMs and interactive programs for that, not to mention shooting coaches. You're buying it because you care about history or because you like pretty books.

> *There sprung a single Partridge—ha! She's gone!*
> *Oh! Sir, you'd Time enough, you shot too soon;*
> *Scarce twenty Yards in open Sight!—for Shame!*
> *Y'had shatter'd her to Pieces with right Aim!*
> *Full forty Yards permit the Bird to go,*
> *The spreading Gun will surer Mischief sow;*
> *But, when too near the flying Object is,*
> *You certainly will mangle it, or miss;*
> *And if too far, you may slightly wound,*
> *To kill the Bird, and yet not bring to Ground.*

---

* My copy is not the first one I've seen to have no number in the space where a number is supposed to be.

CHAPTER 43

Pheasants of the Mind:
A Hunter's Search for a Mythic Bird
by Datus C. Proper
1990

Datus Proper was a hunting partner of mine and a funny man. He sent me postcards of Montana trout streams in New Mexico, writing, "This Water. Do you know what water is in New Mexico?" When I knew him, he was a retired diplomat who owned a bit of trout stream in the Gallatin Valley with his Irish wife and their son. He was very tall and thin with a shock of white hair, a long, lean grasshopper of a man who simply walked over barbed wire fences that I had to crawl through. He taught me a bit about fine guns, and would have taught me more about trout fishing had I been interested enough. But he taught me one lesson I still take very seriously: *Listen to my dogs.*

He drowned in a trout stream while fishing in his seventies. He wrote a good book about trout fishing, which is also in this book, and a better one about Portugal, where he had spent many happy years. But I think this one is his best—180-proof triple-distilled Proper.

It purports to be a how-to hook-and-bullet book, and it actually is, if by that you mean a useful manual. He divides the subject into sensible sections: a slightly mysteriously titled intro, "Pheasants of the Mind"; one called "Love and Death," which recollects his roots in New Hampshire and Pennsylvania before moving through Nebraska and the plains; and ones on dogs and . . . well, who but Datus could call the section on equipment and cooking "Armor, Gun, and Flavor"?

One of the odd things this book did for me was redeem the pheasant. Before reading Datus, though I would hunt them happily, my New Englander's latent snobbery transitioned neatly from ruffed grouse and woodcock to desert quail and prairie grouse, while, despite the best efforts of friends like Steve Grooms (who wrote the *other* good pheasant book), I continued to see pheasants as some sort of gaudy, alien chickens. Datus, whose New England roots were as real as mine, revealed the pheasant to me as a bird worthy of obsession.

He applied his original esthetic standards to everything, to hunting and guns and his dogs. I had thought German pointers to be ugly compared to the English breed, but his Germans were beautiful. His big old male was the essence of dignity; his little female was the prettiest dog I ever saw before I acquired my first tazi, Lashyn, from Kazakhstan.

Here he explains the Why and the What. But before Datus discusses the beauty of the ideal dog, he veers in an odd direction. Just a little older than I am, he says he started noticing cars in the 1950s when "a nation that had once made beautiful vehicles started making them with chrome jowls, droopy eyes, atrophied muscles . . . I bought a used Jaguar XK-120 coupe. It was a hawk among barnyard fowl, a protest against corruption. It was what my dog has to be now that I would rather walk than ride." *YESSSS!!!* The rest of this chapter, in a section called "A Pointer of the Veronese School," is a celebration of beauty in the dog and a rebuke to anyone who denies that beauty and sport inhabit different worlds.

Other than the above, and my nostalgic wallow in his New Hampshire memories, I love his gun stuff best. What sporting fanatic could not thrill to a chapter on guns that begins with the flat statement: "Myths have blood." I don't think Datus was a rich man in any serious sense of the word. He bought his London Best Woodward in the 1970s, when any name but Holland or Purdey was so cheap that if I had known anything I would have bought one of each. He did not collect guns—to my knowledge he owned three 12-bores, the Woodward, a Birmingham gun of similar dimensions for backup, and a clunky Model 24 Winchester he bought in his teens. His constant defense of the London Best was that he needed the great gun to be able to hit anything at all. I feel the same way.

But there are perks: not the recognition of those who can buy anything they damn well please, but that of fellow artists and artisans. In this book he talks about going to an old gun-maker's shop in Portugal to be restocked. A Perazzi, which probably cost its owner five times what Datus had paid for his Woodward, was on the gunsmith's bench. Datus, fascinated as we all are by mechanical things, admired the Perazzi. "Then the gunsmith—a cranky old artist, like many of his kind—did something embarrassing. He swept Mr. Perazzi's best to a corner of the counter, put Mr. Woodward's down in the middle, and gazed with devotion. '*Esta sim é espingarda,*' he said. 'Now this is a gun.'"

It's strange after all these years how Datus comes striding back into the room with his ever-present twinkle as I quote his words. I will remember him as a man who had the most beautiful dogs, and listened to them, and taught an impatient younger man to listen to his.

ALSO READ:
The Last Old Place, by Datus Proper

CHAPTER 44

Cross Creek
by Marjorie Kinnan Rawlings
1942

Do people still read Marjorie Rawlings's *The Yearling?* It's a good children's book, a realistic if rather sentimental novel about raising a baby whitetail deer (and why that's a bad idea). But it is scarcely her best work, which may well be the memoir *Cross Creek.* The only version that my generation seems to know is the 1983 movie with Mary Steenburgen, which is (sort of) about her life rather than the book, and inaccurate about that.

Luckily, I bought my nice first edition, with a dust jacket at that, when I was in Florida in 1979 visiting Charlie Waterman and wanted to learn something about the countryside. I don't think I've ever spent a better five dollars.

Marjorie Rawlings had a farm once in Florida. She's not as romantic as Karen Blixen; her actual line is "I bought a Florida orange grove with my inheritance." Rawlings is no better a writer than Blixen, but she was a more practical countrywoman and a better naturalist. A chapter called "Toadie-frogs, Lizards, Antses, and Varmints" may be the best chapter on such small monsters in literature, from stinging ants to the relic Florida panther, rare even in her time. She had an anachronistic ease with snakes as well; in the chapter "The Ancient Enemy" she describes first playing with and then reluctantly killing a beautiful snake to make an ornament of its skin. When she shows the hide to a naturalist friend, he looks at her and says, "God takes care of fools and children." She had not realized a coral snake was deadly.

In "Our Daily Bread" she shows herself to be a proper Florida hunter-gatherer. She eats crabs, opossums, blackbirds (she uses #10 shot and gives a recipe); a limpkin that her Cracker neighbors correctly told her was delicious; and enough bear to describe one as "the finest bear meat I have eaten."

In that chapter she describes herself as "torn on the matter of bird shooting." But in "Winter" she reveals herself as a true bird hunter, the reason I have placed her here. "Game birds have an added flavor when you have shot them yourself, or have at least been on the shoot. I am a poor shot, and

106

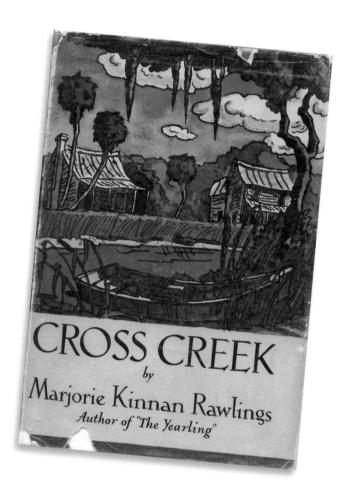

hypocritically have little true desire to be better. What makes the sport is the magnificent country and the stirring performance of good dogs. Good companions lifted into high adventure, and while there are solitary souls that rove the fields alone with dog and gun, it is one of the pastimes that I, who can do with much solitude and like to walk alone, prefer to share." She covers quail in detail, digressing to describe her Aunt Wilmer, a sentimental pre-PETA animal rightist who keeps trying to rescue the dead quail. (Her friend Fred said, "If you can keep your Auntie here, we got no use for a bird dog.")

Her description of wildfowling is ever better.

On days when the sun rose visibly, the gray was slowly infiltrated with lavender, then with pink, until the sun lifted before us and sky and water blazed with salmon and orange and red, and all the world of lake and shore came to life . . . then we settled quietly in the blind, each listening for the other's "Mark!"

I love the swift whir of the approaching ducks, the sharp slicing of the air overhead. I lifted my hypocritical gun obediently and fired, usually to hear, "Diana, damn it, the birds almost took your hat off." It was good to be ravenous in early mid-day, to open a lunch basket and eat the whole length of a Cuban sandwich—eight inches long, four inches thick, stuffed with layers of chicken and ham and roast pork and cheese and chopped sweet pickle—and to digest such a preposterous affair as easily as though it was baby food. A flight of ducks, of course, always came over when one's mouth was full and one's hand was on the beer bottle or the coffee cup instead of the shotgun . . . then the sun was low and egrets came in to roost and the ducks were arrows against the sky. Home was good then, with supper of red wine and biscuits and quail from yesterday's hunt, or a roast guinea, and afterward, good talk by the blazing hearth-fire. These are the things my mind holds dear of hunting.

No man has ever written better about the civilized hunter's life. Hemingway, who knew her slightly through their mutual editor Max Perkins, had good things to say about her. Rawlings eventually left Cross Creek, embroiled in complicated conflicts, but she stayed in Florida and never lost her love for the land or its products. Today another good writer, Guy de la Valdene, lives in that habitat. I hope one day he writes the story of *his* farm.

CHAPTER 45

A Sportsman's Sketches
(Also Known as *A Sportsman's Notebook*
and *A Hunter's Sketches*)
by Ivan Turgenev
1852

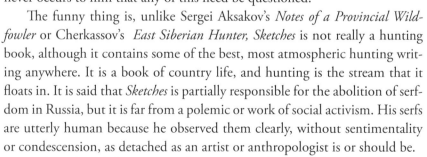

A Sportsman's Sketches is one of the best-known books in this collection, and one of the best. Critic Frank O'Connor says it "may well be the greatest book of short stories ever written." It is a favorite of at least five writers in this collection: Thomas McGuane, Vance Bourjaily, Guy de la Valdene, Jim Harrison, and Ernest Hemingway. Bourjaily catches Turgenev's attitude exactly. "The image one gets of Turgenev's hunting, from his sketches, is one of straightforward enjoyment, and perfect, simple adjustment; he is hunting because he likes to, likes the exercise and the countryside, and it never occurs to him that any of this need be questioned."

The funny thing is, unlike Sergei Aksakov's *Notes of a Provincial Wildfowler* or Cherkassov's *East Siberian Hunter, Sketches* is not really a hunting book, although it contains some of the best, most atmospheric hunting writing anywhere. It is a book of country life, and hunting is the stream that it floats in. It is said that *Sketches* is partially responsible for the abolition of serfdom in Russia, but it is far from a polemic or work of social activism. His serfs are utterly human because he observed them clearly, without sentimentality or condescension, as detached as an artist or anthropologist is or should be.

In fact, though his peasant characters may have heartbreaking lives, his most emotional writing is in his last chapter, "Forest and Steppe"; even in translation* it is one of the most perfect pieces of writing about nature and hunting in any language. I try to read it every fall.

Ideally, I would now quote about six pages, but one paragraph might give you the flavor:

It is a blithe thing to be making your way over a narrow path, between two walls of tall rye. The ears of grain flick your face gently; the corn-flowers catch at the horse's legs, the quail are calling all around you; your horse is going at a lazy trot. And here is the forest. Shade and silence. The graceful aspens babble high above you; the long, drooping branches of the birches barely stir; a mighty oak stands, like some warrior, close to a beautiful linden. You are driving over a green path mottled with shadows; great yellow flies hang motionless in the aureate air and then suddenly fly off; the midges whirl in a pillar, growing lighter in the shade, darkening in the sunlight; the birds are singing peacefully. The golden little voice of the hedge sparrows sounds with innocent, garrulous joy; that voice is in keeping with the fragrance of the lilies of the valley. On, on deeper into the forest. It becomes thicker. An inexplicable quietude falls upon your soul—and all around you, too, everything is so slumberous and still. But now a wind has sprang up, and the treetops have turned noisy, and their noise is as of waves subsiding. Tall grasses grow here and there through last year's dark-brown leaves; there are mushrooms, stand-ing aloof under their small caps. A white hare may leap out unexpect-edly—your dog, barking resoundingly, will dash off after it.

---

* It is impossible to talk about Russian works without talking about translation. *Every Russian translation into English is different.* I currently own two editions of *Sketches*, an Ecco Press *A Sportsman's Notebook,* translated by Charles and Natasha Hepburn in 1948, and a pretty Soviet-era hardback from the foreign languages publishing house in Moscow, called *A Hunter's Sketches,* no translator given. The "Forest and Steppe" chapter is completely different in each. The excellent one I used here, by Bernard Guilbert Guerney, was taken from my anthology *The Art of Shooting Flying;* I no longer have the book! When I helped translate a Russian work, we leaned toward the literal except when an English colloquialism seemed perfect, taking our orders from no less a master than Vladimir Nabokov. If you like language, look for a translation that suits your ears.

ALSO READ:

Notes of a Provincial Wildfowler, by Sergei Aksakov

Notes of an East Siberian Hunter, by A. A. Cherkassov (translated by Vladimir Beregovoy)

CHAPTER 46

The Fragrance of Grass
by Guy de la Valdene
2011

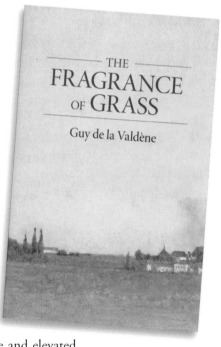

Guy de la Valdene's memoir of his life with dogs and birds and hunting on two continents, *The Fragrance of Grass* (the title comes from a line in a Jim Harrison poem), is even better than his first two good books.

It is an unusual combination of a candid, personal, almost Proustian childhood memoir and a sporting reminiscence with echoes of Turgenev's sketches, haunted by time's accelerating passage; an account of growing up in France and America as a part of a virtually vanished culture, with dogs, a lot of food (good food, not as a luxury but as a natural part of life), and enough shooting both humble and elevated to allow it to be reviewed in hook-and-bullet venues. As I am sure he would admit, he has had a fortunate life.

I find his recurring emphasis on the importance of dogs and the sadness inevitably induced by their short lives especially touching. He isn't weepy—no "I knew an old dog who died" tales, as we used to call the genre at *Gray's,* soon warped into "I knew an old Jeep that died" and worse—but just an honest love for our necessary companions, something he shares with his friend Tom McGuane, who once sent me a letter of condolence on a seventeen-year-old spaniel's death. Some people just get it.

The details of his early, earthy, far more rustic than fancy life in Brittany are fascinating and not at all, to use that word again, "elevated." Of course my mother never shot an elephant with "Pop" Percival—her first and last game animal, incidentally.

His tales of farmers' drives in France, now long gone, beat those of later stuffy high-dollar ones. His set piece and tour de force is the story of a perfect day in his twenty-first year. He has had his uncle's gift pair of Holland Royals modified, and finally shoots magically with them at the book's fanciest driven bird event. For the first time, he does so well that his raffish mentor doesn't "poach" his birds.

He also summered one year in his teens on a Highland estate in Scotland, where he was given a choice of a Holland 7mm Royal and a 6.5 Mannlicher bolt (*without* "un-sporting" scopes) for stags. He wounded one and acquired a lasting distaste for deer hunting, though he honestly admits he still loves venison, if not haggis ("shit pudding").

These days he shoots partridge in Montana behind easygoing dogs like working cockers, and quail on his Florida farm. At a certain age, close or familiar begins to look exactly right. "The past is a different country."

The only thing I don't love about the book is one blurb. Former *New York Times* editor Howell Raines says *Fragrance* "confronts the haunting question of whether the beauty of the hunt can ever justify its savagery." Shut up!—or read Gary Snyder. That is *not* what a hunter's ambivalence is about, and treads a remarkably fine line between ignorance and pomposity. I very much doubt this hunter and his dogs will ever turn vegetarian.

When I first read *Fragrance,* I wrote Guy the next day: "Got it yesterday and sat up reading with a couple of glasses of vodka, marking passages and reading aloud to Libby, until I finished at 1 a.m.

"It is your best I think. It is bravely honest about things nobody talks about, and funny and sad and haunting. You get dogs exactly, and being an aging hunter and lover of our world and all the vanishing things."

ALSO READ:
Guy de la Valdene's *For a Handful of Feathers* and *Making Game*
A Hunter's Road, by Jim Fergus

CHAPTER 47

Gun Dogs & Bird Guns: A Charley Waterman Reader
By Charley Waterman
1986

Charley Waterman was born in Kansas and lived in Montana and Florida. He was the outdoor writer's outdoor writer. Everybody read him, from rank beginners and those who prided themselves on being practical, to novelists, poets, and stylists, who knew he could teach them things about their craft.

Charley and his wife, Debie (if I ever meet you face to face, I'll tell you about the fatuous editor who dared correct her name to "Debby" when he first edited Charley), were short, deadpan, dauntingly competent partners in sport. I first met them in the 1970s in Brookline, Massachusetts, when I was still callow enough to find a country accent unsophisticated, and sat amazed at Charley's tales of some infamous young literati who were his friends. He described them fairly as "Good boys, good writers, good sportsmen" while recounting tales of chemically fueled hijinks that would have made most over-forties of that era run out the door.

Charley "walked the walk." He could tell you the exact point on the mighty St. John's River in Florida to cast for shad, and what fly to use. He had been a champion pistol shooter in his youth and knew enough to prefer fine English shotguns, though not "name" ones. Despite hilarious tales of chasing tightly wound pointers and other problem children, he preferred dogs with the same sane competence as he demonstrated himself. His old Brittany, Kelly, pointed all eighteen species of North American game bird and did everything right; he has two chapters here. He told us about another prodigy, a seven-month-old pointer offered to him as a "bird dog," like this. "He said to me 'The pup is a *bird dog.*' I asked what he knew so far. He said 'He finds a bird, he points the bird, you shoot the bird, he goes and brings the bird back to you.' So I went out and he did just that. I called the guy up and told him and he said 'I know; *he's a bird dog!*'"

There are a million Waterman books and no duds, but he did upland hunting and dogs best, perhaps because he loved them best. This book would be worth buying just for five of his best essays: "False Points. . . ," "Kelly, He Got Them All," "Greying Hunters Hunting Greys," "Shadows on the Prairie," and "Going Up Under the Mountain." These are so deceptively simple you'd think there's nothing special about them until you try to duplicate their clarity and humor.

That last one is a perfect example of the other Waterman: lyrical and slightly haunted in a way that sneaks up from behind and grabs you. Charley was the master of last lines that read like Japanese poetry in demotic American. I used one years ago to cap my shooting anthology. Another ends this collection, about Kelly's last bird: "the last pheasant is always there, hanging in suspended motion, with the benches, the distant pines, the streaks of yellow stubble, and the mountains in the background."

Part 3

GENERAL HUNTING, GUNS, TRAVEL, MIXED, AND MISCELLANEOUS

"One should not talk to a skilled hunter about what is forbidden by the Buddha."

—GARY SNYDER, ATTRIBUTED TO HSIAN-YEN

CHAPTER 48

Across Mongolian Plains
by Roy Chapman Andrews
1921

Roy Chapman Andrews was Indiana Jones, of course; a hero in my youth, he cut an almost ludicrously romantic figure in his knee-high boots and campaign hat. With an adult's colder eye, I sometimes see him as half scientist, half a mixed bag of hustler, socialite, and charlatan. But he had a fabulous life, one blessed by luck both deserved and gratuitous (his autobiography was called *Under a Lucky Star*). He discovered genuinely important things, often while looking for different ones. We should all be so lucky.

Most of Andrews's scientific and sporting life was spent in Asia, starting in China and culminating in his series of famous expeditions to Mongolia. His fame rests on those trips, where he organized caravans of cars to run off hidden caches of gasoline and supplies as far as the remote southern Gobi in "Outer" Mongolia, where there are still no paved roads. Searching for human ancestors (though he never found any; that honor went to the Jesuit paleontologist Pierre de Chardin, who discovered the *Homo erectus* fossil known as Peking Man), he instead found the greatest dinosaur site ever known at the Flaming Cliffs of the Gobi. Ninety-some years later it still yields fossils, but Andrews's dinosaur eggs and his "raptor" battling a Ceratopsian are the most famous. The originals are on display in Ulaan Bataar. Western museums don't let you touch the plastic models, but I got to touch the real ones, as does every Mongolian schoolchild.

Much as I love dinosaur hunting, it is beyond the scope of this book. Fortunately for lovers of adventure, he hunted almost everything else, feathered or furred, for science and sport. He posed constantly with his rifles, so we know his favorites were a Savage 99 in ".250-3000" and a bolt action in the same caliber. He hunted mountain game in China, stalked man-eating tigers with the missionary Harry Caldwell, shot obscure hoofed mammals like goral and serow, and collected magnificent specimens of the Sambur stag. He even hunted monkeys and gibbons.

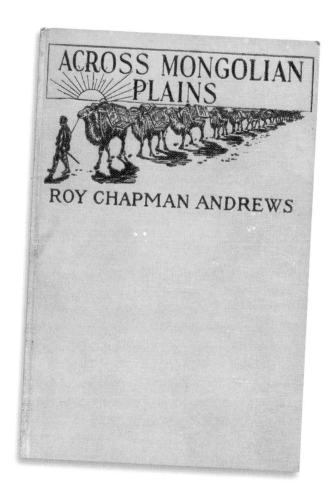

His favorite quarry in his most entertaining book were the swift gazelles of the Asian plains, which he mostly stalked, but couldn't resist chasing with horses and cars. (He filmed the second more than once.) He had his era's fascination with hunting and chasing wolves, which I am sure earned him points—the Mongols are still at war with stock predators. "We were bowling along on a road as level as a floor, when we saw two wolves quietly watching us half a mile away. We had agreed not to chase antelope again; but wolves were fair game at any time . . . They separated almost immediately, and we raced after the larger of the two, a huge fellow with rangy legs which carried him forward in a long, swinging lope."

His friend Coltman wanted to shoot one with his 1911 .45 pistol, so they began to chase the wolf at forty-five miles per hour.

Leaning far out, Coltman fired quickly. The bullet struck just behind the brute, and he swerved sharply, missing the right front wheel by a scant six inches. Before Charles could turn the car he had gained three hundred yards, but we reached him in a little more than a mile. As Coltman was about to shoot a second time, the wolf suddenly dropped from sight. Almost on the instant the car plunged over a bank four feet in height, landed with a tremendous shock—and kept on!

We stopped an instant to inspect the springs, but by a miracle not a leaf was broken. The wolf halted, too, and we could see him standing on a gentle rise with drooping head, his gray sides heaving . . . These wolves are sneaking carrion-feeders and as such I detest them, but this one had "played the game." For twelve long miles he had kept doggedly at his work without a whimper or a cry of "kamerad." The brute had outgeneraled us completely, had won by strategy and magnificent endurance.

There are more-scientific Andrews books, rarer ones, ones with better illustrations, and not a few trashier ones. Start with *Mongolian Plains*, full of fossils, hunting, encounters with bandits and wolves, set in a time and place when *life* could still be a "boy's own" tale. One must hope that, in the words of Ted Hughes, "Life has not really stopped and the world is not really a museum, yet."

ALSO READ:
Roy Chapman Andrews's *Camps and Trails in China, On the Trail of Ancient Man,* and *The Ends of the Earth*
Blue Tiger, by Harry Caldwell
Dragon Hunter, by Charles Gallenkamp

CHAPTER 49

Dersu the Trapper
by V. K. Arseniev
1941

When I first saw the Akira Kurosawa's majestic late film *Dersu Uzala,* around 1975, it reinforced my childhood belief that the last great secret places were in Asia. I did not realize that it was based on a book until, years later, a chance conversation with grizzly researcher Doug Peacock led me to it.

Until John Vaillant's *The Tiger,* this was practically the only book in English about "Primorye," the huge area southeast of Siberia known as the Russian Far East. Primorye is *not* Siberia. A huge area with few roads, savage winters, several indigenous tribes, and a unique mixture of subarctic and tropical animals and plants, it is the home of the great Amur tiger, now nearly exterminated but still lord of the forest.

Arseniev, born in 1872, was a military officer, scientist, and explorer. He made twelve expeditions in Primorye, wrote sixty-some works about it, and never returned to European Russia. He used local guides, showing them unusual respect in an era when Imperial officials often treated subordinates as lesser species. That, and his humble background (his grandfather was a serf), may have kept him out of Bolshevik prisons; a sardonic biographer remarked, "Among other sagacities, Arseniev had the good sense not to be old."

A few critics complain that *Dersu* depicts the friendship between the tribal hunter and the Russian gentleman as patronizing and unequal; that Dersu is a simple-minded "Noble Savage." I think this is an artifact of translation and the conventions of the time. I have bored my readers already with the problems of Russian translation, and adjectives like "primitive" were common in all literate cultures seventy years ago. Dersu does speak in a crude "Me Tonto" pidgin, but I doubt Arseniev, whose respect became genuine affection, intended any insult.

Dersu first appears when he walks in to sit by the fire during Arseniev's first expedition. He calls Arseniev "Captain" and fills his belly as though it were a matter of course; by his custom it was. He explains he is a "Gold," a member of a hunter-gatherer tribe; "more Buddhist and heathen than Orthodox," says Arseniev; stays the night, and without further arrangement accompanies the party on a hunt the next day. He never left. The morning hunt depicts a last, nearly intact ecosystem, almost Pleistocene in its abundance; seeing a spot in the distance, changing shape as it moves, Arseniev declares

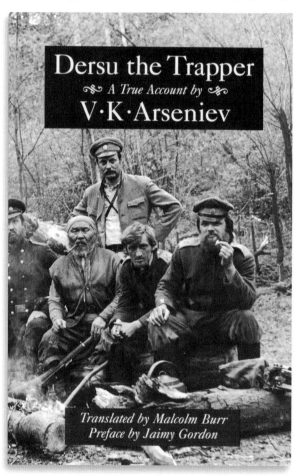

it a cloud's shadow. Dersu looks at him and says, "You know nothing."

Incredibly, the "spot" is an immense herd of wild pigs. Amidst them is a boar, whom Dersu describes as "one man, very big." His choice of pronoun is significant. When he shoots a two-year-old sow, the "Captain," thinking of trophies, asks why. Dersu explains, "Him old man . . . bad to eat." Arseniev questions his insistence on speaking of the pig as a man. Dersu replies, "Him all same man; only different shirt. Him know everything, know traps, know angry . . . all same man."

Arseniev's moment of illumination informs the rest of the book. Dersu, an animist, "humanized his whole environment." While I might say Dersu believed that everything had souls rather than "was human," Arseniev understood.

The complicated bonds between humans and animals are most apparent in their unnerving encounters with "Amba." The first time they meet a tiger, they are waiting at a salt lick to shoot camp meat. Arseniev is unhappy.

"Around reigned the silence of death, only broken by the constant buzz of the mosquitoes. Such silence has a depressing affect on the soul." Apparently not on Dersu's, though. "The serene face of Dersu brought me back to reality . . . Dersu sat like a marble statue. He kept his eyes on the shrubs near the salt-pan and quietly awaited his prey."

Instead of a deer or a pig, a tiger's voice comes rumbling out of the dark. Arseniev is terrified, and even Dersu thinks they have made a bad decision. He stands up and addresses the tiger. "All right, Amba. No be angry . . . this your place. We not know. We go now quick to another place."

The tiger leaves. Arseniev still doesn't quite get it, asking whether they should have waited for a shot. Dersu is annoyed. "Me tell you now, in [my] company will now never shoot Amba! Never! You hear this well, Captain. You shoot Amba . . . you not my comrade." Through three expeditions, the rest of the book, they never kill a tiger. One grabs a dog from the camp. In Dersu's cosmology it is permissible to shoot a tiger who "steals," but they discover the culprit is a tigress with cubs and abandon the chase.

Dersu's end, like that of many wild people and wild animals challenged by civilization, is tragic. He attempts to live in town, but is arrested after he cuts down a tree in the park. Although Arseniev rescues him, "he realized that in a town a man can not live just as he wishes." Arseniev gives him a new rifle, but before he can return to the wilderness he is murdered for it. The "Captain" mourns, "that night I could not sleep. The crushing grief lay on my heart. I felt that I had lost my nearest friend."

Dersu's humble grave disappeared in Arseniev's lifetime. Primorye, still impressive, seems wild, but as its uncrowned king disappears it becomes a tamer, lesser, place. Arseniev's testimony stands as a memorial, and a unique account of friendship in a savage Eden.

ALSO READ:
Notes of an East Siberian Hunter, by A. A. Cherkassov (translated by Vladimir Beregovoy)

Snow Tigers, by Peter Matthiessen

Tigers in Red Weather, by Ruth Padel

CHAPTER 50

The Life of the Hunt
by John Barsness
1995

No equivalent of the old O'Connor-Keith rivalry (perhaps tongue-in-cheek, but taken very seriously by their fans) exists today; today's environment makes it impossible for two individuals to dominate such a fractal, fragmented field. Nevertheless, otherwise sensible people have asked me if John Barsness and Thomas McIntyre (chapter 79, *Seasons and Days*) are today's O'Connor and Keith. My first rude question is: Which is O'Connor and which is Keith? Barsness, a born westerner, started out as a poet and refers to himself as a "third generation Montana . . . *academic.*" McIntyre, who wears big hats and lives in Wyoming, was born in Los Angeles of Irish descent, channels James Joyce and Myles na Gopaleen, and quotes Nabokov and Evelyn Waugh. Between them, they have hunted almost every big game animal on earth. Barsness started at home in Montana as a young teenager, under the guidance of the late Norm Strung (a fine hunter and writer born in New York) and Ben Burshia, an old Dakota. McIntyre enjoyed the last legal safari in Kenya at only twenty-one. At around sixty both are still going strong. The older curmudgeons were talented writers, but I am not sure either's experience was greater.

So let's look at Barsness, the only poor man of our generation who has done nothing but hunt, fish, and write about it. He and his wife, Eileen Clarke, a novelist and former vegetarian who writes great cookbooks and owns three dedicated "gopher" rifles, lived entirely on game and garden vegetables long before "locavory" became chic and Berkeley professors wrote nervously about hunting feral pigs; I doubt either has eaten domestic meat at home in twenty years. From his first paperback about hunting the plains to the recent *Born To Hunt,* he has lived his dream, and described it to inspire others. If a writer is "a reader moved to emulation," how many are made better hunters by emulating John B?

Barsness's style is so simple many readers don't think he has one. Similar charges have been leveled against the great Charley Waterman (chapter

47, *Gun Dogs & Bird Guns*) and the thriller writer Elmore Leonard. Fellow writers know better. He may also be the only "literary" sporting writer who can write eloquently on technical matters, the esoterica of ballistics, loading, barrel-bedding, and gunsmithing in general. His ability to do this is evidence of a real talent that snootier types dismiss. I bet none of them have published poetry.

It's hard to choose a single best from Barness's books. He wrote a good fishing title, *Montana Time,* two books of mostly hunting essays, a book on shotguns, and one on rifles and the obsessive tech freaks he calls "Rifle Loonies." If I am forced to choose one, I nominate his 1995 *The Life of the Hunt.* Even his brilliant new *Born To Hunt* may be a little narrower (more fish and birds in the earlier book), and constant rereading has long since engraved many of its wonderful lines in my brain.

Some of the best are about the sagebrush steppes of the Basin and Range. Barsness is deeply rooted in Montana, as I think nature and sporting writers should be in their chosen or inherited homes; it gives you a base for comparison if nothing else.

It's when your eyes shift above the badlands that the Space begins to be felt, totally and certainly. At first, more stars exist than ever have before, brought so close by the last clear air of a continent that, quite possibly, a sweep of a hand could rearrange a galaxy. But then, in the next perceived instant, the stars move back and back and back, so far that the massive mesa to your right shrinks, to something much smaller than a breadbox and then to something even smaller than the grains of sand beneath your Vibram soles. Somewhere a coyote talks—whether beyond the sleeping bison or the nearest sky you cannot tell. That is the kind of Space where antelope play.

His hunting is rooted in family too. His father hunted but was not serious about it; his grandmother was. "Grandma had married a hardware store owner in the middle of Judith Basin after the war. And he bought her (wholesale, of course) a new .257 Roberts, a *ladies* rifle." With it, according to Barness, she outshot everyone else in the family. Of course Barness has it now.

I have Grandma's .257, though now it wears a scope sight and a custom stock. I suspect she'd disapprove of the first modification but approve of the second since it involved doing things the hard way. Both are very practical, though, because I have used the rifle to take several pronghorn and mule deer . . . And I do these things the hard way, too, walking the coulees and ridges, always wanting to see what lies on the other side, elk jerky in my pocket and the rifle on my shoulder.

Don't neglect his travels outside the country either, to Africa, Alaska, and even Europe; Alaska in particular is a Bigger Big Sky. His love of the hunt doesn't blind him to the comedy inherent in being a paying hunter, nor to its serious side.

Barness's sporting priorities may change, but his writing continues to inspire. His gun advice is more practical than that of most who cover guns these days, who spend their time shooting the Next (commercial) Big Things. Who else other than the wealthy, brilliant connoisseur Ross Seyfried writes seriously about how to modify old guns? His and Eileen's cookbooks and newsletters teach us to waste nothing and enjoy every bit. At not quite sixty, he has achieved every writer's goal; he is not O'Connor or Keith or even Charley Waterman, but 100 percent John Barsness. If you are a self-consciously highbrow hunter who does not know his work yet, start here.

ALSO READ:
John Barsness's *Montana Time, Shotguns for Wingshooting, Obsessions of a Rifle Loony,* and *Born To Hunt*

CHAPTER 51

The End of the Game
(1988 Edition)
by Peter Beard; first published
with different material in
1963

In the late 1950s a very rich young man in love with the idea of Africa arrived in Nairobi to live the life he had dreamed of. He was already taking pictures and keeping diaries, which became works of art in themselves, collages both nightmarish and beautiful. In the intervening years he bought land and built an extravagant tent camp near Nairobi, befriended Karen Blixen and the remnants of the old white-hunter aristocracy, worked game control, and studied crocodiles with the iconoclastic biologist Alistair Graham.

He also romanced and married and divorced models (Cheryl Tiegs, Iman), and jetted back and forth across the Atlantic to Montauk and to London where he socialized with the talented and the notorious—Roger Bacon, Andy Warhol. Yet somehow the playboy managed to produce an enormous body of work, with real depth behind the baroque, even decadent, facade; work that included not just a number of solid books but visual art: photographs and the ever-more-complicated diaries.

His first book bore the name *End of the Game,* but it was a very different book from its final incarnation. Published in 1963, it was a coffee-table-size celebration of the hunter's life in Africa. Not the aboriginal hunter, of course, but rather the adventurous brand of big game hunting pioneered by Europeans, brave romantics who also seemed to possess the ability to write well about their exploits. Their arc started in late-Victorian Africa and descended through the works of Hemingway and Ruark in the mid-twentieth century; their last heirs may be Tom McIntyre and John Barsness. Many of these hunters are in this book, but Beard actually met a lot of the old legends toward the end of their careers. His honest hero-worship and access to their photographs

makes the first *EOTG* a classic. And note well: Many of the photographs in *this* edition are in brilliant color.

Gradually Beard's vision gathered shadows; while his 1975 *Longing for Darkness* is still a celebration (of the life of Blixen's servant Kamante), all was not well in Eden. An expanding population was pressing on the gates of the great reserves, and the ban on hunting in Kenya after Jomo Kenyatta's death actually escalated the poacher's war on elephants. In the early 1970s Beard collaborated with Alistair Graham in a study of the crocodile populations of Lake Turkana, a study that offended more conventional conservationists because they killed over five hundred crocodiles to study and to fund their study. That this did not hurt the population of crocodiles seemed never to have occurred to these people. The resulting book, *Eyelids of Morning* (from a line in the *Book of Job*), was a first indication of where Beard's work was going. Magnificent two-page color spreads mingle with grotesque images of death and decay, naked breasts, medieval woodcuts, Victorian cartoons, maps, textural photos of crocodile skin, and such odd things as the party fishing for Nile perch, or Beard, submerged in mud, aiming what appears to be a .458 over an inner tube. The text moves from an explorer's history of the region to a sober assessment of the crocodile's chances. Other decorations include images by New York pals like Andy Warhol, Saul Steinberg, and Charles Addams, and facsimile pages from his diary showing photos of RFK with a Colt revolver laid on the page. It was a brilliant but disturbing book with an ominous underlying message: Africa, and possibly everything else, was in trouble.

Beard had met the legendary Phillip Percival in 1961. He was Beard's living link to Roosevelt, Selous, and Hemingway. It was Percival who first pointed him toward Tsavo, where he had hunted elephants and where the infamous man-eaters stopped the construction of the railway. In the 1970s Beard heard rumors of massive die-offs in Tsavo. He went there and eventually rented a plane to fly over the once-fertile plains, where he began to document an ongoing disaster.

The results became a horrifying but compelling exhibition of sepia-toned black-and-white photographs in New York and Paris galleries, and were the inspiration for a new edition of *End of the Game*. In it he retained much of the material from the first, but rearranged and changed. Large colorful photos became small monochrome ones, and the overall tone changed from romantic nostalgia to swerve from elegy to horrified witness. Try to imagine the Goya of "Los Caprichos" and the "Horrors of War" with a camera for a tool and elephants as the subject.

After a steadily darkening reworking of the first book, he quotes Percival: "Why don't you take a good look at Tsavo." The next two pages show a great grey plain, flat to the limit of the horizon, with ten ant-tiny elephants concentrated in an inch of space by the centerfold. On the next page the image of a single dead elephant shot from the air with the caption, "Nor Dread nor Hope Attend."

What follows is a portfolio of death. No image is gory, though some are repellent; some are almost geometric; some, like the one of vultures from above, uncomfortably fascinating; some are so abstract and out of context you would not know they are bones. A few are of roads and trackways, the patterns humans impose on chaos. The purity of the dry landscape and leaching away of color make them strangely clean; you forget what the smell must be like on the ground. There is very little vegetation. Some even look like they could be fossils, left behind by some unimaginable catastrophe in a former epoch. Although gigantic images on gallery walls might be individually more impressive, the cumulative power of their numbers in the book is hard to argue. In some moods I might hang one on my wall, but their beauty does not deny their mortal weight.

And I did not say, but you should know: Not one of these elephants was killed by sport hunters, subsistence hunters, or "poachers." Both of the last had been removed by Colonial authorities because they killed elephants. Without predators, the elephants ate their environment and died.

The last image is of an immense pile of bones. These days, the Kenya Game Department has been known to burn piles of ivory this big to "stop the illicit ivory trade," even as some colleagues profit by selling the ever-more valuable banned ivory. And so it goes.

Beard has gone on, and continues to make his art. His enormous two-volume Taschen portfolio called simply *Peter Beard* is a magnificent and still often disturbing tribute to Africa, his life, and his art. All his books are worth a look, and most are prettier than *End of the Game,* but it has the most impact. I will leave you with his own words in the foreword: "Man and his ways have intruded with little regard to Africa's ways, its customs, and privacy. She has been pursued and despoiled. *The End of the Game* has told part of this story because it deals with the essence of African life, the animal. And with that very license of humanity by which we have presumed to conquer we are challenged to reflect upon our defeat."

ALSO READ:

Peter Beard's *Longing for Darkness* and *Peter Beard* (Taschen two-volume set)

Eyelids of Morning, by Peter Beard and Alistair Graham

The Gardeners of Eden, by Alistair Graham

CHAPTER 52

The Wanderings of an Elephant Hunter
by W. D. M. Bell
1923

African big game hunting has spawned such a disproportionate amount of hunting literature that picking titles for a hundred-book collection is difficult. The English and other Europeans (but little of their literature is yet translated) were an unusually literate bunch, not just (for the most part) upper-class, but the kind of rebels, romantics, and misfits that have the need, as well as the ability, to write down their stories.

My final choices are doubtless eccentric. Real writers who loved Africa are easy—Hemingway, Ruark, the Baroness Blixen—beyond that I could have chosen thirty or forty African titles, all enjoyable. Instead, I have concentrated on writers who have something significantly different to say or are otherwise unusual. Among the ones with lasting legacies is this genial Scot, one of whose rifles is still being shot today, though he retired in the early part of the twentieth century.

Walter Dalrymple Maitland Bell was born in Edinburgh in 1880 and, being an independent sort, left school at twelve to work on a boat to Tasmania. His first trip to Africa was at sixteen; he worked as a meat hunter, using a single-shot .303. After brief stints in Canada and in the Boer War, he organized himself to return to Africa to hunt ivory, soon abandoning the conventional heavy double for a .303 SMLE, a petite .256 Mannlicher, and, to eventual notoriety, 7-millimeter ".275 Rigby." He worked as a professional until World War I, where he fought in several theaters including the Middle East, and allegedly tried or succeeded in shooting down an enemy aircraft with a Broomhandle Mauser pistol. He then hunted commercially again until the mid-1920s, but found the modern scene unattractive. He retired to Scotland where he spent his twilight years shooting red stags with a .220 Swift and sailing. In his lifetime he was alleged to have killed over 3,000 elephants. As a witty friend said, his was "a history of succeeding with superficially inadequate calibers."

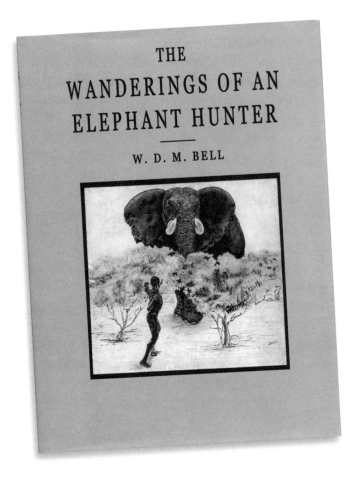

Bare bones, but bones one could weave an epic from. Any reading of Bell, whether of this book or his more famous *Karamoja Safari,* leaves one with the impression of a calm, witty, self-deprecating man with no ego to speak of and an unusual, all the more apparent because understated, appreciation for the locals as neither noble savages nor faceless servants but as rather interesting fellow humans. But these virtues were not enough to make him famous.

The first thing incomprehensible to moderns is that he killed all those elephants with neither remorse nor, apparently, much reflection. As I say to people who find my predatory birds morally lacking, it's what he did. The second difficulty some up-to-date types have with Bell is that, but for some early experiments, he shot all his elephants with rather small deer calibers, and in his retirement killed what we think of as elk with a "varmint rifle," something westerners would call a prairie dog gun. Probably by now an enterprising editor could make a thick book about this controversy alone. Those not familiar with African hunting trivia must take my word that no other such controversy exists in all of hunting literature.

The number of his kills does not concern me. When Bell hunted, he had no effect whatsoever on the population of African elephants; see this book's entry on Peter Beard (chapter 51, *The End of the Game*) to see how unthinking *protection* may have done them more harm. The caliber matter is interesting, and I'll return to it in a moment. But first, read his cheerful account of meeting and befriending a future guide, to show his straightforward attitude to cultural matters.

At first I thought that he was come to show me elephant. That was his intention, he said, but first he wanted to become my blood-brother. He said he could see that I was a kindred spirit and that we two should be friends. He said he had no friends. How was that? I asked. Pyjalé answered in a whisper that the lion never made friends of jackals and hyenas. And so we became friends. I was not going through the blood-brother business, with its eating bits of toasted meat smeared with each other's blood, sawing in two of living dogs or nonsense of that kind. I took his hand and wrung it hard, and had it explained to him that among us that was an extraordinarily potent way of doing it. That seemed to satisfy the old boy, for the act of shaking hands was as strange to him as the act of eating each other's blood was to us.

Despite such virtues, Bell's lasting fame rests on some numbers: .275 (Rigby) and .256 (Mannlicher-Schoenauer). The first, better known as 7 X 57 or 7 MM Mauser, though greatly appreciated by the likes of Jack O'Connor (albeit for his wife) and more significantly by Jim Corbett for man-eating tigers, is now dwarfed by most of the modern magnums and postmodern *short* magnums that your average three-day-a-year hunters think are necessary for mule deer. (Please understand the little caliber, first used as a military alternative to fat black powder loads in the ninetenenth century, will not stop an elephant that is charging at you with the intention of stomping you flat. The biggest proprietary loads of the London gunmakers, up through .600 Nitro in a sixteen-pound double rifle, may not do that.) Bell was a commercial hunter with the skills of a poacher, and he shot his quarry standing, unawares, sometimes even sleeping, at very close ranges. He was so skillfully sneaky, and the report so relatively soft, that he sometimes shot four or five before the herd became alarmed. He sawed elephant skulls in half lengthwise, to better understand what obstacles his little bullets must traverse.

"For the style of killing which appeals to me most the light calibers are undoubtedly superior to the heavy. In this style you keep perfectly cool and are never in a hurry. You never fire unless you can clearly see your way to place the bullet in a vital spot. That done the caliber of the bullet makes no difference."

Sure, the elephants were easier then; yes, he picked his shots; yes, there are technical ballistic properties, including such things as "sectional density," that give subtle advantage to the 7 X 57 and the smaller Mannlicher cartridge (Bell, trying to push a .256 out of the breech: "Calibre [sic] .256 is very small when you come to try poking sticks down it"). Bell was a Zen swordsman's ideal of the Rifleman, and anyone who thinks those cartridges are too small for deer deserves to pay big dollars for a modern piece of crap. Not only O'Connor and Corbett but Harry Selby and contemporaries like John Barsness know the oldies' virtues.

Which book of Bell's to recommend is a milder conundrum. If you like pure narrative, try *Karamoja Safari* instead. It still has plenty of ballistics for the gun geek, but is the tale of one extended safari. I slightly prefer these connected essays because they were written soon after Bell's retirement; the later *Karamoja,* "recollections in tranquility," can seem a little hazy in comparison.

I have owned a .275 by Rigby, and loved it. It now resides with a friend who deserved it more than I did, and we eat elk from his bounty every year. Bell's rifle passed from him to (after his death) Robert Ruark, thence through the great hunter Harry Selby. It has recently passed into the hands of an acquaintance, and I suspect it will actually see Africa again, though governments no longer allow anyone to use such a puny weapon on thick-skinned big game. Modern time, mon, as Peter Matthiessen said in *Far Tortuga.* . . .

ALSO READ:
African Rifles and Cartridges, by John Taylor, for an informed but different ballistic philosophy

CHAPTER 53

In the Pink
by Caroline Blackwood
1987

This is a book about capital-H Hunting: riding across the countryside on horses in pursuit of mammals, the only pursuit the English dignify with the term. It is especially interesting because, if she were to vote on the matter, Caroline Blackwood might well vote against hunting, or, these days, to keep the ban that now exists in England. But maybe not: See what she says at the end.

Although she was born to the foxhunting classes, she never hunted. She first thought about the subject when, in 1986, two young "antis" were caught trying to dig up the tomb of the Duke of Beaufort, a prominent master of foxhounds, and cut off his head. As a journalist she was intrigued: "I was told that the whole issue of foxhunting in Mrs. Thatcher's Britain contains a paradox: the sport has never been so popular as it is today; perversely, never in its history has it been so violently unpopular . . . I felt that I was learning about a class that has many similarities to a religious war."

She set out on a quest to talk to hunters and antis to find out why they believed what they did. She succeeded, I would guess, because her background fit well with one and her intellectual sympathies with the other. She also covered related matters: hunt clothing, the 1971 statistical survey of the beliefs of Masters of Foxhounds by Professor Hans Eysenck, and "drag-hunting" to artificial scent (Montaigne: "To hunt without killing is like having sexual intercourse without orgasm.").

She identified with the fox; what she could not seem to do is identify with the antis. And she tried. After dutifully quoting a rare country-bred spokesman ("Bryant insists that those who work for his organization come from both the city and the country; they have only one factor in common—they were all bullied at school."), she meets a vegan who advocates killing hunters. "Tim Morgan is a vegan who runs a sanctuary for animals in northern England . . .

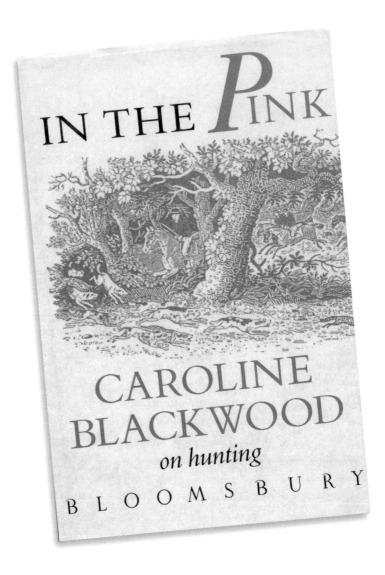

he keeps turkeys and hens, but believes that it is cruel to eat eggs . . . 'I don't see anything wrong with killing a huntsman.'"

Their personalities and social milieu offend her. Against the spokesman above, she quotes Seamus Heaney: "Prevention of cruelty talk cuts ice in town, where they consider death unnatural." They seemed rooted in Puritanism:

"Under the Protectorship of Oliver Cromwell, hunting was disapproved of socially. The deer parks were broken up, and the sport of stag-hunting in England never really recovered . . . the deer was threatened with extinction . . . 'Nothing remains,' lamented a Cavalier, 'except rabbits and Roundheads.'" When an undercover agent for the antis releases a photograph suggesting that some packs feed the bodies of hounds who have died to other hounds, she observes that "the undercover agent with his duplicitous nature might have planted the dead hound in a feeding trough in order to take a snap of it."

Eysenck's poll might give a clue to her sympathies. His findings don't map well with current American cultural polarities, but do describe a certain old class of Englishmen very well. The packs' Masters were pro-church *and* pro-adultery; fiercely patriotic, threatening to resist any occupation by a foreign power at any cost; and utterly libertarian in the American sense of the word. For a British group they were also unusually philo-Semitic, perhaps in celebration of such grand old Jewish hunting families like the Sassoons. I suspect she found the hunters congenial sinners.

In her last chapter a retired Master says, "They think that hunting is to do with cruelty—but it's nothing to do with that—it's to do with beauty." Strange? It is not so strong a statement as the one just above it, by a woman (Karen Blixen) at that: "The person who can take delight in a sweet tune without wanting to learn it, and a beautiful woman without wanting to possess her, and a magnificent head of game without wanting to shoot it, has not got a human heart." The best she can do to oppose these is from a worker for the Campaign for Nuclear Disarmament: "Fox-hunters and nuke-lovers—they all have the same mentality."

Her last sentence puzzles over the apparent paradox: Humans can derive pleasure from causing pain. But in the penultimate paragraph, she quotes John Masefield: "Hunting makes more people happy than anything else I know. When people are happy together I am quite certain they build up something eternal, which weakens the power of all evil things upon the life of men and women."

ALSO READ:
On Hunting, by Roger Scruton

CHAPTER 54

The L.L. Bean Game and Fish Cookbook

by Angus Cameron
and Judith Jones
1983

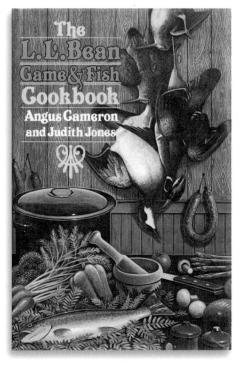

The L.L. Bean Game and Fish Cookbook, by the late great Knopf editor and sporting character Angus Cameron and his friend Judith Jones (legendary in cooking circles), was, when it came out in 1983, the most encyclopedic volume of game cookery since the days of Derrydale. Its authors were larger-than-life, novelistic characters out of the romantic era of American publishing. Cameron, Old Left in politics if often patrician in tastes (I inherited one of his Pezon et Michel bamboo rods; Jack O'Connor, one of his writing stable, arranged for AyA to build him bespoke double guns in Spain), left the firm during the McCarthy years and supported himself hunting and trapping for a spell. Judith Jones discovered Julia Child's and Anne Frank's diaries and edited, among others, John Updike, Anne Tyler, and Marcella Hazan. Their combined and unique combination of intellect, sophistication, and experience resulted in what may still be the best and most useful single volume available today.

That is: *If* you must have only one fish and game cookbook (I could no more own one than one shotgun), this is the one to get. First, it passes all the simple dumb tests. Don't buy a game cookbook that doesn't know that prime wild ducks, unlike the fatty domestic version, should be roasted for twenty minutes in a hot oven; don't buy one that doesn't at least *know* that snipe and woodcock are classically cooked with their entrails in, whether or not the writer likes them that way being of lesser import. Most important, any book that thinks rabbit is the same as hare would confuse chicken with duck or beef with pork (and should be thrown away lest it lead budding game cooks astray!).

But *Bean* goes far beyond these small necessities. It doesn't just list recipes but gives careful details on methods. It is readable, with anecdotes and recipe histories. It is beautifully illustrated with pencil sketches of birds and fish and tackle—I mean, recognizable equipment is the rarest feature in any sporting book, and the gun on page 203 is without a doubt an Ideal Grade L. C. Smith! It is actually fun to read, including such nonessential but fascinating asides as "How to get the most out of juniper berries" and "Hanging game birds, French style." It is encyclopedic, including sunfish and pike and coots as well as the more aristocratic game, with chapters on sausages, sauces, and dishes made with already-cooked game. Finally, it is practical, telling you how to cook such things as shad so that the bones "melt."

My only reservation is that this book seems to think that ambitious game cooks all live on the Eastern Seaboard. As a source for the English "Harvey's Sauce" it recommends *Bloomingdales*—tough if one lives ninety miles from Albuquerque as I do. Oh well, such quibbles are worth mentioning only because the book is otherwise so fine; the availability of mail order and the Internet makes quibbles about ingredients less important now than when it was written.

ALSO READ:

The Derrydale Game and *Fish Cookbooks,* by Louis De Gouy (classic)

Anything by Rebecca Gray, the best cook I know besides my (former professional cook) wife, Libby

Slice of the Wild, by Eileen Clarke: hard-core! She and her husband, John Barsness, were living the locavore hunter-gatherer life before it was cool.

Hunt, Gather, Cook, by Hank Shaw: best of the new California locavory; more technique

The Omnivore's Dilemma, by Michael Pollan: why hunt, culminating with a Berkeley professor deciding to hunt hogs

CHAPTER 55

Man-Eaters of Kumaon
by Jim Corbett
1946

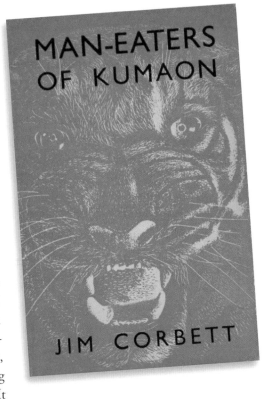

Jim Corbett, a gentle Indian-born British Edwardian, was the only expert tiger hunter who ever wrote a bestseller. He was also a man, when you study him, who seems the utter antithesis of the stereotypical big game hunter. Although he attained the rank of colonel in the British Indian Army and killed a ridiculous number of man-eating cats, he spent most of his life working alongside his Indian employees. It is said that, when he was a shipping contractor, he helped the workers carry their loads from the docks; he almost seems a less neurotic version of Tolstoy, one who did not just play at labor. A humble man, unself-consciously so. But the national park in northern India now known all over the world as the Corbett was originally called the "Hailey" after Lord Malcolm Hailey; who remembers Lord Malcolm today?

But if he were only a worthy official who shot an occasional bothersome tiger, or even (as he was) a premature Green and an unlikely defender of big predators, we might not remember him. Time hallows those who write well, and their tales outlive them. When he published *Man-eaters of Kumaon* in 1946, Corbett jumped to the bestseller list and stayed there as long as he lived. I suspect it surprised him, but maybe it shouldn't have. His man-eater "trilogy," collected in the *Jim Corbett Omnibus*, taps into the deepest subconscious fears and obsessions in the human psyche. Before and even after we hunted, we were prey; beasts still lurk beyond the circle of the campfire, waiting to stalk us.

Corbett maintains a unique balance. He is not dismissive about fear, dread, even terror; nor does he lean the other way, speaking in hollow tones to make your flesh creep. He carefully paints a picture: Here is the land and its people; this is the nature of the beast. Then he introduces a historical circumstance: A tiger encounters a porcupine, or is shot with an inadequate, wounding weapon (like the monstrous tiger in Vaillant). That tiger, while convalescing, is surprised by a woodcutter or a cowherd, kills him, and finds that this odd animal is edible. A year or two passes, the tiger eats a few tens or hundreds of humans, and finally some Colonial administrator picks up his phone and calls Colonel Corbett, working on the railroad.

As the narrative unfolds, Corbett walks alone, observes, thinks, studies tracks; he listens to the birds. He talks to the relatives of the slain. Eventually he may stake out a young goat and sit over it in a bare tree; not for him the ostentatious "machans" of the typical Colonial trophy hunter (he imagines the tiger watching the villagers build such structures, then going away for a few months). Gradually, through hardship and fascination, he gets close to the tiger or leopard. Perhaps he succeeds in shooting it. If he does, he will skin it out and show you the broken teeth or the suppurating flesh around the old muzzleloader ball that caused it to choose a life of easy predation.

Or, more likely—for man-eaters do not earn their deserved reputation by recklessness—he fails, and ponders, and tries again. He walks lonely dirt tracks at dusk, and in his plain prose, without a trace of braggadocio, he lets you know what *that* feels like. He never claims to be anything but observant, but his bravery is manifest. Nor is his narrative pure stoicism. In his civilized way, Corbett deftly mixes self-deprecation with feats so daring I can only conclude he thought anyone might do them. At least one is so over-the-top that satirical sporting writer Ed Zern parodied it in his collection *To Hell With Hunting*.

Corbett is hunting a family of man-eaters in a part of the Himalayan foothills known as Chowgarh. As he is also a bird collector, one morning, already on the hunt, he is delighted to find the nest of a nightjar. He notes that the eggs were of "a most unusual shape, one being long and very pointed, while the other was round as a marble; and as my collection lacked nightjar eggs I decided to add this odd clutch to it." As he had no container he went on, carrying the eggs in one hand and his little .275 Rigby in the other.

Naturally, he slides into a ravine. Naturally, he comes around a corner to see the tigress sleeping on a ledge with her tail toward him. Naturally, he contrives to wait and kill her; just as naturally, for Corbett, he worries about the ethics of shooting her sleeping, but justifies the lapse because she was a man-eater. And, in a paragraph that could only have been written by Jim Corbett, he explains:

"Three things, each of which would appear to you to have been at my disadvantage, were actually in my favor. These were (*a*) the eggs in my left hand, (*b*) the light rifle I was carrying, and (*c*) the tiger being a man-eater." Only Corbett could make you see how *sensible* these observations are, and I will leave the rest to your future reading.

He doesn't do this kind of thing to be funny, though I think he saw the humor of the eggs. In a later volume, *The Temple Tiger,* he was forced to hunt a difficult man-eater while suffering from a huge abscess in his head, the result of some idiot who shot close to his ear on a drive and ruptured his eardrum. The medical procedures of the day gave him no relief, the man-eater was racking up a terrible score, and he began to hunt night and day as an escape from his pain. Close on the track, he wounds the tiger. As he bends down to look at her tracks, he realizes he has made a mistake.

I had only run a few yards when I was overcome by vertigo. Near me were two oak saplings, a few feet apart and with inter-laced branches. Laying down my rifle I climbed up the saplings to a height of ten or twelve feet. Here I found a branch to sit on, another for my feet, and yet other small branches for me to rest against. Crossing my arms on the branches in front of me, I laid my head on them, and at that moment the abscess burst, not into my brain as I feared it would, but out through my nose and left ear.

Being Corbett, he counts his relief as being another advantage. And of course, when he skins her he finds twenty old porcupine quills embedded in her leg.

Read them all. Corbett's books are both the cordial memoirs of a genial naturalist and, simultaneously, true accounts of terror that embody the spirit of Kipling's fearful Everyman: "Comes a breathing hard behind thee—*snuffle-snuffle* through the night—It is Fear, O Little Hunter, it is Fear!" We have all been there, at least in our dreams.

CHAPTER 56

Life with an Indian Prince
by John J. Craighead and Frank C. Craighead Jr.
2001

John Craighead and his twin brother, Frank, lifelong naturalists and conservationists, are best known for their studies of the grizzly in Yellowstone in the 1960s and '70s. But their work started in the 1930s, as teenagers, when they studied and photographed birds of prey and sold an article on their work to *National Geographic.* This good fortune led to a book contract for *Hawks in the Hand* (1939, and a more recent Lyons Press reprint) and an invitation from an Indian prince, R. S. Dharmakumarsinjhi ("Bapa") to visit and see how falconers in India still carried on a tradition that was hundreds, perhaps thousands, of years old.

They passed into a world that, despite Daimlers and swimming pools, was still medieval. From October 1940 until April 1941, they traveled, photographed, and filmed everything from falconry and coursing with trained cheetahs to a royal wedding. They never dreamed that, soon after their return, the flames of World War II and the passions of Indian Independence would sweep away the entire society they had glimpsed. The brothers published a short article, "Life with an Indian Prince," in *National Geographic* (still often available in old bookstores and on the Internet), and went off to train naval pilots for survival in the South Seas.

They also made a film for *National Geographic,* but it was never released. Perhaps its straightforward hunting scenes with bird and even cheetah, not to mention the shooting of a lion, were considered too rough for postwar sensibilities. About fifty years later, Frank Craighead delivered a detailed day-to-day diary of the trip and hundreds of color slides to S. Kent Carnie of the Archives of Falconry in Idaho. Colonel Carnie realized that he had his hands on a virtual time machine, an intimate glimpse into the lost culture of the Raj. The Archives made every effort to produce a book worthy of the material, and succeeded with *Life,* an oversize volume on fine paper with color photographs on practically every page.

The diaries begin at the trip's start in Pennsylvania. The brothers drive across the country and embark from San Francisco on the *President Cleveland*. During the crossing they paint vivid, innocent pictures of prewar South Seas travel and photograph such things as a Hong Kong still dominated by forested hills, reminders to contemporary readers of how the world has changed.

The bulk of the book details a sporting season in western India. The Craigheads participated in trapping and training a princely plentitude of falcons and goshawks (Bapa alone had a team of thirty-three birds, all attended by professional falconers), using methods unchanged since the dawn of falconry. They rode on bullock carts with trained cheetahs after blackbuck antelope. The brothers crossed India on a private train to attend a royal wedding complete with a retinue of costumed elephants and attended a ritual lion hunt in the formally managed Gir forest. Finally, they took their birds out to hunt hare and partridge, heron and plover, even such medieval quarry as ibis and kite.

Modern readers should realize that, *because* of hunting, British India's wildlife was intensely managed and conserved. The Gir forest lions survive to this day because they were preserved for the Maharajas' hunts, though one might argue they are more like domestic animals in a very large cage. These days post-Independence chaos and unrestrained population growth have reduced the wildlife of Bhavnagar to a ghostly remnant of what existed in 1940.

Life remains a testimony to a time when the particular horrors of the late twentieth century were still invisible, just over the horizon. The lives of the upper classes were the same as they had been for centuries, and it was possible to believe that their ways could go on indefinitely. This unique window into the past is not just for hunters and naturalists; it is a time machine for anyone curious about lost worlds.

ALSO READ:
Hawks in the Hand, by Frank and John Craighead
Falconry in the Land of the Sun, by S. M. Osman

CHAPTER 57

Out of Africa
by Isak Dinesen
(Baroness Karen
von Blixen-Finecke)
1938

Out of Africa is one of those perfect works, one embedded in my generation's cultural DNA because of the popular movie made from it. It may be the only movie in existence in which modern politically correct figures like Robert Redford and Meryl Streep appear to shoot and kill lions using the correct rifles, like Bixen's 6.5 Mannlicher-Schoenauer. (That the short American Redford does not resemble the towering, bald Anglo-Saxon aristocrat and esthete Denys Finch Hatton is another matter.) The book also embodies a perfect "Jane Chord"*: "I had a farm in Africa, at the foot of the Ngong Hills. / The outline of the mountain was slowly smoothed and leveled out by the hand of distance." The version that uses the first and last paragraph is even better . . .

As I said, perfect, a work that makes Ruark and even Hemingway (who, with his customary generosity toward female writers, said in 1954 that she should have won the Nobel Prize) look a little pedestrian. It is harder, and less necessary, to explicate great works than to simply point at them. *Out of Africa* is a carefully crafted gem of autobiography rather than a hunting memoir per se, but it is also a work of the hunter's art.

Much of the hunting in *Out of Africa* is typical upper-class trophy hunting, beautifully rendered. But Blixen and her peers were also farmers and ranchers, who had to deal with practical matters. This matter-of-fact account of shooting cattle-killing lions at night will demonstrate her intrepidity. It is interesting that Finch Hatton expects no less.

---

* See *A River Runs Through It;* using the first and last sentence (word, paragraph) to stand for an entire work.

We walked a little again and the deep growling was repeated, this time straight to the right. "Put on the light," Denys said. It was not altogether an easy job, for he was much taller than I, and I had to get the light over his shoulder on to his rifle and further on. As I lighted the torch the whole world changed into a brilliantly lighted stage . . . First the circle of light struck a little wide-eyed jackal, like a small fox; I moved it on, and there was the lion. He stood facing us straight, and he looked very light, with all the black African night behind him. When the shot fell, close to me, I was unprepared for it, even without comprehension

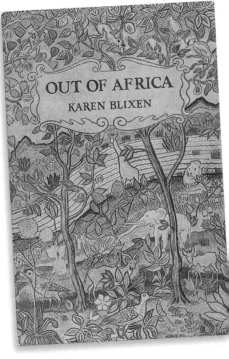

of what it meant, as if it had been thunder, as if I had been myself shifted into the place of the lion. He went down like a stone. "Move on, move on," Denys cried to me. I turned the torch further on, but my hand shook so badly that the circle of light, which held all the world, and which I commanded, danced a dance. I heard Denys laugh beside me in the dark—"The torch-work on the second lion," he said to me later, "was a little shaky."—But in the centre of the dance was the second lion, going away from us and half hidden by a coffee-tree. As the light reached him he turned his head and Denys shot. He fell out of the circle, but got up and into it again, he swung round towards us, and just as the second shot fell, he gave one long irascible groan.

ALSO READ:

The Flame Trees of Thika, by Elspeth Huxley, a memoir of growing up in the same Kenya society as Blixen, with much hunting

CHAPTER 58

Big Woods
by William Faulkner
1931

No reader can ignore the two alpha writers who dominated American literature in the twentieth century. Despite my penchant for dependent clauses and long sentences, I am more a Hemingway-ite than a Faulknerian. We can argue about why two; the human brain seems to strive for dualities, yin and yang, black and white, *Time* and *Newsweek,* but no one who grew up in the second half of the century has not read Ernest Hemingway and William Faulkner. Hemingway seems to be undergoing a mild revival, and Faulkner an eclipse; idiot reviewers on Amazon complain about things like his "run-on sentences"—! Faulkner need not worry. As a young man, Hemingway once said of Conrad, then unpopular and newly dead, that he didn't know about critical value, but he thought that if by grinding up T. S. Eliot and sprinkling the resulting powder on Conrad's grave, that Conrad would rise from the dead and write one more novel, then he was heading for London with a sausage grinder. If people continue to ignore Faulkner, I've got my grinder. . . .

Both wrote of hunting. Hemingway specialized in bird hunting and big game hunting and fishing for huge fish from expensive boats, and minored in fly fishing. These are now the sports of the wealthy and literate. Faulkner did not write of the things that are monopolized by the wealthy today, but of the elemental, of hounds chasing deer and predatory quarry. In the South everyone followed hounds, rich man and poor, often together. The southern hunting tradition came to the "New" world when its landed aristocrats and independent yeoman fled their old one. Southern settlers were countrymen, unlike the bourgeoisie of New England. As Europe's noble quarry disappeared, its hunters carried the tradition to the South. (And southerners brought it to the West; where will the hounds go when all is forbidden?)

Meanwhile, Faulkner's hunters live. "The Bear," embedded later in *Big Woods* and earlier in the shaggy collection *Go Down Moses,* which some still think is his best work, is America's iconic hunting saga. Without it would writers like Bill Humphrey ever have written their tales?

The battle between a heroic feral Airedale mix, Lion, and the wounded bear, Old Ben, is a clash of titans.

This time the bear didn't strike him down. It caught the dog in both arms, almost loverlike, and they both went down. He was off the mule now. He drew back both hammers of the gun but he could see nothing but moiling spotted houndbodies until the bear surged up again. Boon was yelling something, he could not tell what; he could see Lion still clinging to the bear's throat and he saw the bear, half erect, strike one of the hounds with one paw and hurl it five or six feet and then, rising and rising as though it would never stop, stand erect again and begin to rake at Lion's belly with its forepaws. Then Boon was running. The boy saw the gleam of the blade in his hand and watched him leap among the hounds, hurtling them, kicking them aside as he ran, and fling himself astride the bear as he had hurled himself onto the mule, his legs locked around the bear's belly, his left arm under the bear's throat where Lion clung, and the glint of the knife as it rose and fell.

Faulkner is often accused of not being able to do action; the last paragraph should cure any thoughts of that. He is justly celebrated as the master of southern impressionism. Let me leave you with his land and the hunter's place in it:

The Big Woods, the Big Bottom, the wilderness, vanished now from where he had first known it; the very spot where he and Sam were standing when he heard his first running hounds and cocked the gun and saw the first buck, was now thirty feet below the surface of a government-built flood-control reservoir whose bottom was rising gradually and inexorably each year on another layer of beer cans and bottle tops and lost bass plugs; the wilderness itself, where he had served his humble apprenticeship to the rough food and the rough sleeping, the life of hungers; mean and horses and hounds, not to slay the game but to pursue it, touch and let go, never satiety; —the wilderness, the Big Woods themselves being shoved, pushed just as inexorably further and further on until now the mile-long freight trains were visible for miles across the cotton fields, seeming to pass

two or even three of the little Indian-named hamlets at one time over
the ground where every November they would run the ritual of the old
warp-footed bear; —the Big Woods, shoved, pushed further and further
down into the notch where the hills and the Big River met, where they
would make their last stand.

Any reader of my book will have read this before. As I said in my notes
on Norman Maclean, read it again.

CHAPTER 59

The Art of Falconry: Being the De Arte Venandi cum Avibus

by Emperor Frederick II

Translated by Casey A. Wood and F. Marjorie Fyfe

1244 to 1250

Emperor Frederick II of Hohenstaufen was born in 1194 and died at only fifty-six in 1250. His family was from Swabia (as one wit said, the Holy Roman Empire was not holy, Roman, or an empire). His mother, Constance, was over fifty when she bore him; she was Sicilian by royal inheritance, a princess of Norman descent from the House of Roger d'Hauteville. His father was German, son of Frederick Barbarossa, but Frederick was, like his mother, Sicilian by choice, as eastern and southern as he was northern.

He grew up running wild in Palermo, a virtual street kid, but reclaimed his heritage at eighteen. He was reputed in his lifetime to be the Antichrist, and was known as Stupor Mundi, the Wonder of the World. Dante, of the opposing political party, wrote him into Hell in the *Inferno*. He was excommunicated four times and married three.

Myths, slander, and truth mingle in his legend. He is said to have experimented on humans, raising children without speaking to see what tongue they spoke, weighing bodies before and after death to attempt to discover the weight of the soul. He may have been the first rationalistic observer in pre-Renaissance Europe; he was without a doubt the first to describe migration, which the rest of the world didn't catch up with until about 1800. He invented an early form of the sonnet and founded the University of Naples. He also tempted St. Francis of Assisi with naked dancing girls.

He defeated a Moslem guerilla army in Sicily, then made them into his personal mercenary guard, settling them in the walled city of Lucera on the mainland and building them a mosque. He kept a harem and employed Moslem and Jewish philosophers, artists, and physicians; although he gave lip service to the persecutions of the time, he hired exiled troubadours from heretical southern France to sing for him.

He made a reluctant crusade and ended up crowning himself King of Jerusalem, where he visited the Great Mosque, shook hands with Saladin, and discussed falconry. He died of malaria back in Italy, too young, worn out from his struggles. When they opened Frederick's tomb not long ago, they found he was sharing it with an unknown young woman. Today he is remembered mostly by falconers and Sicilian patriots, allegedly including some elderly Mafiosi.

He left a son who was soon to die defending his cause and bloodline, a strange castle in Puglia, and the first scientific ornithology, a book of advanced science and art in the form of a falconry manual: *De Arte Venandi cum Avibus*. He was one of the greatest falconers who ever lived, and can still teach us everything lost we need to remember.

John McDonald is good on Frederick. "If modern writing on sport had only one originating point—unlikely as that assumption might be—a claim to it could be made on behalf of Frederick II's *Art of Falconry* . . . *The Art* . . . was the most important and influential treatise on hunting in the early Middle Ages."

There have been three modern editions. The rarest is a two-volume Latin version published in Leipzig in 1944 while the bombs were falling. This fascinating edition has a certain fame among booksellers and is mentioned in Bruce Chatwin's short story "The Estate of Maximilian Tod." There is also a more recent Latin edition, a facsimile that costs about as much as a shotgun. But the accessible edition, still in print, is the translation made by Casey Wood and F. Marjorie Fyfe of McGill University in the late 1930s.

It's a peculiar book, a "curate's egg." Wood and Fyfe were not falconers, and their understanding of the details of the sport is often suspect. Despite the wonderful translation, the book includes a lot of irrelevant and some ludicrous supplementary material, including poor-quality redrawings of nineteenth-century bird illustrations, inaccurate lists of falconers' favorite birds, ornithological mistakes, an account of modern US falconry that names only one falconer, and entirely too many photographs of the Nazi's state hawking news.* To be fair there are also photographs of Frederick's buildings and contemporary portraits of him, but it is best to treat most of this material with caution.

---

* Goering sent a falcon trapper to Iceland to bring him gyrfalcons. In an almost medieval gesture, the trapper defected to the United States and brought the falcons as tribute to Col. Luff Meredith, the American falconer mentioned by Wood and Fyfe.

The text is another matter, fascinating and still completely useful, not least because Frederick concentrates on the great gyrfalcon and its close Eurasian relative—the saker—rather than the peregrine. From Frederick's time to the 1820s in the west, and always in the east, these "great falcons" were considered the best; only now are westerners beginning to rediscover their superiority.

Modern equipment has improved, but the nature of the bird is unchanged. One of the most important and difficult things for a falconer to learn is how to place a hood on a falcon's head. Frederick devotes *five pages* to this subject alone. Newcomers to the sport could do worse than to commit these to memory; they describe every possible reaction of the bird to the hood and what the falconer's answer should be. He also tells you how it looks when you have done things right. "The signs that the falcon is no longer displeased with her hood are that she occasionally shakes it, rearranges and anoints her feathers, and holds the falconers fist lightly and does not try to sink her talons into it. She sometimes goes to sleep with her hood on, especially after she has been awake on the falconer's hand for a long time or is hungry or tired."

I won't bore you further with falconry esoterica, though Frederick's command of detail is astounding. That one would do something so odd as to fly big falcons at hares before you start them on large waterfowl or cranes is counterintuitive, but it is now being done with success in New Mexico, as Frederick advises. Read *De Arte* and inhabit the mind of a cool, shrewd, strangely "modern" thinker as he calmly refutes the status quo, remarking on the birds he sees migrating through Sicily or describing the body language of a bird. The older I get, the more I can see that Frederick has been down all my roads before me.

ALSO READ:

Observations on Modern Falconry and *The Taming of Genghis,* by Ronald Stevens, who was the first modern master of the gyrfalcon and read Frederick

Frederick the Second, by Ernst Kantorowicz

An Accidental Autobiography, by Barbara Grizutti Harrison, in which she wrote an essay titled "Frederico Secundo," the best short modern treatment of Frederick I know

CHAPTER 60

The Last Running
by John Graves
1974

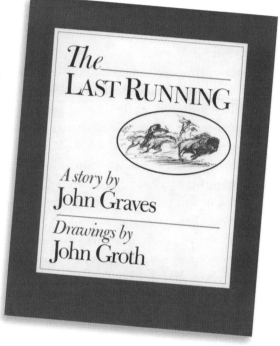

When *The Last Running* was first published as a book, they used my blurb: *"The Last Running* may be my favorite short story of the last thirty-five years, and contains my all-time favorite last line." A part of me is tempted to let it go at that, but I will tell you more so you'll understand that this statement is neither over-the-top nor dictated by literary friendship.

John Graves, who despite obvious contenders would be my pick for the best Texas writer, is alive in his nineties in the Hill Country, probably still rolling his eyes at being called "the sage of Glen Rose." His entire body of work might fit between the covers of an overstuffed airport potboiler, with the difference that every word he ever wrote is worth reading. He first achieved general notice in 1960 with *Goodbye to a River,* a naturalist's narrative about canoeing down the Brazos before it was dammed, with good hunting and fishing and a little history. He has also written the occasional article and essay, two good nonfiction books, *Hardscrabble* and *From a Limestone Ledge,* and this iconic piece of fiction.

On the surface it is the simplest narrative in the world: A ragged band of Comanches rides from the reservation in Oklahoma in the early part of the twentieth century to the ranch of an old Texan who they call Tom Tejano, and ask him if they can have a buffalo. When he eventually, grumpily, turns one over, they don't take it away for meat. They run it, kill it with arrows and lances, and ride away, while the old man and a young boy, later to be the narrator, watch.

That's it. In *Goodbye to a River*, Graves gives us the bare bones, saying that it happened to Charley Goodnight, the pioneer cattle driver. Those notes take up less than a page, but the story must have fermented, to be transmuted into this haunted tale.

The stand-alone edition is a handsome book, with drawings throughout by John Groth (illustrator of Gingrich's *The Well-Tempered Angler*, chapter 9). I liked it so much that I decided to give it to Leonard Parker, a tough old Comanche who was one of the legendary Quanah Parker's many grandchildren, very much in the mainline of what he called, not without irony, Indian aristocracy; there is a well-known photo of Quanah's reburial in 1956 with Leonard standing by the grave in his army uniform. He is now in his late eighties, retired back to Oklahoma, but when he was in Magdalena he worked for the Bureau of Indian Affairs (BIA)—he had a college degree—managed the bar, and ran a firewood business with me. As I once said to a friend in a letter, "He is The Trickster and an evil old bastard, but I am very fond of him." I got Graves to send him a copy of *The Last Running* inscribed, "To Leonard, whose ancestors gave mine a hell of a time on the Texas plains." It was the only time I ever saw him cry.

John wrote back, "Glad for your friend's response to *The Last Running*. Sometimes I don't think that story is really mine. It's unlike anything else I've done, it just came to me whole & sort of wrote itself in a day or two . . ."

And that last line? The boy is standing beside old Tom, who is holding the lance as he watches the Indians ride away. "He felt my eyes and turned, the bloody lance upright in his hand, paying no heed to the tears running down the sides of his big nose and into his moustache.

"'Damn you boy,' he said. 'Damn you for not ever getting to know anything worth knowing. Damn me, too. We had a world, once.'"

CHAPTER 61

The Nature of Paleolithic Art
by R. Dale Guthrie
2005

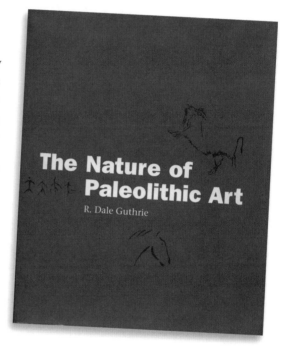

I would love to do a review book even odder than this one and review Guthrie by reprinting only a selection of illustrated panels, and let that stand in place of my words. A fair percentage of readers would immediately go out and buy it, and the others probably wouldn't want to read it anyway.

Among other things, *The Nature of Paleolithic Art* is an ambitious academic work by a paleontologist who is both intellectually and physically adventurous. Dale Guthrie is a paleontologist, an Alaskan, a big game bowhunter, an artist, and a sculptor. He found the frozen paleo-bison popularly known as "Babe," and ate part of its meat; the story is included in his earlier book, titled *Frozen Fauna of the Mammoth Steppe*. He is probably the greatest expert on the fauna of the Bering land bridge.

This sprawling, massive book, profusely illustrated by Guthrie's interpretations of the classic cave paintings, is his masterwork. It is apparently controversial, especially because he is impatient about the prevailing popular view of cave art as primarily religious or shamanic; his view is earthier and more biological. I will leave such arguments to the professionals. The book is both enlightening and delightful whether you agree with his interpretation or not.

What is hard to argue about is the illumination that his experience as a modern Paleolithic hunter brings to his interpretations. He indicates how much the experience of the ancient hunters informs their portraits on such things as the marking on horses or lions or *Megaceros*. Anyone who has ever lung-shot a big game animal would agree with his interpretation of the many portraits of hemorrhaging hoofed animals. Many interpreters either insist the blood is "breath of life," somehow tied to shamanism, or recognize it and say that the old hunters were "morbidly focused on pain, blood, and death."

Guthrie has a brusque rejoinder: "For me, these scholars fail to appreciate the extent to which human well-being, survival, and happiness depend on the demanding and erratic successes of killing large mammals. I suspect Paleolithic artists included these details as integral parts of the ensemble, as an expression of beauty and excitement."

You don't have to agree with every one of Guthrie's conclusions to find this remarkable book the best view yet into the minds of our ancestors. I will leave the last word with Guthrie:

Like the gravedigger, those of us who are grave digger-uppers are often aware that we too do not have forever—that our now-vivid times will also pass, like those halcyon days around the campfires with skewered shelk roasts and extravagant sunsets. A seer throws the old ivory carvings, kneels, and reads them thoughtfully: "They say, 'Wake up, you are on; we have had our time and this is yours.'" She smiles and—I thought she was mocking, but perhaps not—goes on to say that the truly good message from Paleolithic art is "that one would be wise to play: play physically, play mentally, and, above all, play artfully."

ALSO READ:

The Dawn of Art: The Chauvet Caves, by Jean Marie Chauvet

Deer of the World, by Valerius Geist

The Quaternary Extinctions, by Paul S. Martin and Richard Klein

For an utterly different point of view, *The Shamans of Prehistory: Trance and Magic in the Painted Caves,* by Jean Clottes and David Lewis-Williams

CHAPTER 62

The Stars, The Snow, The Fire: Twenty-five Years in the Northern Wilderness
by John Haines
1989

The Stars, The Snow, The Fire by John Haines is an utterly unique little book, a backwoods Alaskan memoir by an award-winning poet who was also a fur trapper. It is philosophical, episodic, and sensory, marked by the narrator's haunting and sometimes harrowing encounters with wildlife. Haines knew, as only someone who has lived a subsistence life may know, that to kill to live is a serious business, touched by guilt and satisfaction; how many contemporary poets know that truth in their bones?

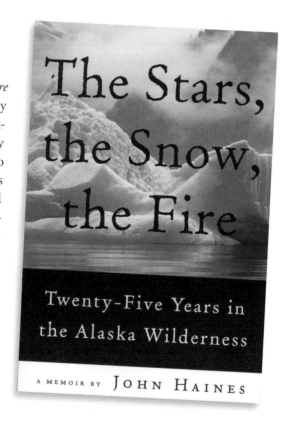

The hunting and fishing, the wild fruit, the trapping, the wood that we burn and the food that we eat—it is all given to us by the country. The fur of this marten is lovely when held in the light, shaken so that the hair stands from the pelt. And meat of the moose is good to have; it keeps us fed and warm inside, and I pay no butcher for it. Yet I cannot trap and

kill without thought or emotion, and it may be that the killing wounds me also in some small but deadly way . . . It can be hard and cruel sometimes, as we are prepared to see it clearly. I put the beast to death for my own purposes, as the lynx kills the rabbit, the marten and the squirrel, and the weasel the mouse. Life is filled with contradictions—confused and doubting in the heart of a man, or it is straight as an arrow and full of purpose.

There's more here than just the hunter's paradox. "Of traps and snares" and "Three days" are almost the only literate essays on trapping I've ever seen. Add tales of north-country eccentrics that remind me of Norman Maclean, and pieces—"Burning a porcupine" and "Death is a meadowlark"—that delight by their titles alone, though their content is every bit as good. And a final bonus for you if you enjoy handsome books for their own sake: Graywolf Press did a beautiful job of book design on *The Stars, The Snow, The Fire.* Under a subtle and handsome photographic dust jacket, the cover is of deep midnight blue cloth, adorned by three gold wolves and three gold stars (there is also a paperback if this does not move you).

Besides, you won't find many other poems about trapping.*

ALSO READ:
Florida East Coast Champion, by Rod Taylor (*which has the only other good trapping poem I know, as well as several on hunting)

CHAPTER 63

Is She Coming Too?
by Frances Hamerstrom
1989

Born to a prominent Boston family in 1907, Frances ("FRAHN
not Fraan!") Flint became fascinated with hunting and falconry
at an early age. She met and married her lifelong soulmate Frederick Hamerstrom, a kindred spirit,
when they were in their teens, and
together they became part of a
select group, the first class of Aldo
Leopold's students: America's pioneer wildlife biologists. Along the
line she found time to save the
prairie chicken, be a debutante,
a model, a hunter, and a serious
eagle falconer; raise children in
a Victorian farmhouse in rural
Wisconsin with no modern plumbing; and write eight or nine books
including a game cookbook. I don't know why she wasn't famous, but then
she was one of only two friends of mine who made it to Letterman . . .*

Her books form a composite memoir. *Birding with a Purpose* is about
bird-banding; *Strictly for the Chickens* chronicles their years studying the prairie chicken. *My Double Life* deals with her childhood, shooting and preparing "specimens" and hiding them in a hollow tree. But in *Is She Coming*

---

* That snide Indiana-born pseudo-Manhattanite grimaced and made "covert" faces at the camera when
she cleaned a pigeon, as though she were a toothless inbred Snopes grammaw cooking aged roadkill for
his audience's smug derision. I called to complain about his rudeness and she laughed: "Stephen, for
writers, *all* publicity is good publicity!"

Too?—referring, of course, to the reaction of most male hunters when she arrived with Frederick—she gives the most complete portrait of her hunting life. On one of her first "dates," if the word applies, with Frederick, she swims out naked to retrieve her first duck—a scoter—and is accosted, half-dressed, by a policeman who objects to her parking illegally. She goes on to shoot on quail plantations and over live decoys, still legal in the 1920s; then to "game school," where she is, as often, the only female; finally to her and her husband's apprenticeship under Leopold, who taught her to cook woodcock with their intestines still inside.

In the Midwest they found their true *Querencia,* hunting sharptails and prairie chickens near home and Montana sage grouse under big skies. She writes eloquent chapters on these incomparable birds and, for equipment junkies like me, adds one on their Parker 20-bores and how they acquired them. *My Double Life,* her broader autobiography, followed, even better if less of a hunting book. (The bound galleys startled me with the late revelation, suggested by a drawing and abundantly confirmed by photos and data, that her childhood estate eventually became my extremely odd grammar school. I shot crows there with the Mother Superior's permission; FFH to SB: "We collected our first *specimens* on the same ground!")

The passion, commitment, and matter-of-fact intelligence she brought to her particular adventures make these books endlessly readable. Listen to her prologue: "For me, hunting is so much more than the high point of delight of any one sense. I use all five senses—and all the knowledge I have accumulated up to that time—and besides I hunt with my man. For me hunting is not symphony, not a painting, not to be defined. It is a long, fascinating road leading to moments of ecstasy."

ALSO READ:
All the above, plus *An Eagle to the Sky*

Just Before Dark
by Jim Harrison
1991

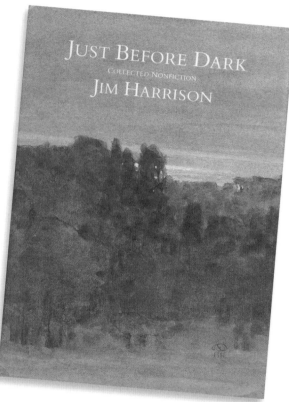

Is there anyone out there these days unfamiliar with Jim Harrison's novels, essays, poetry, even screenplays? Some of his books are epics, some bawdily humorous; the very best (*Dalva,* for example) contain both elements. He is a man of enormous appetite and—it doesn't seem paradoxical to me, though it seems to puzzle some critics—of great sensitivity. He hunts birds and fishes in Montana, his native Michigan, and the tropical flats of the Caribbean; eats (as I once wrote of his friend and publisher Russell Chatham) like a nineteenth-century Parisian; can be crude or poetic; writes humorously of lust and gluttony; got so far inside the head of his great female hero, Dalva Northridge, that *Dalva* is the favorite contemporary novel of several tough literate women that I know; aches for the Great Plains tribes and has written more movingly about their passing than any other recent novelist I know; studies Zen Buddhism . . . well, you get the point.

    Just Before Dark is divided into three parts—"Food," "Travel and Sport," and "Literary Matters"—though there's plenty of tasty mixing between the sections. The one that most concerns us here is, of course, the second; but before we pass on to such matters, I can't resist quoting a description (one of many) of his larder in his former home place in Michigan, from the first chapter. "Until recently, my home base . . . was over sixty miles from the nearest first-rate restaurant . . . This calls for resourcefulness in the kitchen, or what the Tenzo in a Zen monastery would call 'skillful means.' I keep an inventory taped to the refrigerator of my current frozen possibilities: local barnyard capons; the latest shipment of prime veal from Summerfield Farms, which includes sweetbreads, shanks for osso bucco, liver, chops, kidneys; and a little seafood from Charles Morgan in Destin, Florida—triggerfish, a few small red snappers, conch for chowder and fritters. There are two shelves of favorites—rabbit, grouse, woodcock, snipe, venison, dove, chukar, duck, quail—and containers of fish fumet, various glazes; and stocks, including one made from sixteen woodcock that deserves its own armed guard." As Harrison used to call his *Esquire* column, "Sporting Food," cubed. . . .

But the broadest range of pieces in the book is in the second part, which ranges in time, space, and, I guess, esthetics, from "Ice Fishing, the Moronic Sport" and "A Plaster Trout in Worm Heaven" (both set in Michigan in the early 1970s, both from *Sports Illustrated*) to "La Venerie Francaise" (stag hunting at a friend's ancestral estate in France). The very best ones may be in the middle of the scale—an old favorite, "A Sporting Life," which wanders around the world, and the more recent "Bird Hunting," which manages to say some fresh things about that overdone subject.

> *Hearing distant shooting I climb to a bare hillock and look through my monocular (I'm blind in one eye so in a moment of brilliance gave up binoculars after thirty years). The Dogman and Count approach a swale perhaps a thousand yards distant. My monocular is a small round movie screen focused on three pointers on tightly honored point. There is a flush and the Count swings left and right and two birds fall. Unlike the artist and I the Count and Dogman take turns. Now I see my own dog, Sand, streaking toward the real action as the Count's retriever fetches the birds. I turn with the monocular and focus on the artist dozing under an oak tree, his left hand brushing acorns from beneath his ample bottom. I am not exactly "one with the earth" but I'm feeling good.*

Is this too robustly bucolic for you? Then try this piece of surreal tropical natural history, from "A Day in May":

Here, a few years back, we saw an explosion up on the flats and checked it out. It was a hammerhead shark, nearly as long as the seventeen-foot skiff, chasing tarpon in the shallow water. He paused to investigate us and we teased him with the push pole. The shark circled the skiff with one goggle eye raised and tried to figure out if we were a meal. There was a stiff wind, and the sun focused him in brilliant flashes under the swiftly fleeting clouds. The water only intermittently covered him, and his long, thick, gray body glistened in a bulbous wake. Aside from a mostly imaginary danger, I could no more kill one of these creatures than I would a house pet. He belongs where he is and we are merely visitors.

This collection is *all* "good parts." Like all Clark City books, it's a beautifully designed cloth-bound volume, with a Chatham dust jacket. Since *JBD*, Harrison has gone on to write a daunting amount of novels, two rather different stabs at autobiography, and at least two more collections, one including his notorious over-the-edge Paris meal that allegedly cost over $30,000. If pressed I would still call this my favorite; a few more, written over many years, are below.

ALSO READ:
Jim Harrison's *Legends of the Fall, Dalva,* and *The Raw and the Cooked*

CHAPTER 65

The Shotgun
by Macdonald Hastings
1981

"*The* Shotgun"; not just any shotgun. This book is about the London capital-B Best game gun, a working tool that has attained a level of perfection (and stasis) achieved by very few human creations. In the middle of this celebratory volume, after explaining some of the processes that create a unique object of desire, Hastings underlines that point:

> *I doubt whether there is any mechanical skill that equals the love that is put into a Best Gun. It is arguable that the effort is wasted . . . yet, as the poet Keats argued, "beauty is truth, truth is beauty." I am inclined to think that not since the fifth century B.C. has anything been made functionally better than a London Best gun. You need not shoot it. Just look at the lovely thing it is.*

Those of us who have shot such magical artifacts know that he's right. *Nothing* handles like a bespoke game gun, even someone else's. The best float through the air to their targets as though possessed by deadly predatory spirits.

Their unarguable beauty and their vast expense give them a certain mystique. They have inspired a body of commentary, some hagiographic or nearly pornographic, featuring salivating portraits of guns that cost more than my house. A lot of English volumes assume prior familiarity with the English double, making them difficult reading for Americans; some Americans don't know enough to have opinions. A few texts are very good. Several are better in detail than *The Shotgun*.

So why give it first place? Most of the others are for committed gun nuts; none tell you what a Best gun *is*, how it came to be, why you should care, even if you're a sane person who never thought or knew of the existence of such a thing before. Macdonald Hastings was a reporter and ace magazine editor who wrote sporting books, mysteries, and biography; a writer's writer

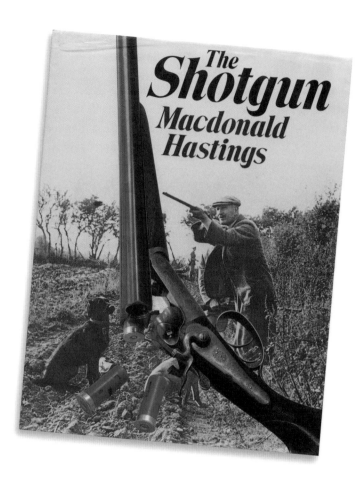

and an intimate of the gunmaker Churchill; and could tell a story and knew his subject from top to bottom.

In *The Shotgun* he shows how the Best evolved contingently from the conjunction of unique forces, like a biological organism. The London Best appeared once, in one place, when prestige and prosperity met a rising social need for large bags and difficult shots, and new materials from the Industrial Revolution coincided with a migration of skilled craftsmen to a couple of big English cities. It appeared in England because, although the Continent and America produced quality doubles, their environments demanded different solutions. (Hastings tried to contrast the English sporting shotgun and the Colt revolver, as they applied to England and the frontier; give him an "A" for effort and forget that he missed the Winchester repeater.)

The Shotgun also covers everything from shooting school and poaching to live pigeon shooting and house parties. The last, as is obvious from such productions as "The Shooting Party" and "Gosford Park," was an important factor in the evolution of the Best.

There are a few puzzling mistakes. Writing in some sort of demented or drunken despair, he laments, "It is sad that so many of the great names in the English gunmaking trade are gone. There is no Greener anymore, no Purdey, no Holland, no Lancaster, no Boss, no Churchill, no Manton." *WHAT?* Purdey, Holland, and Boss have never ceased production since they were founded in the nineteenth century. Greener did, but is in business again. Churchill, a twentieth century latecomer, has flickered on and off. English Mantons died in the 1830s. Of these names, only Lancaster died in the twentieth century and has not been revived.

Still, Hastings wrote delightful, accessible history. I have listed some more reliable references below. If you enjoy him as a writer, you should try his *Game Book,* his biography of Robert Churchill, and his son Max's bemused biography *Did You Really Shoot the Television?*

ALSO READ:

Shotguns and Gunsmiths: The Vintage Years, by Geoffrey Boothroyd

The Shotgun (three volumes), by Major Sir Gerald Burrard

Vintage Guns for the Modern Shot, by Diggory Hadoke (most practical)

Double Guns and Custom Gunsmithing, by Steven Dodd Hughes (an American custom gunsmith who gets it)

British Gun Engraving, by Douglas Tate

The Best of British, by Vic Venters

British Vintage Shotguns, by Terry Wieland

CHAPTER 66

We Live in the Arctic
by Constance and Harmon Helmericks
1947

Often, though I don't like it, I know why a book I love is neglected; not so for this one. *We Live in the Arctic,* published in 1947 by a major publisher, is a straightforward adventure classic that should be read by anyone who loves wild things. Its plot, if plot can be attributed to a nonfiction book, is the soul of simplicity. "Bud was with the Army Engineers and then served with the army of the Alaska Defense Command . . . when he returned we retired from the business and industrial world at the age of twenty-six, obtained a tent and a canoe and struck out north . . . 'How long will we be gone?' I asked, just once for I didn't much care. 'Oh, two, three, or more years, maybe,' he replied. 'We should get a pretty good hunt out of this trip anyway.'"

They did. I have occasionally and not too inaccurately summed up the rest of the book when recommending it to friends as: "Wander around the backcountry, shoot everything with a .30-30, and eat everything including the fat and the guts. Repeat." It is a *little* reductive, if only because it makes a book of cheerful adventure sound repetitive. But both points are worth making. Like Bell and several other writers quoted here, they never seemed to realize that a .30-30 was inadequate. Their entire armory consisted of two Winchester 94s, a 12-gauge pump, and a .22 automatic Colt Woodsman pistol—and they shot grizzlies for food. Constance put it succinctly: "there is too much discussion altogether given to the caliber of guns, for when it comes to hunting, nine-tenths of that sport is just what it says—hunting and not shooting."

Re food: The Helmerickses were either ahead of, or behind, their times; they knew the value of fat and stomach contents, and knew they had to kill fat animals or risk dietary deficiencies or even starvation.

> . . . *raw animal fat is the most easily available and most easily assimilated food from which the starving hunter can gain quick energy if he has nothing else. This precious substance is, moreover, something no wild animal can have too much of for the hunter's needs. It is known that native peoples living by hunting eat first of all the fat and the fattest parts of the animal, and this holds true from Alaska to Africa, where hippopotamus fat is loved by the black hunters in the same way certain fats are prized by the wild foragers of the arctic.*

These days the Helmerickses probably look pretty "primitive." Living off the grid is presented as a grim and serious step; adventuring in the wilderness takes more and more expensive "essential" equipment. The whole enterprise seems so daunting that an entire industry has been built on the helpless stupidity of an idiot that starved himself in a school bus in Alaska, far closer to an industrial civilization than the Helmerickses ever ventured. They make it all look easy.

Because, of course, with the right heart and half a brain, it is. The hunter-gatherer's life, the old way, is full of delight. Constance, with several more years ahead in the Alaskan wilderness, looked back and said it well:

> *We think now of our roaming days in the present American arctic. They were great days, living by hunting and loafing in the solitudes, the prodigal existence of those who wander and are not bound. Our tale is spiced with arctic suffering—a little—but then there were also strange delights. We think of it as the story—for our generation in the mid-twentieth century—of the hunter of all ages and climes, who wanders endlessly and forever, over happy hunting grounds, always young and joyous and carefree.*

CHAPTER 67

Green Hills of Africa
by Ernest Hemingway
1935

The hardest chore in this project has been cutting, and perhaps the hardest case of that has been the various works of Ernest Hemingway. How do you pick *one* book? Not only was he among our finest novelists, whose reputation finally seems to be recovering from the attacks of yapping post-1960s academics, but he also lived an exemplary sporting life—fished for trout in Michigan and Europe and marlin off Cuba in the Gulf Stream, shot birds everywhere, loved Africa with a passion, and wrote well about it all. Finally, I have gone with *Green Hills of Africa,* his only explicitly sporting book, which was done with the conscious aim of writing a hunting book as a work of literary art. It even looks good. I love Ruark's romantic tales, but *GHOA* is a subtler and more fundamental work.

Today, barring some attitudes of Hemingway's character that might be dismissed as retrograde, *Green Hills* seems utterly modern or even postmodern, but this is after the journalistic revolutions of the 1960s and '70s that brought us the New Journalism and Truman Capote's "Nonfiction Novel" *In Cold Blood.* By the standards of the 1930s, it is a damn strange book. Hemingway explicitly warns the reader in his three-sentence "foreword": "The writer has attempted to write an absolutely true book to see whether the shape of a country and the patterns of a month's action can, if truly presented, compete with a work of the imagination."

He tells good hunting stories first. In that straightforward task he succeeds, though those who take literature to bits to see how it works seem to find *Green Hills* annoying. His framework is a monthlong safari in Kenya, concentrating on his hunt for a trophy kudu in (mostly) friendly rivalry with the younger friend he calls "Karl," with asides to grumpily but perceptively discuss literature or mutter darkly about being shown up. "I was, truly, very fond of him and he was entirely unselfish and altogether self-sacrificing I

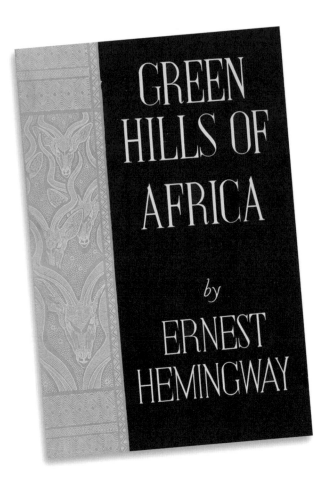

knew. I could outshoot him and I could always outwalk him and, steadily, he got trophies that made mine look like dwarfs in comparison."

Those without irony deplore the narrator's compulsive drive to compete with his friend, ignoring the fact that he consciously documented it. If he is a reporter so honest that, at times, he makes himself the least attractive character in the book, he should win points for remarkable honesty. If he is doing slightly tongue-in-cheek fiction, using real characters, award him more points for doing that so well that every other reader thinks it reveals him to be a jerk. Most likely he was aware he was putting himself in an unattractive light, but did so anyway in fealty to his vision of honest writing. Is the reductive version of "theory" so pervasive that these critics doubt he could hold all these ideas at once? Closer readers might intuit that all interpretations can exist simultaneously; Hemingway, like that other "simple" writer, Kipling, contains multitudes. I choose to think he placed every word like a brick in a wall.

His slightly boozy campfire lectures on writing, with more lit-crit than he allows in any other book, are usually sounder than his envious ramblings and often worth the price of admission, though some of his remarks are notorious for their boastfulness. This rigorous observation beats some of his better-known snark:

> *First, there must be talent, much talent. Talent such as Kipling had.*
> *Then there must be discipline. The discipline of Flaubert. Then there*
> *must be the conception of what it can be and an absolute conscience as*
> *unchanging as the standard meter in Paris, to prevent faking. Then the*
> *writer must be intelligent and disinterested and above all he must sur-*
> *vive. Try to get all these in one person and have him come through all*
> *the influences that press on a writer. The hardest thing because time is so*
> *short, is for him to survive and get his work done.*

Turn away from the petty rivalry and savor this wonderful passage (just *two sentences,* for those who insist that Faulkner wrote better ones) on the hunter's life in our oldest home:

> *I'd make some money some way and when we came back we would*
> *come to the old man's village in trucks, then pack in with porters so there*
> *wouldn't be any damned car to worry about, send the porters back, and*
> *make a camp in the timber up the stream above the Roman's and hunt*
> *that country slowly, living there and hunting out each day, sometimes*
> *laying off and writing for a week, or writing half the day, or every other*
> *day, and get to know it as I knew the country around the lake where we*
> *were brought up. I'd see the buffalo feeding where they lived, and when*
> *the elephants came through the hills we would see them and watch them*
> *breaking branches and not have to shoot, and I would lie in the fallen*
> *leaves and watch the kudu feed out and never fire a shot unless I saw a*
> *better head than this one in back, and instead of trailing that sable bull,*
> *all gut-shot to hell, all day, I'd lie behind a rock and watch them on the*
> *hillside and see them long enough so they belonged to me forever.*

Hemingway could easily have earned four books here, plus at least two about him; don't neglect his other writing. Here is another African bit, from the novel-within-a-novel—postmodern surface again!—nested in his posthumous *Garden of Eden.* Despite some simpletons calling that part a "boy's book," this late writing is as fine as ever:

It was not very long before they came on the secret. It was off to the right in the forest and the tracks of the old bull led to it. It was a skull as high as David's chest and white from the sun and the rains. There was a deep depression in the forehead and ridges ran from between the bare white eye sockets and flared out in empty broken holes where the tusks had been chopped away. Juma pointed out where the great elephant they were trailing had stood while he looked down at the skull and where his trunk had moved it a little way from the place it had rested on the ground and where the points of his tusks had touched the ground beside it. He showed David the single hole in the white bone of forehead and then the four holes close together in the bone around the ear hole. He grinned at David and at his father and took a .303 solid from his pocket and fitted the nose into the hole in the bone of the forehead.

Hemingway's ghost haunts us all.

ALSO READ:

Ernest Hemingway's *Byline Ernest Hemingway, Islands in the Stream, The Garden of Eden,* and *True at First Light.* The last African work was edited by his literate son Patrick, who worked for many years in Africa as a hunter and wildlife biologist. He was comfortable enough with the result to sign his name on the flyleaf at least once. The other posthumous book, culled from his last safari, is *Under Kilimanjaro.* It is unwieldy and reads as unedited, though full of nuggets and details of animals and people and guns.

As for works about him, there is a thriving Hemingway industry. For reasons too numerous to detail, I recommend the biographical and scholarly books below over many more I have read. Unlike most of them, these are accurate.

Running with the Bulls, by Valerie Hemingway

Hemingway's Guns, by Silvio Calabi et al. Calabi did first-rate detective work: Among other things Hemingway did *not* kill himself with a Boss pigeon gun, though the thoroughly debunked rumor persists.

Hemingway's Boat, by Paul Hendrickson (Best modern critical work; reads like a novel. Still buys the Boss myth.)

CHAPTER 68

Bull Cook and Authentic Historical Recipes and Practices

by George Leonard Herter

1969

I'd like to evoke for your amusement if not edification the eccentric ghost of George Leonard
Herter—entrepreneur, innovator,
author of, among many writ-
ings both ephemeral and collectible, *Bull Cook, The Truth About
Hunting in Today's Africa,* and
George the Housewife, and holder
of . . . odd opinions. He should
be remembered for at least one
serious reason: He was a real pioneer in outdoor mail order, who
published endless catalogs of
fishing and reloading tackle and
garrulous advice; those catalogs
were an inspiration and "dream
book" to my generation of fly
fishers and hunters. A lot of
this more pragmatic advice, like

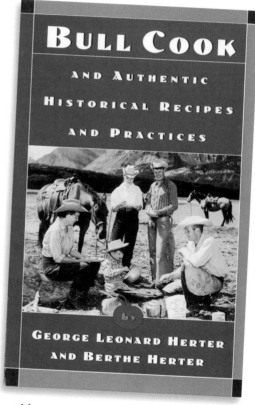

that in his guide manuals, is still sensible
today, but sensible nostalgic how-to has a rather limited appeal. It was in his
cookbooks and "lifestyle" manuals that George approached a level of, if not
genius, inspired lunacy.

George the Housewife can be described as a male Heloise for the barking
mad (I'm not sure that Heloise doesn't approach that point herself). I will

deal with the African book's wonders below. But *Bull Cook and Historical Recipes* is his essential classic, worth owning both to read aloud for entertainment at any table where the wine flows, and because many of the game and fish recipes, the reason the book exists—"Doves Wyatt Earp," for one famous instance—are pretty good. In a time when game cookbooks and male cooks were both uncommon, Herter presented himself as a plain man who was comfortable in the kitchen, a knowing mentor with a backwoodsman's zest and a European's breadth of taste.

But the history, or George Leonard's version thereof, is why anyone with a sense of the absurd must buy the book. My favorite line in all the Herter oeuvre is "The Virgin Mary was very fond of spinach," closely followed by "It is a *well known fact* [a constant Herter locution] that Beethoven was fond of Spam." Other immortal quotes include "Sauerbraten was invented by Charlemagne . . ."; "Henry the VIII actually never amounted to anything and would not have made a good ditchdigger . . ."; "In 1212 St. Francis went to the Holy Land. When he came back he taught his followers a simple way to poach eggs . . ."; "Pate De Foie Gras was first made for Joan of Arc by one of her army cooks . . ."

The African book (1963), which features a zebra-striped cover and many photos of dead birds being thrown upside down to re-create the author's son's shots, also has at least one immortal line: "Most people don't realize that being eaten by a hyena doesn't hurt very much."

It is well worth getting any of the above and reading them aloud to friends and family. We raised a generation of literate young outdoorspersons on them, and every one can complete sentences beginning "Being eaten by a hyena" and "Beethoven was fond of . . ." Many actually own *Bull Cook*. I can only hope it didn't warp their lives too much.

"Real" editions of the books mentioned are collectible and can bring startling prices; I still don't have the legendary *How to Live with a Bitch* for that reason. It is a tribute to GLH's inspired weirdness that Ecco, a haut-lit press, brought out an affordable paperback of *Bull Cook* in 1995.

CHAPTER 69

Hunting American Lions
by Frank Hibben
1948

Until the 1960s hunting mountain lions and bears with hounds was a main-stay of sporting literature, even in the Big Three. Invisible cultural forces seem to have erased it from the media, if not from life. Houndsmen continue to hunt, and a few eccentric writers continue to report, but the subject is off the contemporary radar screen. Even some hunting writers these days seem to be taking cues from the Humane Society of the United States, though why any big game bowhunter thinks he is any less a target for the likes of Wayne Pacelle is beyond me.

Hunting with hounds, the way a few mavericks still do in the United States, is perhaps the oldest form of hunting that still exists; we will be the poorer if it vanishes. I'll mention a few contemporaries in the "Also Read" section, but books from the innocent time before it was condemned will give you an unclouded look at the houndsman's life, properly celebrated. In America the greatest predator hunter, though no writer, was the strange Old Testament character Ben Lilly, who started out in Louisiana and ended his life in southwestern New Mexico.

The best account of lion hunting in the first half of the twentieth century, *Hunting American Lions* includes not only the best portrait of Lilly ever painted, by someone who hunted with him, but contains many other well-written tales of lion hunting across the West.

Frank Hibben was a controversial archaeologist as well as a big game hunter. A friend who studied under him summed him up: "A hell of an entertaining teacher, but a bad archaeologist." He championed the so-called "Sandia Man" site, with its dubious early dates, threw spears in the classroom à la Indiana Jones, and used his influence to introduce most of the exotics we are blessed with or plagued by in this state; I can drive for half an hour and see an African oryx more easily than I can see an elk. But he was "present at the Creation," and he could tell a hell of a tale.

Hunting American Lions would be worth keeping for Ben Lilly alone. In 1934 some prematurely perceptive conservationists in Albuquerque hired Hibben to study the lion because they were worried about its population. All of his rancher and hunter friends agreed that he must seek out Ben Lilly. But by this time Lilly was ancient and possibly senile, and he had always been feral and half-mad. When Hibben goes to his ranch, Lilly admits, "I've killed a heap of them," and, still talking, starts walking toward the mountains. They walk for the next three days. As he told Hibben, he had been walking since he was a young man, when his then-wife told him to go out and kill a hawk and he, like the bird, "just kept going."

Lilly's nominal fundamentalist views obscure the fact that he was a hunting mystic, more like Dersu than a hired gun. While he regarded predators as "cursed," he simultaneously thought of himself as their friend and equal, and would speak of them as such. "A man has to be accepted into the family . . . You can't live with them and you can't hunt them if you aren't a member." After listening to him for a while, Hibben wrote, "I had the distinct feeling that he talked with animals more easily than with man, and if I had been one of his lion dogs, I would have learned even more."

For three days they walk, talk, and camp cold, only breaking for the Sabbath, eating mostly venison they steal from the lion's cache. Though they do not kill a lion, the hunt stayed with Hibben for the rest of his life. "We tracked down no game and we fired no shot, but on that chase I learned more about lions than on any other subsequent hunt. Certainly it was on those three days with a half-mad old hunter that I caught the true spirit of the hunt."

There are plenty of successful hunts in the book, and good scientific information as well. Hibben examines the still relevant question of lion predation on humans ("Certain of the people of Vancouver Island with long memories might give a very dire account indeed of the mountain lion . . ."), and even hunts locally, twelve miles from my present house, with a "young man" whom I know, now in his eighties. Get his good book and then read more; I list several good selections below, some more "serious." But for better or worse, you'll not see the likes of Ben Lilly or Frank Hibben again.

ALSO READ:

The Beast in the Garden, by David Baron (man-eaters in Boulder)

The Ben Lilly Story, by J. Frank Dobie

Eyes of Fire, by Warner Glenn (a second-generation houndsman, guide, and tree conservationist who releases the first official US jaguar in a decade)

The Longwalkers, by Jerry Lewis (professional Montana hunter)

Soul Among Lions, by Harley Shaw (a naturalist's perspective from a biologist and lion hunter)

Meet Mr. Grizzly, by Montague Stevens (another local, a one-armed English gentleman, who hunted grizzlies with hounds he kept in his house, then lobbied, too late, for their protection)

Almost anything—too little on his lions and hounds collected—by E. Donnall Thomas Jr. (Montana medical doctor, bowhunter, and houndsman, who has been known to eat lions).

CHAPTER 70

Dance of the Dwarfs
by Geoffrey Household
1968

Geoffrey Household, my choice for the greatest suspense story writer of the twentieth century, was the master of . . . not hunting exactly, but of Being Hunted. A born sportsman and a good field naturalist with an understanding of animals better than that of many scientists, he wrote brilliantly from the viewpoint of prey. This paragraph about sensing the attention of a predator is from *Dance of the Dwarfs*, but its theme recurs through decades of his novels.

> *I am becoming a connoisseur and analyst of fear. There is a definite distinction between that unconscious warning and the Declaration of Intent; the latter produces a conscious terror in every way the equivalent to that caused by the classical ghost, whether or not the ghost is an illusion.*

I knew I would have a Geoffrey Household book here; my problem was to pick one and resist the temptation to load the list with Household titles. The most obvious choice was his first bestseller, 1939s *Rogue Male*, in which an English hunter goes to ground in the English countryside after attempting to assassinate a Hitlerian dictator; others might argue for *Watcher in the Shadows*, in which an English zoologist flees to the countryside after an attempt on his life in London, or *The Courtesy of Death*, with its hidden Paleolithic cave paintings.

I went with *Dance of the Dwarfs* because of its seamless blend of natural history, hunting lore, and sheer terror. It purports to be the posthumous journals of a genial English agronomist on assignment in an isolated site in southern Venezuela where the grasslands meet the forest. His comfortable life of work, sport (he shoots a 16-bore Spanish double and an SMLE, naturally), and romance, is interrupted by a mystery that slowly expands into

obsession and terror. A perceptive teacher uses this book in a
course in the writing of history
to illustrate "how to lie with a
primary source." He is being
"writerly." Owen Dawnay,
Household's narrator, doesn't
lie; he is perplexed, and never
quite understands until the
last what is happening.

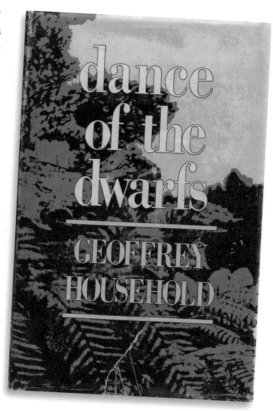

It is difficult to say
too much about the story
without giving "spoilers."
Dawnay becomes aware of
disturbing phenomena in
the jungle just outside his
vision. He tries to investigate and hears legends of
spirits, dancing dwarfs,
and other seeming impossi-
bilities. Are there unknown
tribes, or species, hovering
on the edge of his perception, or is he imagining things?

I'll leave you hanging. One of the joys of reading Household is discovering how subtly he builds his structure, delighting you with details of a life you
wouldn't mind living, as something ominous approaches just out of your line
of sight. Even after he reveals his secrets, you will read him again and again,
though this time you know what's coming. . . .

ALSO READ:
All titles above

Geoffrey Household's *The Sending, Sabres on the Sand* (short stories),
and *Against the Wind* (an early exercise in autobiography). He wrote
many more, but these in particular are concerned with country and
sporting matters.

CHAPTER 71

Home from the Hill
by William Humphrey
1958

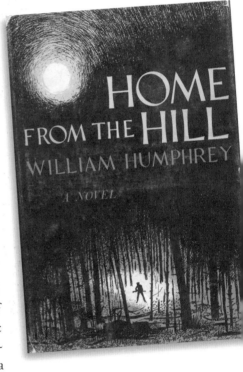

Home from the Hill was Bill's Big Book, his first novel, and his first movie sale*—heady stuff for a thirty-four-year-old New Yorker from East Texas. It is in some ways a young man's book, but in a good sense; it's a country epic, the tale of a young man's struggles in mythic Faulknerian country with his formidable father. It is by no means a "hunting book," but it could not exist without its hunting scenes; few books have been as permeated with the essence of southern sport.

In the book's keystone hunt, the boy, Theron, faces down a wild boar out of classical mythology. Even his dog's name evokes greater days.

> *Deuteronomy had leapt and sunk his teeth into the pig's ham as he shot past and had been lifted off his feet and carried along like the tail of a kite, the pig oblivious of him. Theron fired, and nothing happened. He felt the kick of the gun and heard the blast, and looking down the barrel saw the boar come on without faltering, but seeming actually to have gained momentum, seeming to have no legs or feet, but to be skimming a foot above ground. He kept the gun to his shoulder, but did not think to*

---

* "If they ever want to pay you to make a movie out of your book, take the money, run, don't walk, and don't look back."—Bill Humphrey to author.

work the lever for another shot. It had all happened too suddenly; he had neither thought nor felt. Now terror hit him like a blow to the chest, like the impact of the beast hurtling at him, and his sour gorge rose into his mouth. The next second the boar stopped, emerged from the gray blur of his speed into a distinct object; legs appeared on him, only to disappear in the next instant as his huge body collapsed and sank on them.

Even some of the guns are larger than life.

In the gun cabinet were five guns, two shotguns, two rifles, and a pistol. The bird gun was English, a Purdey, a famous make, a double barrel 12 gauge, and had been custom built for his father at a cost of over a thousand dollars. But it was the other shotgun that was really fabulous. It too was a Purdey. It too had been custom built. It had cost nearer two thousand dollars. It was a magnum 10 gauge double with barrels thirty-three inches long and weighed just under fourteen pounds. No man but the Captain, it was said, could take the punishment it dealt the shoulder in a day in a duck blind, and on the still damp foggy air of a good duck day in the marshes it could be heard for miles, like the boom of a cannonade.

There's plenty more; Humphrey wrote as observantly of life and comedy and bitter tragedy as he did of guns and hunting (there's plenty more of that too, from a squirrel scene good enough that you could learn something about the sport to the ethic of catch-and-release that seemed to be evolving among coon hunters when the book was written). You should read *Home from the Hill* because it is an American classic, but you could do worse than read it for the hunting.

ALSO READ:
William Humphrey's *Farther off from Heaven*, the autobiography of the childhood that formed the novel, with no Purdey, but a lot more fishing, and a gator. . . .

CHAPTER 72

Pale Horse Coming
by Stephen Hunter
2001

This will be the shortest account in my list of one hundred; you will either want to read it or not. Stephen Hunter is one of America's best suspense novelists and the former movie critic for the *Washington Post.* Unusual for a staffer at one of our great urban papers, he is also a dyed-in-the-wool gun nut who grew up reading the same 1950s gun writers as did many hunters of my generation.

He had been writing a series of novels about the Arkansas-born father and son, soldiers and lawmen, Earl and James Lee Swagger. In 2001 he decided to write a slightly tongue-in-cheek tribute to the old gun writers, enlisting them in Earl Swagger's attempt to bring down the corrupt empire of a backwoods prison warden and his sadistic minions.

Pale Horse Coming is not exactly a hunting book, but to appreciate it fully you need some knowledge of hunting and firearms, and to appreciate its sly wit you really need to know something about the personalities of O'Connor and Keith and their friends and rivals. Think of it as the *Magnificent Seven* meets The Old Boys ("the old gun writers"), with maybe a little bit of *The Wild Bunch* thrown in. A single paragraph will tell you whether you want to read it or not. Notice that he does not even change the first names of his two chief rivals.

> *Elmer hated Jack. This had to do with a philosophical issue, to be sure: Elmer was a believer in the theory of the big, slow bullet, while Jack only cared for small, fast bullets. But it was more than that, and if one had switched to the other argument, the other would counter-switch just to be not on the same side. Basically, each felt entitled to the leadership of what might be called the gun world. Each was a king. Each had a magazine*

*that published his comments and research, each had a retinue of follow-
ers (who hated each other too, even more than the two old rulers), each
had connections with certain gun manufacturers (Jack with Winchester,
whose products he used exclusively, Elmer with Smith & Wesson, like-
wise). Each said nasty things about the other whenever it was possible.
Each acted with arrogance and majesty. Each had killed over six hundred wild game animals, and while Elmer had once busted broncs and
was very cowboy in his way, Jack saw himself as an aristocrat or even an
intellectual of the rifle, and had no popular gifts and no interest in them.
Elmer could spin a yarn, Jack could deliver a lecture. Each held to his
positions as fiercely as rival party chairmen, which of course they were.*

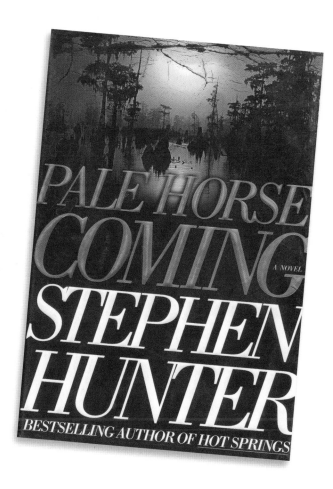

CHAPTER 73

Illumination in the Flatwoods
by Joe Hutto
1995

It is safe to say that Joe Hutto is not your regulation biologist. For one thing he is affiliated with no university; for another he has been the subject of a *New Yorker* profile by Bill Buford. He is also an archaeologist and a cowboy and a lot of other things; Buford lists both zoo and ranch manager and adds "an elk hunting guide, a competitive springboard diver, a dog handler (Labradors), a horse trainer, a landscape painter, an antiquities scuba diver, and a venomous snake catcher ($3.00 a foot for rattlers, $1.00 for water moccasins)." The last time he drove through here, knowing of my interest in the Pleistocene, he gave me a 12,000-year-old tooth from a young mammoth that he had retrieved while fossil diving in a Florida spring. Did I mention that he makes furniture?

But what he is above all is a naturalist and writer who knows more about wild turkeys than anyone alive. Reviewers routinely compare every scientist who works with animals to Konrad Lorenz. In Hutto's case the compliment may for once be deserved. Everyone interested in animals has seen photographs of Lorenz swimming with his geese, of imprinted geese and ducks following him down a path, but only Joe Hutto has lived as a peer and flock member in a group of wild turkeys.

Hutto, a turkey hunter (he opens the book with a vivid memory of calling up a tom when he was twelve), acquired his feathered family by accident. He was managing a north Florida quail plantation when he idly mentioned that it would be interesting to get some wild turkey eggs. A tractor driver soon delivered him a stainless steel dog bowl full. Little did he know that they would change his life, in fact become his life, for the next couple of years.

Figuring he could be at least as good a turkey mother as a chicken, he makes sure he is present for the hatching so the youngsters will imprint on him. "I spend a very pleasant hour or two greeting new arrivals . . . Each time one of these little birds comes into the world and identifies me as the object of his complete devotion, I am deeply moved. They are so small and vulnerable, but they represent something to me so rare and extraordinary, even powerful."

As the turkeys grow and begin to explore their environment, this remarkable respect and sensitivity allows him to enter into their world, and they change his perception, not just of turkeys, but of the natural world, even of color. "The turkeys are very concerned about my appearance and choice of clothing. Colors of red or purple are totally unacceptable; strangely, they also find a particular beige shirt annoying and try to remove it." He worries about being a dangerous influence; when he sees a beautiful but deadly coral snake nosing through the leaf mulch, a creature he would normally pick up, he says, "Exercising great restraint, I refrain from handling this living jewelry. I am afraid of setting a bad example, and so keep my hands to myself."

Some people perceive birds as being reflexive, hard-wired automatons, unlike mammals. Hutto, like many of us who live intimately with birds, learns that they have ideas of their own. The turkeys' reaction to bones is fascinating.

> . . . they seem . . . to be intrigued by the unusual shapes and textures. I once saw one of the hens casually transporting the skull of an opossum. Eventually, she lost interest and dropped it without looking back. Several others immediately begin playing with it . . . we visit several sites with regularity where skeletons lie, and the birds never seem to tire of studying them. When approaching a particular skeleton for the first time, however, they can be extremely cautious.

Hutto shepherds his little herd from adolescence to young adulthood, through adventure and amusement and occasional tragedy. His best friend among them, a male he calls "Turkey Boy," becomes fixated upon him, transferring all his "social attention" to Hutto and his wife. Suddenly, in January, something inside him changes and he sees Hutto as a rival male. "All his switches flipped—all his lights came on—and through what I gathered to be some sort of transference, he completed my evolution from parent to companion to adversarial brother. Turkey Boy had discovered that his mission in life was to fight."

It was no joke; Hutto could not leave his cabin without being attacked at eye level. Confrontation could have turned into tragedy. A desperate Hutto was forced to defend himself with a pine bough. When that didn't work, he attempted to inject the furious bird with the hormone Depo-Provera. The turkey then nearly died of a bacterial infection, but Hutto nursed him for three weeks near death's door. Amazingly, when he recovered, he had ceased to be aggressive or fearful, and they resumed a cautious friendship.

The book ends with a haunting evocation of his avian friend.

Perhaps one day a seasoned and wary old bird will answer and come to my call, and as he stands cautiously observing the odd lump that sits propped against the base of an old oak, there will be some peculiar element of familiarity that will cause him to remain for a moment longer. I might observe a crooked toe or mandible that imperfectly occludes or receive a subtle message conveyed by some language that we both understand but cannot speak, and I could say: "I know you, old friend. I recognize you by your iridescence, your incandescence, your illumination—I recognize you by your loneliness—you must be my brother."

ALSO READ:
Joe Hutto's most recent book, *The Light in High Places*. It takes place in Wyoming's Wind River Range, an environment as different from Florida as any on the planet, and deals with such diverse species as bighorns, deer, and eagles. In addition, it is one of the few books about cowboying written from the inside.

CHAPTER 74

A Hunter's Story
by C. J. P. Ionides
1965

With all the possible candidates for the "white hunter"* spot in this book, my choice of Constantine John Philip Ionides might seem a perverse one. More famous hunters may seem more romantic or typical than a short, sardonic, ethnically Greek ivory poacher and snake collector. I differ, for several reasons. First, he's not as atypical as he likes to think. Neumann, Selous, Hunter, Taylor, and of course Bell, just to name a few popular saints and idols, all poached ivory; not all of them became game rangers the way Ionides did; only a couple wrote honestly about it. Cranky "Old Iodine" did, about that and everything else. His reminiscences are probably the least-censored account we are likely to have from these reticent Edwardians.

Today Ionides is best known from the fascinating biographical sketch by Margaret Lane, *Life With Ionides,* an almost necessary companion volume to his excessively *un*-analytical autobiography; Ionides was a psychological mystery to himself as much as to his puzzled friends. Lane thought that his sense of self as an outsider, which he attributed in part to his "non-U" Greek heritage, was partially to blame. She said she was "puzzled, listening to his

---

* The pre-PC but then utterly accurate term for professional hunters.

uninhibited talk and considering the extreme respectability of his family and upbringing, that he should refer to his Congo ivory-poaching and his youthful adventures of pheasant-poaching and chicken-stealing as though they were a regular part of middle class experience, something that could happen to any young man, a schoolboy of normal spirit." But if you read the accounts of others closely, one begins to suspect such experiences *were* normal. As usual, Ionides was just more candid.

Asked why he killed so many elephants he would simply answer, "For money." He told Lane, "In those days there was really no stigma attached to poaching, you know; the only rule was that you mustn't be caught. One wasn't conscious, then, of the diminishing number of animals, and the thing was dangerous and probably had a certain glamour." He added, hauntingly prefiguring Beard, that elephants "go on breeding and increasing in spite of everything, and always have to be controlled."

He was as blunt about professional hunters. "They're a breezy lot, devil-may-care, excellent company, if inclined to inaccuracy, generous, kind, tolerant. But from what I have noticed, the deadly eye is often rather bloodshot, and I have met few hunters who can identify any but the commonest trees, or can be relied upon to provide proper nature notes from their observations of wildlife . . . to be a success a hunter must charm and entertain his clients, most of whom are rich, sophisticated city people: usually a middle-aged couple, a bored wife who wants to be amused, and an out of condition husband who wants very big trophies but is barely able and still less prepared to work for them . . . I am afraid I worked my clients too hard to survive as a white hunter." Any wonder Ruark liked Harry Selby better?

So he became first a game ranger, with an autocratic style that I can report still survives among his black successors in post-Colonial Africa (a head ranger near Kariba in Zimbabwe once told me with a diabolical grin that he was the best ranger because, "I kill more poachers.").

Then Ionides discovered the mysterious allure of dangerous snakes, and collecting them for scientific institutions became his most famous career. Oddly, the story most often attributed to him, about a mamba that drops through the roof of a hut and kills a family of five, is one he absolutely denies: "That incident has now been translated to Neriya where I live, the number of people killed has increased to eight, the black mamba has become a green mamba, and I have become the five-star hero who captured it." Be that as it may; Lane's description of his catching a Gaboon viper may give you a better portrait of Ionides and his snakes than his own blunt prose.

The interior of the mass looked the same, all leaves and compost, but he quickly handed the stick to Rashidi and squatted on his hams, though I could still see nothing. He groped beside him for a pair of tongs, and screwing up his eyes against the cigarette smoke (he was still smoking) extended his hand and gently touched a leaf in the centre of the nest. And then I saw it, for the leaf flinched, and was not a leaf at all but the creature's head, and the whole centre of the hollow, dusty and brown and black like all the rest, suddenly revealed itself as the richly sober coils of a large snake . . . He rocked on his knees, finding a firm balance, and to the sound of breathing from the onlookers hovered for a moment over the body before swooping to a powerful grip at the back of the neck. The movement was so quick that neither I nor the snake had been prepared for it; the next instant he was crouching back on his heels with the head held well away from his and his left hand firmly grasping the arched body, which one now saw was about four feet long, compact with power-ful muscle and as bright as a tapestry.

Ionides never compromised, and lived out his life alone with his servants and serpents on a high plateau overlooking Mozambique, where Robert Jones once encountered him having an evening drink with a pet viper in his lap. Read both books, his own for history and poaching and pungent opinion and his oddly cerebral "rarity hunting"; Lane's for a brilliant snapshot in a present tense and her usually futile efforts to probe his recalcitrant brain for motive. It is permissible to think he was aware of, and enjoyed, his own outrageousness (on a man-eating lion, in his book: "He is, as it were, the instrument of poetic justice, exacting dire retribution for the indiscriminate slaughter of the great herds of beautiful creatures."). But I think Margaret Lane had his number. He was an ascetic hunter-monk who devoted his life to his peculiar idea of the chase, and lived it to the end.

Ionides' thirst is a primitive one, concentrated and disciplined by intel-ligence. It is a passion for getting down to the bed-rock of existence, for meeting a challenge unaided, with every faculty at full stretch and life consciously felt through every sense because of the proximity of death. The satisfactions he has achieved are not, I believe, so very different from the release and exhilaration which many people find in danger and war, in the creation of works of art, in all solitary and difficult forms of self-expression.

CHAPTER 75

Blood Sport
by Robert F. Jones
1974

In 1982 I opened a package sent through *Gray's Sporting Journal* to discover a paperback horror novel titled *Blood Root,* with a cover featuring a gnarled tree with a hole in it, through which a monstrous face stared. Opening the first cover disclosed a second one, where the "tree" hugged a naked woman with its roots. The author's name was Thomas Mordane. But on the title page was a long inscription stating that writing such things kept the pot boiling, thanking me for kind reviews, offering to show me secret grouse coverts, and ending "Thomas Mordane, a.k.a. Robert F. Jones."

It was the first time I'd ever received fan mail from someone I admired. I wrote back immediately, and Bob and I commenced a long-distance friendship, soon cemented by a first visit with him in Vermont, that didn't end until his final e-mail.

By the time he wrote *Blood Root,* Bob Jones was the author of three utterly original novels. But this was only the second career of a man who was already a legend in the world of magazine writing. Bob was born in Milwaukee on May 26, 1934, and grew up in suburban Wauwatosa. He went to the University of Michigan, where he met Louise, who would be his wife for forty-six years. He graduated in 1956 with honors in journalism. From 1956 to 1959 he served as an officer in the Navy out of Long Beach, California, and all over the Pacific. When he left the Navy, he had a letter of reference from a journalism professor to *Time. Time* told him he needed experience on a small paper before they would hire him. He spent ten months at the *Milwaukee Sentinel,* then went directly to *Time.*

He had found his niche, and the legend began. You will hear many stories from this time—some of them true. Though he didn't coin the word "hippie," he was responsible for its general usage. When an editor looking for a tag to apply to the people of the counterculture for Bob's cover story asked what

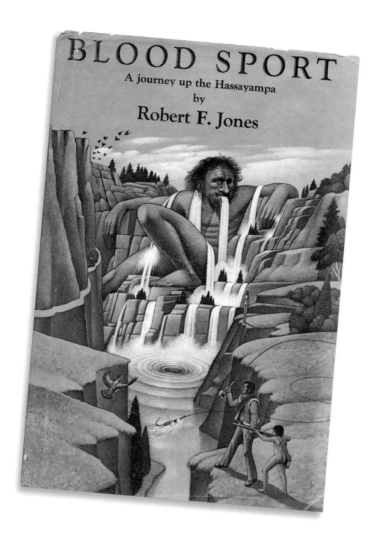

they called themselves, Bob answered "hippies," among several other suggestions. The rest is history.

Before he left *Time,* Bob wrote an incredible, still unmatched, twenty-two cover stories. The natural progression there was from writer to editor, but Bob preferred to write. In 1968 his friend Bill Johnson, who had moved to *Sports Illustrated,* suggested that Bob would be happier there. *Sports Illustrated* was then edited by a wild Frenchman, Andre Laguerre, who preferred horse racing and boxing to more conventional sports. Under Laguerre and, later, the legendary Pat Ryan, Bob was to write a new and more vivid kind of sporting journalism.

These days it is hard to believe the freedom that writers had at the Laguerre/Ryan *Sports Illustrated*. Bob, Tom McGuane, Jim Harrison, Dan Gerber, William Hjortsberg, Russell Chatham, William Humphrey, and many others wrote stories that stretched all boundaries. They were the glory days of so-called New Journalism, and all of life seemed fair game. I believe the first hunting piece of his I ever read involved his killing a wolf on a sandbar in the Yukon, an act about which he would always be ambivalent. Shortly thereafter he wrote a story on an elk hunt in Montana, graced with details, like a guide's bad lungs and a backyard peacock, that you would never have seen in, say, *Field & Stream*. He reported from a drunken shoot at Lord Alexander Hesketh's in England, a piece with echoes of Waugh and Wodehouse, with a little motor racing on the side. Who *was* this guy?

He upped the ante in the early 1970s with a surreal short story in *Harper's*. It began with this memorable line: "The Hassayampa River, a burly stream with its share of trout, rises in northern China, meanders through an Indian Reservation in central Wisconsin, and empties finally into Croton Lake not a mile from where I live in New York State." The story, in which a father and son catch an eighteen-inch cop car on a speeding Camaro lure, was the seed from which Bob's first novel, *Blood Sport,* grew. His wife, Louise, says the first image came to him in a dream.

Blood Sport is utter surrealism with all manner of field sports from fly fishing to big game hunting, sex and private wars, moving obscene tattoos, mastodons, fried maggots, and an immortal reincarnated outlaw named Ratnose, illuminated by dark humor and flashes of lyricism. It is simultaneously a collection of sportsman's tales by a man who knew all his field sports, a meditation on civilization and chaos, and a story about a father teaching his son, but it is strong medicine. Still, if I must pick one of his books, it somehow embodies all the others. The first edition has a cover by Roger Hane, the guy who did the Carlos Castaneda books. I have a Spanish one with a Tyrannosaur on the front and an obscene inscription in Spanish by Bob (*Con pazienza y saliva el elefante se culo la hormiga*)—which has no relevance to the story whatsoever.

Bob's other novels make a closer approach to the actual world. *The Diamond Bogo* is African satire with a Cape buffalo and intelligent priapic naked apes, and true safari stories. *Slade's Glacier* is Alaskan adventure with

Jones-esque details. *Tie My Bones to Her Back* is my favorite novel of the buffalo hunters, ever. There is a scene of train tracks leading between two walls of
buffalo bones that almost out-Cormacs the McCarthy of *Blood Meridian*. In
The Run to Gitche Gumee, Bob's last, humor leavens the chill of mortality. You
should also read his nonfiction, which includes African tales, bird hunting,
and dog books. My favorites are *African Twilight*,* *Hunter in My Heart*, and
his anthology *On Killing*.

Bob had a genius for friendship. Although he was one of the most combative humans I have known, his ferocity was driven more by his intellectual
intensity than any tendency to be a bully. His erudition was formidable; he
read and had read everything—not just novels and sporting stuff, but history,
anthropology, and science. He could hold forth on Col. Richard Meinertz-
hagen in Kenya or the scalping practices of Plains Indians. Geoffrey Norman
said he once described Bob's intelligence and curiosity as "omnivorous." "A
friend quickly corrected me. 'More like *carnivorous*, I'd say.'"

In memory it is his kindness that shines through. My wife, Libby, who
had been apprehensive to meet someone called Bad Bob, always told people
he was "a gentle man and a gentleman." He lived a wonderful life—lived,
loved, created, married, fathered, befriended, fought, played hard, battled
cancer once and won, twice and couldn't.

In the last lines of *Gitche Gumee*, Bob said of life, "It never ends in comfort." He would never yield without a fight to Death, a figure he personified
as "La Grande Puta." But always knowing it must end, he wrote an epitaph
for himself when writing about a friend's death in *Hunter in My Heart*. Sub-
stituting his name for his friend's, let me end with Bob's own words: "I'd like
to think that sooner or later an atom of the force that was once Bob Jones
may permeate every body of water on this wild planet he so dearly loved. The
world will be better for it, as the world is surely better for his having lived."

---

* The book is dedicated to me in part, but I had read much of in places like *Audubon,* and praised it in
  print, before I ever knew that.

CHAPTER 76

A Sand County Almanac
by Aldo Leopold
1966

This set of essays by the conservationist, reformed wolf killer, pioneering wildlife biologist, and patron saint of modern wilderness preservation Aldo Leopold may be the most important single book in the collection. It also includes some of the best writing in English about natural history, hunting, and the essence of country. When I open my copy to find quotes, it falls open in all the "good spots."

Sand County includes immortal essays on cutting in time through the rings of an oak, on the sky dance of courting woodcock, on the passenger pigeon, on a lonely peak not too far west of my home that is "only a mountain now," on a vanished delta on the Mexican border, on falconry, and on a certain "fierce green fire." If you have not read any of these, please put my book down and go out and buy this one; if you do, my work has been worthwhile. Here are some things that Leopold said:

The woodcock is the living refutation of the theory that the utility of a game bird is to serve as a target or to pose gracefully on a slice of toast. No one would rather hunt woodcock in October than I, but since learning of the sky dance I find myself calling one or two birds enough. I must be sure that, come April, there be no dearth of dancers in the sunset sky.

• • •

The pigeon was a biological storm. It was the lightning that played between two opposing potentials of intolerable intensity; the fat of the land, the oxygen of the air. Yearly the feathered tempest roared up, down, and across the continent, sucking up the laden fruits of forest and prairie,

burning them in a traveling blast of life. Like any other chain reac-
tion, the pigeon could survive no diminution of his own furious inten-
sity. When the pigeoners subtracted from this number, and the pioneers
chopped gaps in the continuity of his fuel, his flame guttered out with
hardly a sputter or even a wisp of smoke.

—•—•—•—

For one species to mourn the death of another is a new thing under the sun.

—•—•—•—

Escudilla still hangs on the horizon, but when you see it you no longer think of bear. It's only a mountain now.

—•—•—•—

For two and a half cents one can buy and shoot a cartridge that will kill the heron whose capture by hawking requires months or even years of laborious training of both the hawk and the hawker.

—•—•—•—

We reached the old wolf in time to watch a fierce green fire dying in her eyes. I realized then, and have known ever since, that there was something new to me in those eyes—something known only to her and to the mountain. I was young then, and full of trigger-itch; I thought that because fewer wolves meant more deer, that no wolves would mean hunters' paradise. But after seeing that green fire die, I sensed that neither the wolf nor the mountain agreed with such a view.

Do yourself a favor and get a real old-fashioned edition, with the pencil illustrations by Charles Schwartz.

CHAPTER 77

A Sporting Chance: Unusual Methods of Hunting

by Daniel P. Mannix

1967

A Sporting Chance inspired more people to embark on a life of adventure with animals than any other book of its time. I can't count the number of friends and acquaintances who read this book, along with maybe Seton, and claim it as a primary influence. Daniel Mannix and his wife and life-long partner, Jule, were wealthy kids from respectable Main Line Philadelphia families who at some point decided to spend their lives keeping and playing with animals. Their families and peers were either appalled or amused. (In the 1970s Betsy and I had an upstairs neighbor who had been a sorority sister of Jule's in the 1930s. We learned this when she stared at a hooded merlin on my fist one day and remarked, "I used to room with a girl who had one of those, but it was rather *larger*. Do you know Jule Mannix?" When I answered that I knew who she was, she replied, "It was an *eagle* I think—*rather* larger . . .")

Whether it was the time or just boundless self-confidence, they also expected to make a living writing about their adventures. A patrician background probably didn't hurt. In Jule's memoir, *Married to Adventure,* she mentions in passing that "Dan had a small income left to him by an aunt, which was just sufficient for us to live on." I pause to note that their first apartment was half a block from 5th Avenue, but it *was* another time; they kept an eagle in it. And the money was thin enough that they soon decamped to Mexico to make money by filming themselves catching iguanas from horseback with two eagles, a bald and a golden.

The late Ray Bradbury is credited with saying that you must jump off cliffs and trust yourself to grow wings. The Mannixes evidently lived by this credo, and never looked back. Dan produced scores of books on subjects from sword swallowing to the Roman games to juvenile novels about animals, one of which was ruined by Walt Disney. His best work includes this book and his earlier memoir *All Creatures Great and Small,* but don't forget Jule's memoir with the remarkable cover photo of her on horseback in Mexico with a hooded bald eagle.

All Creatures Great and Small made me want to be Mannix when I was thirteen, but *A Sporting Chance* made us all want to *do.* Every off-trail sport mentioned in the book you are reading pops up in *A Sporting Chance:* hunting with cheetahs and other wild cats, falconry in many aspects, bow hunting, terrier and hound work (formal and informal), ferreting, snake hunting, harpooning big fish, and fishing with cormorants and otters. He adds such oddities as blowguns, crossbows, boomerangs, bolas, catching things with toads, and even historical "man-trapping." There is nothing remotely like it in twentieth-century literature.

The Mannixes' joy in their activities shines through. Daniel's light touch never leaves him. His first remark on falconry is a paraphrase of Wodehouse, who remarked, "as far as he could see, the only things the hawk didn't have to learn was Sanskrit and the use of the trap drums." But like most light writers, including Wodehouse, he had serious things to say between the lines. "To many people, a great difficulty with the old methods is that they are arts rather than sciences, and anyone using them must be an artist—or at least a highly trained craftsman. By the end of boot camp, any normally capable GI can be a reasonably good shot, but to be an archer requires years of practice."

Read this one for sheer biophilic delight and a certain nostalgia for a time when it was easier to have fun playing with animals. Sometimes I fear for the next generation.

ALSO READ:

Daniel Mannix's *The Wolves of Paris, The Fox and the Hound,* and *The Killers*

Chulo and *Our Nature,* by Bil Gilbert, a younger writer and star member of Pat Ryan's *SI* lineup, who lived a similar life without being a rich kid

CHAPTER 78

An Outside Chance
by Thomas McGuane
1990

How can this book not be full of writing by Thomas McGuane? A polymath of sport, known almost as well for his fly fishing as for his prize-winning fiction, he also hunts birds and trains dogs and has owned more Best-quality English shotguns than anyone I have known. His passion for horses ("Horses are my falcons," he once wrote to me) is such that he is still competing in cutting-horse events past his seventieth birthday; he has written enough about them to compose an entire volume, *Some Horses,* perhaps the only book about horses I have read cover to cover, with real interest. He wrote "Heart of the Game," perhaps my favorite big game essay ever. But if I had to pick one (nonfiction) work to stand for him, I'd pick this sporting collection.

An Outside Chance is a book to delight the generalist rather than the specialist. McGuane has hunted and fished (and trained those quarter horses) all over the country, from his native Michigan to his longtime home in Montana, with stops along the way in Rhode Island, California, and Key West. There may be a few other people who have pursued as many sports; maybe even a few who have done as well. But very few of them have been his equal in writing. He has a gift for the odd yet appropriate metaphor:

> *. . . the tarpon when hooked and running reminds the angler of a piano sliding down a precipitous incline and while jumping makes cavities and explosions in the water not unlike a series of pianos falling from great height. If the reader, then, can speculate in terms of pianos that herd and pursue mullet and are themselves shaped like exaggerated herrings, he will be a very long way toward seeing what kind of thing a tarpon is.*

An Outside Chance—as a reader rather than collector, I prefer the second, 1990 edition, even if the first is more "collectible," as it includes several new essays and omits none—is an irresistible book, full of humor and

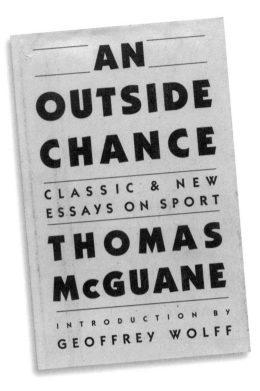

excitement and precise observation, rooted in a conservation ethic so deep that McGuane does not have to preach about it. It includes the essay I alluded to above, mostly on hunting mule deer out of his home ranch, "The Heart of the Game." If you have a friend who is adamantly anti-hunting and can read, you might try this essay on him or her; someone who is opposed to any killing may be too impatient to sit through a book-length defense, but still be moved by this piece. I've been handing it around since it first appeared in the first issue of *Outside* magazine what seems like—hell, *was*—a generation ago. McGuane lays out a collage of scenes from a hunter's life and concludes in his woodshed, late on a winter's day, after a long and successful hunt: "I stopped the twirling of the buck, my hands deep in the sage-scented fur, and thought: this is either the beginning or the end of everything."

ALSO READ:
Thomas McGuane's *The Longest Silence* (fishing essays) and *Some Horses*

CHAPTER 79

Seasons & Days
by Thomas McIntyre
2003

Disclaimer: I have known Thomas McIntyre for nearly thirty years, and I am a declared partisan of his writing. We met when we were in our early thirties, word-drunk, ambitious Catholic schoolboys from opposite coasts with shared, unlikely twinned passions for books and hunting, and have maintained a long-distance friendship punctuated by marathon phone calls, letters, and, later, e-mails ever since. I think we have actually hunted together only once, chasing jackrabbits with sighthounds through a capital-A Art "Installation" situated in remote ranchland west of here, which gave Tom the memorable opening line for a *Sports Afield* story not reprinted in this collection: "They wouldn't let us run the dogs in the Lightning Field."

Tom has been fortunate enough to afford some memorable adventures; his first safari at twenty-one may have been one of the last in Kenya. He has killed so many Cape buffalo that he gave me a spare skull. He has a chair made out of musk ox hide that looks like Cousin It. But there are plenty of rich hunters, and not one, not omitting Hemingway and Ruark, writes like Tom. He argues quotes from Nabokov with crusty uber-editor and gun maven Dave Petzal, as well as calibers. He reads and has long since assimilated both of those old safari writers, and Nabokov of course, and Joyce, and Waugh, and Myles na Gopaleen (look it up). Stretching for something to say about his forthcoming book, a fable about a shape-changing snow leopard, I groped for comparisons: the Victorian Jesuit poet Hopkins for language, Kipling and Patrick O'Brian and the classical Chinese poets for content. When I reviewed his first book and called him "the thinking hunter's poet laureate," I was being pretty accurate.

So, consider anything I might say about him biased, but know that writers make friends (at least with fellow writers) in part because of shared views. This 2003 collection is something of a "Best of McIntyre." The pieces he has assembled go back as far as the 1970s, and though I might have added a

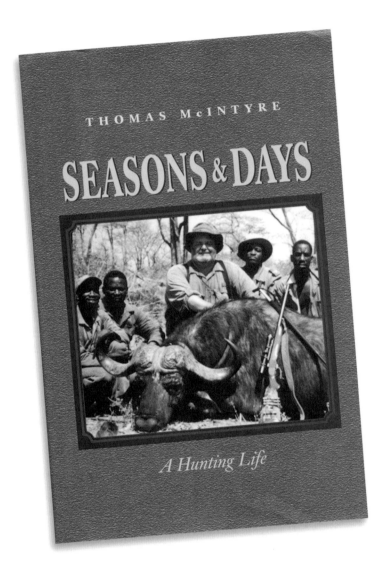

few more, every single one is good. Some are lyrical, some are funny, some are dead serious if not solemn, and every one is worth not just reading, but rereading. I am more inclined to point to favorites or quote than analyze. Here are a few.

"The Bandtail Above All," about Bandtail pigeons in the Pacific Northwest: "At shooting light there will be a Bandtail on the wing, looking for all the world like a cross between an F-15 and the Paraclete." "The Fire In the Beast," about hunting wild pigs in his native California and the cult of pigs in general: "As for there being a fire in the beast, this I know to be unquestionably true." "Presbyopia, Pronghorn & Blood on the Poet," about pronghorns in Wyoming: "The pronghorn was still there, turning in the wind, almost cooled out. At this distance, she resembled something or someone, quite-robed, floating above the ground. Floating, or maybe ascending." And more and more and more; the hilarious piece on gators, a dark, haunting one on Cape buffalo called "Old No. 7" ("Do you think there's fear to be seen in a handful of dust?"). His writing encompasses all hunting and a bit of fishing; by subject alone it never bores. In a time when most writing in staff-written magazines consists of product-oriented pieces that stay within the safe boundaries laid down by marketing departments, that may be the most remarkable thing of all.*

In the unlikely event that you have not yet encountered McIntyre, this book is a good starting place. I suspect after you read it you will seek out his other collections. And, if you become a fan, watch for his coming snow leopard novel, where Irish-Catholic poetry meets Buddhism and the Neolithic on the high plateau north of Tibet.

ALSO READ:
Thomas McIntyre's *The Way of the Hunter* and *Dreaming the Lion,* and look for his *The Snow Leopard's Tale*

---

* Every publisher I speak to insists this is what sportsmen want. Every sportsman I know (and my sample includes cowboys at the Golden Spur Bar in rural Magdalena, New Mexico, no salon for artistes) complains that there are no long stories anymore, and that everything is about whitetail deer and "black rifles." Many cite McIntyre and Barsness as writers they would like to see more of. *Somebody* is out of tune. . . .

CHAPTER 80

The Island Within
by Richard Nelson
1991

Richard Nelson is an anthropologist who has spent his life among hunting tribes. *The Island Within* is his first book where his own life, rather than that of traditional hunting societies, is the focus. *The Island Within* is a series of meditations and narratives about the wild coast of the Pacific Northwest where he makes his home, and its rich stew. In fact, like the Pacific Northwest's rain forests, it's almost *too* rich—you must read it slowly. This is a book of natural history, and one human's attitude toward a place where man still fits himself to nature, rather than vice versa. The wild Pacific coast is a place where all human inhabitants are surrounded by an incredibly diverse and complex ecosystem. Nelson states, in his chapter "The Forest of Eyes": "The dark boughs reach out above me and encircle me like arms. I feel the assurance of being recognized, as if something powerful and protective is aware of my presence, looks in another direction but always has me in a corner of its eye . . . I am never alone in this wild forest, this forest of elders, this forest of eyes."

But he is not just an eloquent exponent of modern "green" pantheism; he is, no mistake about it, a hunter. His reliance on deer and fish as sources of food for his family and the rightness of the hunting way are themes that run through the book and continue today in other works; I can only hope his earnest and reverent attitude toward the necessary taking of life will speak to readers who might otherwise dismiss the hunter's role. "It's always this way: the sudden encounter with death, the shock that overrides the cushioning of the intellect. I force away the sadness and remember that death is the spark that keeps life itself aflame: these deer we eat from, and the fish, and the plants that die to feed us."

ALSO READ:
Richard Nelson's *Hunters of the Northern Ice,* a hunter-gatherer anthropology used as a survival text by the military, and *Heart and Blood: Living with Deer in America*

CHAPTER 81

Hunting in the Southwest
by Jack O'Connor
1939

Jack O'Connor, born in Arizona near Phoenix when it was a frontier town rather than a metropolis, was an educated man, a journalism professor, and novelist before gun writing fame and some movie money made him independent. He always cultivated a gentleman's image. He wore three-piece suits in civilization, and his trademark Borsalino fedoras brought a touch of that same elegance to the field. He was literate, sardonic, and understated, the only "gun writer" ever reviewed in the *New Yorker* (see his editor Angus Cameron's letter), and his obituary ran in the *New York Times*. Technical gun books can date, but any hunter can still enjoy this book, his first outdoor title.

His lifelong rivalry with his cowboy counterpart Elmer Keith amused and divided a generation of outdoor readers and hunters. It is unlikely that any two outdoor writers will ever again have the influence and following they earned in the 1940s and wielded through the 1960s. We have writers as good or better, some with comparable experience and skill, but our world has changed. Although we have doubtless gained a bit more sophistication, we have given up the robust flavor of a more innocent time. Could two such oversize characters thrive in the age of blogs, Google, Wiki, and argumentative "fact" checking?

Both were westerners, but they couldn't have been more different. O'Connor's writing was more elegant than Keith's (I have seen some of Keith's manuscripts and letters—he often wrote in one long unpunctuated sentence until editors did their work, and had an odd habit of referring to himself in a sort of royal "we"). O'Connor wrote a memoir, *Horse and Buggy Days,* and two novels, *Boomtown* (made into a movie starring Clark Gable) and *Conquest.* Keith wrote the definitive book on six-shooters and an autobiography, first called simply *Keith,* then released an expanded version more aptly titled *Hell, I Was There!* It is exuberant and utterly outspoken, something

O'Connor, a man of bred-in understatement, never achieved until his post-humous *Last Book*.

Their prejudices and differences in style did not just extend to their ideas about rifles—they were the embodiment of them. O'Connor favored modest, rational, flat-shooting calibers embedded in elegant, classic stocks. He popularized and defended the .270 and was also fond of the .30/06 and the 7 mm Mauser. His *The Rifle Book,* perhaps the most influential of its kind, set forth his credo. A quote from O'Connor's *The Last Book,* from the chapter "Big Bore Boys," pokes some fun at Keith's more fanatical followers: "users of big bores always attack the users of small bores . . . The big bore boys also feel that anyone who doesn't enjoy getting belted out from under his hat by a hard-kicking rifle is not very masculine, if not actually gay."

Keith, on the other hand, demanded and eventually got the .44 magnum handgun cartridge, shot a 10-gauge magnum double at geese all his life, and loved anything above .338 caliber—fans and detractors alike might say, the higher above, the better. People I trust have told me he could hit a target accurately with his famous .44 at six hundred yards and drop passing ducks with the big 10 at eighty. He liked anything with the name "magnum," and all the elephant calibers. He at least once implied that the .30/06 wasn't good for *anything*.

O'Connor never stopped changing intellectually. In 1984 Amwell reprinted *Game in the Desert*, the Derrydale version of his 1938 Knopf *Hunting in the Southwest*. Though more shooters bought things like *The Rifle Book*, this handsome, entertaining, still-useful volume had been perhaps the most important book for introducing the literate American hunter to the modern, post–Teddy Roosevelt West. In his new preface he apologized for his anti-mountain lion attitude in the 1930s. Unrepentant Keith advocated shooting all predators, including eagles and hawks, until the end of his life. (His book *Shotguns* has a full-page photo of his very young son holding a dead goshawk and the famous magnum 10 Ithaca.)

Except for occasional bouts of rhetorical excess on Keith's part, both O'Connor and Keith wrote far more sense than nonsense. They did take potshots at each other (without mentioning names), but this might just have been good business. Think of Keith as a straight shot of sour-mash bourbon and O'Connor as silky-smooth Irish whiskey, and you'll have it about right. Both writers ended up in Idaho's Snake River Country, where both made themselves amazingly accessible to the new generation of sporting writers despite their crusty reputations. It doesn't take too much imagination to see them together at last in some hunter's Valhalla, still deafening each other with shouts of their eternal conflict.

ALSO READ:

Jack O'Connor's *The Rifle Book, The Shotgun Book,* and *The Last Book*
Rifles and Cartridges for Big Game, Sixguns, Shotguns, and *Hell, I Was There!* by Elmer Keith

CHAPTER 82

Lift
by Rebecca K. O'Connor
2009

Rebecca O'Connor's falconry memoir, *Lift,* could live on the merits of its fierce opening paragraph alone:

> *I should kill the duck. I know how to do it. A master falconer showed me with a deft hand. He split the skin where the leg meets the body and with his finger, jammed it inside and found the heart. It dislodged with no sound and laid beating in his palm. He offered it with an open hand to my falcon who took it with dainty bites while the duck stilled.*

The two best recent books with (not about) falconry are by young women, Rebecca K. O'Connor and Helen Macdonald, and there are more coming. Unfortunately, this interesting phenomenon may go nowhere unless potential readers are made aware of the books. Helen Macdonald, a serious falconer, poet, and lecturer in the History of Science at Cambridge, has had some good fortune; *Falcon,* her first book with falconry, was published as a part of a popular series by London's Reaktion Press, and she now has a contract with a big publisher to write a twenty-first-century version of *The Goshawk,* about her adventures with a big female gos named Mabel.

Small presses are more likely to respond to new writers; Red Hen, O'Connor's publisher, is a literary press with a good reputation. But they do not seem to be able to attract attention in today's market. *Lift* was published to great reviews, but until recently at least, it only sold a couple of hundred copies. It's hard to see why. It is good enough that any literate reader not utterly opposed to carnivory should find something unique in it; you don't have to be female, a falconer, or even a hunter.

O'Connor first sees a falconer's peregrine when she is a troubled, dreaming child, and ends up one of the few master falconers and serious duck hawkers left in overcrowded Southern California, hoarding her last available

Lift

Rebecca K. O'Connor

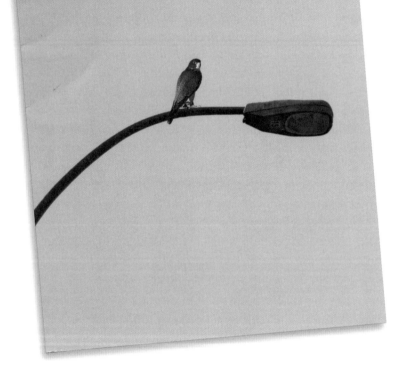

and accessible ponds even as their owners succumb to the irresistible pressure of real estate prices. In between she deals with childhood demons, works in bird shows and strip clubs, and learns the difficult disciplines of training a high-flying bird. It is a tribute to how well she writes that you might imagine that you could too, after you read her.

Lift is about living and losing and coming back and winning, and love, and loss. That "loss" can be more than metaphorical or personal; she flies big true falcons in classical waiting-on flights, the kind of birds who, if they miss, will tail chase a duck for twelve miles. You will learn more about tracking telemetry and its limitations in this book than in any other I have read! O'Connor flies her birds and reads, and writes, and thinks, without the reflexive, almost automatic acceptance that a lot of us guys have, about being a hunter. After her peregrine tiercel Anakin kills a kestrel, she wonders if *she* is a hunter. She has no trouble with killing to eat, but wonders why Hemingway, who she admires, could kill predators. Her conclusion is original:

I would never kill a predator for sport, but watched helplessly when Anakin killed a kestrel, forgiving him instantly. Food is food when you're hungry, but I also know that Anakin wasn't very hungry when he killed the kestrel. Nestled in the tamarisk and clutching his prey I would see that he had done it for sport. I still forgave him. In fact, I was proud— his triumph a guilty contagion.

Lift is one to read for all the good reasons: to learn something new, to support a good writer who is serious about her craft, but above all, always, to delight in good writing. Read it because it is a first-rate celebration of postmodern falconry, and to make sure O'Connor continues to celebrate the things that we all love.

ALSO READ:

Falcon, by Helen Macdonald

Equinox, by Dan O'Brian (best account of a single season's falconry in the United States)

WATCH FOR:

Helen Macdonald's forthcoming book on the goshawk

CHAPTER 83

Meditations on Hunting
by José Ortega y Gasset
1942

Ortega wrote *Meditations on Hunting* in 1942, as an introduction to *Veinte Años de Caza Major (Twenty Years as a Big Game Hunter)* by his friend Count Yebes. It was first published in English in 1972 but sold badly. Gradually its word-of-mouth reputation built up to the point where used hardcover copies of that printing were bringing as much as $150. But as of this writing (2013), there are at least two more editions, and you have no excuse for not owning it.

Meditations is *the* standard "why hunt" text, the source of such much-quoted passages as "one does not hunt in order to kill; on the contrary, one kills in order to have hunted." Ortega writes from a lofty perspective; he is a cultured old European, and those who consider him a "sophistical reactionary," as did some unnamed friend (I am told Ed Abbey) of hunting's intellectual defender John Mitchell, will scarcely be convinced by his frankly elitist arguments. But when read in conjunction with other good biological and anthropological arguments (some cited below and throughout this book), his whole man-as-hunter-and-conservationist thesis acquires the momentum of inevitable logic.

There's a lot to ponder here, some of it controversial. Ortega does not balk at the question of the privilege involved in hunting, but holds a meritocratic rather than an aristocratic view of it. "Argue, fight as much as you like, over who shall be the privileged ones, but do not pretend that squares are round and that hunting is not a privilege . . . It is to be hoped that the West will dedicate the next two centuries to fighting—there is no hope for a suspension of its innate pugnacity—to fighting, I say, for something less stupid, more attainable, and not at all extraordinary, such as a better selection of privileged persons." Other absolutely essential points he covers are "Vacations from the human condition," "Municipal Paleolithic Man," and (see Wilson below) "The hunter—the alert man."

And finally, what reader of this book might not grin in rueful agreement at Ortega's early complaint? "In our time—which is a rather stupid time—hunting is not considered a serious matter."

ALSO READ:
Bloodties, by Ted Kerasote
The Hunt, by John Mitchell
Biophilia, by E. O. Wilson
All works by Richard Nelson

CHAPTER 84

Tales of a Rat-Hunting Man
by D. Brian Plummer
1978

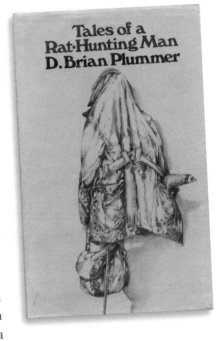

David Brian Plummer (he later dropped David) was born in a scarred village in Wales to a mother whose god was respectability and a father addicted to beer and Karl Marx. His early world was one of streams running black with coal dust and bucket-of-blood pubs, a world of whippets, lurchers, rabbits, hares, poaching, and rat-hunting.

He grew up to be a gifted teacher, and a brawler and gambler who would doubtless be denied any contact with children in these fearful times. He soon began to record the lore and secrets of a shadow England of artisan hunters, gypsies, itinerants, and poachers, an alternate history that stretches back in time to when Saxons and Celts haunted their Norman overlords' estates to reclaim their game; stories the gentry never heard, full of dark humor, pain, and furious enthusiasm.

Sitting Bull said that when the buffalo are gone, we will hunt mice. Thomas McIntyre, in *The Way of the Hunter,* added a modern footnote: "Even in locales where there seems no possibility of hunting *anything* anymore, municipal Paleolithic man hunts on." Plummer's wild men inhabit such a devastated landscape; to quote J. A. Baker, a contemporary observer of England's crowded landscape, a world "as profuse and glowing as Africa . . . a dying world, like Mars, but glowing still."

Which sounds romantic, but tragic. Plummer's world, if you have a strong stomach and a black sense of humor, is comic, even hilarious. I can't be the only one to see in his title an echo of Siegfried Sassoon's upper-class

Memoirs of a Fox-Hunting Man. Plummer begins in autobiography by establishing his workingman's bona fides. He then devotes an entire chapter to rat science and folklore. He tells you more about rats, their love lives, history, and diseases than you might wish; how to hunt them, and how to catch one by the tail, alive.

You will certainly learn reasons *not* to catch one. "[The rat] . . . raced up my arm and disappeared down the floppy neck-hole of my sweater, scrabbling against my naked chest. The night, previously sweltering, suddenly became very, very cold, and my whole body went incredibly clammy with fear. With sweating hands, I reached down and drew him scrabbling and scratching from my sweater. I was twelve short of the number I required, but could not will myself to go on."

As the characters and adventures unfold, you begin to think, against your good sense, that you'd spend a night with Brian Plummer and his cast of ratters, people like Barney Lewis, "the noted warrener and poacher," whom Plummer lamely describes to an academic colleague as having "some advanced views on moles"; or a more nervous volunteer, a self-described lycanthrope who claims not to know what kind of animal he will change into, and panics when he sees a friendly whippet.

Above all he gives us dogs: brave dogs, slow dogs, savage ones, and ones that remain in Plummer's heart forever. Plummer never tires of telling the reader how grotesque his first great dog, Sam, was: "His torso had an ugly hour-glass figure and his shoulders were something shocking." But he eulogizes him with unusual sentiment. "He died in his sleep a few days before his twenty-first birthday. During his life he had traveled most of Europe with me and never made me look a fool . . . Losing him was like losing an arm."

Garm, who he claims was raised on hospital waste, does not fare as well. "I had visions of Garm skulking around the amputation unit looking for pieces . . . a dog who was such a killer that he was dangerous to anything from a pig to a postman. My God, I will remember the time of his coming, and the dreadful seven months I owned him, to my dying day."

The book culminates in a series of hunts at the Mexborough maggot factory.

Mexborough—grim, grisly, great, glorious Mexborough. Home of mills, millionaires and maggot factories . . . Reader, I bid you take note, I do not make up this tale, there are such things as maggot factories . . . Maggots, the grub of the common bluebottle, live on meat, preferably meat that is slightly 'ripe' or 'off'. . . . They also welcome old tripe, condemned liver and dry cadavers of hapless beasts that have died of awesome diseases. Amazing creatures find their way to these maggot factories.

The games played out at this ultimate temple of rat hunting, and the characters that play them—folksingers, terriers, ferrets, an engineer who uses homemade bombs to flush rats—and the puzzled citizens who react to them, compose a comic masterpiece unique in literature. It's tribute to Plummer's storytelling that when you finish laughing you may well look back on Mexborough with a kind of perverse nostalgia. Plummer's paeans to anarchic freedom in a society that was then all but closed to the children of the working-class poor, his deranged version of biophilia, and his defiant joy in his pursuits despite overwhelming poverty and squalor will resonate with anyone who would chase mice and watch starlings in a *Blade Runner* landscape rather than give in to the temptations of a merely virtual reality.

Rat-Hunting Man was Plummer's first successful book, preceded by a manual on ferret keeping. He would follow it with many more, including a diary of his unique hunting and biographies of two of his most famous dogs, the intelligent lurcher Merle and the diabolical terrier Omega. (*New Yorker* writer R. C. Smith thinks *Omega* "contains his most extreme writing," though I would award that honor to the hard-to-find *Rogues and Running Dogs.*) He has been the subject of two documentary films and a *New Yorker* article, and has written three novels, the protagonists of which are a pit-fighting dog, a badger, and a spectral hare that is coursed to its death by every predator in creation but always rises to run again. After *Rat-Hunting Man* I'd suggest you try *Lepus,* the hare novel, utterly different and almost mystical, with its perfect Martin Knowelden ink drawings. I suspect if you like these you'll go on to read all of him, as I have. But first, test your nerves, your sense of humor, and the depth of your biophilia: Join the rat-hunting man and his good companions for a drunken midnight sortie in some forbidden, crumbling abandoned building.

ALSO READ:
Brian Plummer's *Rogues and Running Dogs, Omega, Merle, Lepus,* and *Diary of a Hunter*
"Ratcatcher," by R. C. Smith, *New Yorker,* Feb. 15, 1988

CHAPTER 85

Hunting with the Bow and Arrow
by Saxton Pope
1923

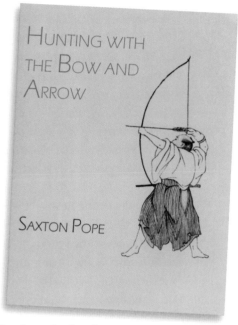

In 1911 a lone native, a man who was said to be "about [sic] 49 years old" emerged from his home in the woods near Oroville, California, and into dubious fame. He was the last (maybe) of the Yahi Indians of California (maybe), and no one ever did learn who he really was. The Berkeley anthropologist Alfred Kroeber, with whom he lived for the next six years, called him "Ishi," the term for "man" in the language of his people, because it was rude to ask his proper name.

Legend surrounds myth surrounds science, and the legend of Ishi may not be exactly what we were told when we were young and things seemed simpler. What is beyond doubt is that the gentle man, who worked as a janitor at the university, was the last "wild" adult hunter-gatherer in the United States. He was befriended by a young professor of medicine, Saxton Pope. Pope became fascinated not just with the gentle, charismatic hunter, but also with his stone-age technology and his knowledge of nature, so much so that he wrote a simple book with a simple title.

All American archery descends from it. *Hunting With the Bow and Arrow* begins with the story of Ishi, and in the second chapter zooms in very specifically on his tools and methods. Ishi was a hunter rather than a technician; his bows were not powerful, but certainly good enough for the job if one could get close to one's quarry.

Pope then skips over the history of archery and goes to the heart of the matter: how to make your own bow. You could follow his directions today.

His instructions are no less detailed than those in *Primitive Archer* magazine, though the technology is better understood today. On backing with rawhide:

> *When the hide is soft, lay the pieces smooth side down on a board and wipe off the excess water. Quickly size them with hot glue, remove the excess with your finger, turn the pieces over and apply them to the bow. Overlap them at the hand grip for a distance of two or three inches. Smooth them out towards the tips by stroking and expressing all the air bubbles and excess glue. Wrap the handle roughly with string to keep the strips from slipping; also bind the tips for a short distance to secure them in place. Remove the bow from the vise and bandage it carefully from tip to tip with a gauze surgical bandage. Set it aside to dry overnight.*

Pope thinks of the bow as a gentle weapon, and says, "We found from the very first that the arrow was more humane than the gun. Counting all hunters, for every animal brought home with the gun, whether duck, quail, or deer, at least two are hit and die in pain in the brush." I'm not sure I buy this, but then Pope always used dogs to trail his wounded animals. He makes an interesting statement: "the sort of dog an archer needs for deer is one that can point them yet will not follow one unless it is wounded." With such dogs he eventually hunts even cougar and bear in the mountains of California, which now bans the practice.

One man's friendship with a reticent Indian janitor on a college campus gave birth to this little book, which in turn gave birth to what is now a multi-million dollar industry. Forgive me if I find more charm in Pope's and Ishi's ways.

ALSO READ:
Primitive Archer magazine
All the books of E. Donnall Thomas Jr. While Dr. Thomas is a bird hunter and a fly fisherman, his most remarkable exploits involve hunting large game animals with hounds, killing them with longbows he makes for himself like Pope and Ishi, and eating them.

CHAPTER 86

Nature's Diary
by Mikhail Prishvin
1951

In 1987, when the Penguin paperback of this book came out, the Eastern Literary Establishment briefly rediscovered field sports. Even before publication of Mikhail Prishvin's *Nature's Diary*, John Updike wrote a long essay about it in the *New Yorker*, then contributed an introduction to the Penguin paperback. Updike was a voracious reader and a perceptive critic who knew Russia and its literature, and could point out the book's oddities—its free-association structure or lack of one, with short essays, tales, and observations suggesting others, in no particular order save that of the seasons; its subjective style, where Prishvin's immediate impressions count for more than his scientific knowledge and a peasant's observation on thunder causing frogs to become active counts as much. He was aware of its real virtues. But he also exhibited a typical urban Puritan's distaste for hunting, whining, "There is a great deal of hunting and killing here—more than any modern nature lover expects."

Hmmm . . . maybe. But one who cannot appreciate hunting will not be likely to love this book. Prishvin was a kind of ranger who ran a field station in the backcountry of central Russia in the 1930s, and like most Russian naturalists to this day, he was a hunter to the core.

Prishvin manifests a healthy coarseness, and a fatalism that holds little kinship with a modern critic's worldview. Searching for an alleged scent of violets on a dead fox, his companion sniffs beneath the tail of a fox and announces in disgust, "It smells just as you would expect an animal to smell there." Prishvin tells us after that fox's death that "There is no need to pity the animal, my kind-hearted readers, we're all due for it sooner or later, I for one am almost ready, and the only thing that worries me is that people might look at me in disappointment 'How small he is.'"

Most of summer and fall is devoted to his dogs, and Prishvin on dogs is as good as it gets. Listen to this description of his hiding to teach a young setter to keep in touch in the woods:

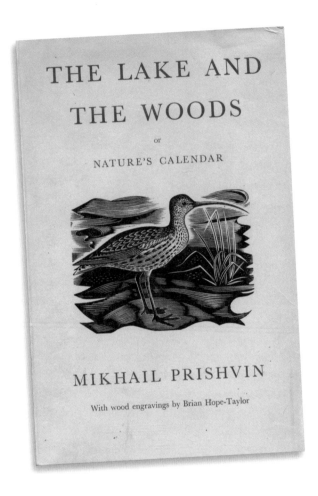

My whistle must have reached him just as he stopped to listen and puzzle things out. He sensed correctly the direction of the sound and made a frantic dash puffing like a steam engine. He stopped short at the edge of the clearing where I crouched motionless in the bushes.

What with his hard run and fright, he was exhausted and his tongue lolled. He could not scent anything in this condition of course, and had to depend on his ears alone. He pricked up his ears but they wouldn't stay erect, the ends drooped and obstructed his hearing. He tried cocking his head to one side—no good, to the other—no good either. He saw what the trouble was, at last: he could not hear his master's signal because of his own breathing. He snapped his mouth shut, but in haste bit his lip and so stood listening with one lip thrust over the other.

I was choking with laughter looking at his funny face and had to clamp my hand over my mouth. But he did not hear me. The woods without his master were a wilderness where only the wolves, his fore-bears, were prowling. They would never forgive him for betraying their cause, for his devotion to man, for his snug cubby-hole and security— they would tear him to pieces and devour him. When one lives with the wolves one must howl like one, says an old proverb.

And he tried it. He lifted up his head and howled.

The last vignette is a tale of a bear hunt with one brief moment of terror so beautifully rendered, fear that comes so fast it is not recognized: "White as a sheet, Godfather came up to me and said, 'Why you're quite white!' Greek said that same to Godfather, though he was just as white as we were. None of us had felt a speck of fear, for the cowards in us must have been still trudging behind us when we were facing the suddenly aroused beast, and had only just arrived when it was all over."

Elemental, and doubtless a rare event in poor Updike's suburbs (where, let the record show, I once pissed on his lawn after an epic night of drinking with Alaska writer Ron Rau). But as Prishvin says, "How infinitely small is the span of the written word as compared with the thousands of years in which man fought the bear?"

ALSO READ:
There is an interesting book by Prishvin, published by Pantheon in 1952, called *The Lake and the Woods,* a handsome volume illustrated by woodcuts. A close read reveals it is *the same book,* but by a different translator and, more remarkably, with hardly any two words the same! I have helped translate another hunting book from the Russian, and know that the languages are different enough that some paraphrase is inevitable, but this edges into funny. Having no Russian edition, I can't tell which seems the better. The new one reads more smoothly and the old is prettier. I am happy to have both.

CHAPTER 87

The Scavenger's Guide to Haute Cuisine
by Steven Rinella
2005

When I first read Steven Rinella's *Scavenger's Guide,* it drove me nuts. I spent half my time cheering him on, a quarter laughing, and a quarter saying "No!" He is a young writer of Italian descent who grew up a hunter and fisherman, just like me. He has tremendous enthusiasm and appetite, and often comes across as a cocksure know-it-all. He has lived on the coast and in Montana and will hunt, fish for, and eat anything that moves.

Hmmm. . . .

Rinella's foremost virtue, other than perhaps intrepidity, is his blunt honesty. ". . . I just like the whole package of wild food: eating, almost being killed, and, yes, killing . . ." and follows that right up: "I'm surprised that I came right out and said that. Even hunting and fishing magazines avoid saying that. *Which is odd, because hunting and fishing are, fundamentally, methods of food procurement* [italics mine]." Then he twists the knife.

> *Fisherman have developed an even more thorough separation from their barbaric parent, the hunter-gatherer. Basically, catch-and-release fishing is a weird paradoxical sort of vein, where you try to poke a hook through a fishes face without causing it unnecessary harm. The most notable distinction between catch-and-release and golf is that the plaything being knocked around in catch-and-release is a sentient being.*

His first book is structured around his deciding to cook a multiple-course meal shaped by Escoffier's *Le Guide Culinaire*. I might be cautious of attempting to replicate anything as relentlessly old-school haute cuisine as Escoffier. But "cautious" is not a word that I would apply to Rinella. Did he really boil a mud swallow's nest to see if he could make soup out of it?

Before we get to cookery per se, let me rant a little. A recurrent theme throughout the book is his attempts to raise and cook pigeons for squab. He grabs them from nests on bridges and attempts to raise them in his Montana yard. He cycles through every urban cliché about pigeons that you ever heard. Pigeons he says, can carry . . . well, every alleged disease devoted to them in popular lore, 90 percent of which have nothing to do with pigeons. He discovers websites that explain "how to raise pigeons just for the hell of it," but claims to find none with recipes, and not one that explains—end of rant promise here—*that squabs are just-fledged young pigeons, not adult birds.* Which is approximately like confusing milk-fed veal calf with an aged Himalayan yak.

Typical—and I still love the book. Rinella chases and eats everything: octopus in the Alaskan Gulf and eels in New York, rabbits everywhere, even a bighorn sheep. His best chapter, though, is on hunting elk in Montana with his brothers. Despite his characteristically wise-assed renaming of their habitat "The Stinkhole Mountains," it is one of the best set pieces on hunting elk I have ever read, perhaps the only one that documents the absolute physical difficulty and almost excruciating level of sheer work that goes into removing an elk from the wilderness after the high point of a successful shot, and the well-earned euphoria that follows that exertion.

Scavenger's Guide culminates in a comic feast I would have been happy to attend. Rinella continues to stretch the boundaries. I would advise those who think themselves too sophisticated or too refined to put up with his occasional obvious lapses of knowledge and slightly monotonous profanity* to get over it and enjoy his continuing adventures. He has more fun than his detractors ever will.

ALSO READ:
American Buffalo, by Steven Rinella, a book-length wilderness version of the elk hunt

---

* Steve, re research: Read up on it, don't fake it! And, though it's okay to say "fuckin'" and "shit" once in a while, it works better in direct quotes than in text *all the frickin time* . . .

CHAPTER 88

The Wilderness Hunter
by Theodore Roosevelt
1893

It is fair to say that we have had several decent conservation presidents in my lifetime, both Republican and Democrat. But what we have not had, neither in my lifetime nor since long before, is a president who knew anything about wilderness or hunting or sport. Allegedly Herbert Hoover was a serious fisherman, and more recently an alleged fly fisherman killed a rabbit with a paddle. But the last president who lived and breathed wilderness, who ranched and hunted, who went to Africa and collected specimens alongside his trophies, who after his presidency embarked on a strenuous expedition in Amazonian headwaters, was Teddy Roosevelt, the president who put conservation on the map.

He also wrote books, naturally and compulsively, without any ghost writers. He wrote military and political history, memoirs, books about books, and books about hunting and ranching. His outdoor books age well; I almost put in his *African Game Trails,* and his *Ranch Life and the Hunting Trail* has many modern devotees. But *Ranch Life* has a lot about cowboys and is marred by some terrible illustrations of wildlife by Frederick Remington (in the war between Remington and Russell, I am an unabashed Russell-ite, and only wish the old cowboy had illustrated Roosevelt. Remington may have "known the horse," but the fat Connecticut bigot's mountain lions resemble emaciated African lionesses, and his elk aren't much better). The African book is good, but *The Wilderness Hunter* shows Roosevelt on his own ground.

Most readers will know that Roosevelt, a sickly eastern kid from a good family, built himself up by strenuous outdoor exercise and, as a young man, ranched for a time on the edge of the Dakota badlands. *Wilderness Hunter* is imbued with a certain Victorian celebration of the character virtues built by living a hunter's life. On Washington, he said, "The qualities of heart, mind and body, which made him delight in the hunting-field, and which he there exercised and developed, stood him in good stead in many a long campaign

Roosevelt on safari in Africa, ca. 1909 to 1919 (Library of Congress)

and many a stricken field." Perhaps he created the Roughriders, a company that consisted of a mixture of socialites and New Mexico cowboys, because he believed that the West created such character.

And he knew the West. After a short introduction of the various big game species of the American West, he gives us two of the best chapters ever on Western hunting, called simply "Hunting From the Ranch" and "On the Cattle Ranges," full of long, lyrical passages that still read true today.

> *When the sun was well on high and the heat of the day had begun we came to a dreary and barren plain, broken by rows of low clay buttes. The ground in places was whitened by alkali; elsewhere it was dull gray.*

Here there grew nothing save sparse tufts of coarse grass, and cactus, and sprawling sage brush. In the hot air, all things seen afar danced and wavered . . . No man save the wilderness dweller knows the strong melancholy fascination of these long rides through lonely lands.

He speaks of animals whose habits seem the same today, like mule deer and antelope, and ones whose habits seem to have changed, like elk, of which he says, "Elk are sooner killed off than any other game save buffalo . . ." I can only say that in my country the booming elk population is driving out the deer. He knows things about my totem bird, the great golden eagle, that have only recently been rediscovered, after years of popular doubt about them eating anything larger than rabbits.

. . . a neighboring ranchman informs me that he was once an eyewitness to such an attack. It was a bleak day in the late winter, and he was riding home across a wide dreary plateau, when he saw two eagles worrying and pouncing on a prong-buck—seemingly a yearling. It made a gallant fight. The eagles hovered over it with spread wings, now and then swooping down, their talons out-thrust, to strike at the head, or to try to settle on its loins. The antelope reared and struck with hoofs and horns like a goat; but its strength was failing rapidly, and doubtless it would have succumbed in the end had not the approach of the ranchman driven off the marauders.

Read *The Wilderness Hunter* for its still-fresh insights and delights, and marvel at Roosevelt's easy familiarity with life and death and big animals. It is probably best not to think of the last three presidents if you care about such things.

CHAPTER 89

Cache Lake Country: Life in the North Woods
by John J. Rowlands
1947

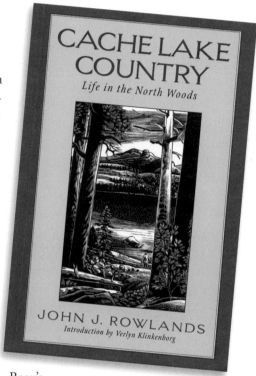

When I was a kid growing up in New England, the essence of wilderness was what we all thought of as "The North Woods." With its semi-familiar inhabitants, deep shadows, and snowy winters, it seemed a large-scale version of what greeted us when we climbed over the stone walls that edged our backyards. In the 1950s, classic outdoor works by many of the writers in this book still lined the children's shelves: Beebe, Seton, Roosevelt, the Craigheads, Dan Mannix; in fishing catalogs, George Leonard Herter. L.L. Bean's emporium was located just to our north, and the local newspaper's outdoor columns were full of canoes and paddles and fly rods and trolling reels and old lever-action deer rifles, all suitable for the northern habitat. Add checked wool shirts and half-rubber Bean boots, and anything southern or western, never mind African, looked pretty exotic. While Alaska, of course, with moose and bear and caribou, was just a bigger, colder variant.

John Rowlands actually worked at MIT in Cambridge, Massachusetts, but his soul lived in the big North. Verlyn Klinkenborg tells us that he worked in northern Ontario, but Cache Lake is a more universal destination.

Klinkenborg has a more specific locus in mind, but adds, "If you want to search for an actual vicinity, just walk across Canada on the 47th parallel." My simpler child's mind thought: head north. I thought it was in Maine, and really, it could have been.

There are a lot of books that tell you how to do everything in the woods; the genre dates back to at least the work of "Nessmuk," over a hundred years ago. But few have the charm of *Cache Lake Country,* and none have the illustrations. The book is arranged around the seasons: In February you can learn about trapping; in May about catching pike and pickerel; in September about chasing moose from a canoe; in October how to cook grouse and duck. Nor is it just a sporting book; Klinkenborg, who like me grew up on it, adds: fry leftover oatmeal, sew moccasins, make a bird's Christmas tree, and "work your way up to the iceboat and outdoor bake oven."

Henry Kane's illustrations are perfect, a combination of line drawings with stylized ink scratchboard full-pagers that remind me of the more formal work of Francis Lee Jacques, but somehow more lively. A snowshoe hare droops from the talons of a snowy owl against a black background; a pike curves across a similar black space, his crocodilian jaws about to grasp a minnow: "The pike are killers." A canoe and a moose cut parallel lines across a white lake, seen from above. There's nothing quite like them.

As far as I know, *Cache Lake* has been in print continually since 1947, and its timeless simplicity still delights readers. It is a genial book and a beautiful one, one you should give to your kids, or someone's kids. And when you venture to the North Woods, as Klinkenborg says, take this book along.

ALSO READ:
Two Little Savages, by Ernest Thompson Seton

Something of Value
by Robert Ruark
1955

Robert Ruark, journalist, south-
erner, boozer, Manhattanite, and
most romantic of the popular African hunting writers, was a best-
selling novelist in the 1950s; his
image, with leopard-skin hatband,
was almost a cliché, parodied in
at least one movie. Today he is
scorned by critics, sometimes
unfairly, and celebrated by sporting fans who ignore his genuine
faults. Many readers from both
categories prefer the simple bird-
hunting tales of *The Old Man
and the Boy,* or his sub-Hemingway nonfiction celebration of the
professional hunter Harry Selby. I submit that his best work is the sprawling,
flawed novel *Something of Value,* a biased account of the Mau-Mau "troubles"
in Kenya, a poignant history of Kenya's historically doomed white tribe, and
one of the best safari books ever.

That history, and that of European hunting in East Africa, is portrayed
by suggestion and in miniature in his description of a settler's gun cabinet,
early in the book. It is a long passage, but so evocative of the book's virtues it
is worth quoting at length.

> *The two rooms formed an exact half of the house. The veranda was
> nearly as deep and fully as long as both rooms. The walls were paneled in
> unvarnished cedar, with the wormholes and deeply bitten grain showing
> through. At the right end of the living room a red-black stone fireplace*

was big enough for a tall man to walk into without stooping. Over it was the head of a Cape buffalo, a big one, forty-eight inches and a bit on the inside curve. A recessed glass-fronted gun cabinet, locked, hugged the corner between the fireplace and the wall. It was framed by the tusks of a big bull elephant. Each tusk weighed a touch better than one hundred and thirty pounds. The butt ends were deeply inset in hammered, oxidized copper. They formed a gleaming parenthesis around the glass which housed the arsenal. The arsenal consisted of a matched pair of Rigby .416s, a matched pair of Jeffrey .500s, and a matched pair of Westley-Richards .470s. There had been a time when Henry McKenzie shot elephant on control, for money to keep his farm alive. There had been a time when Henry McKenzie had poached elephants along the Tana River, and over in the Belgian territory, and in the Karamoja country of Uganda, to keep both the bankers and the locusts suitably fed. In the gun rack there was also a pair of Purdey 10-gauge shotguns, a Westley-Richards .318 rifle, a Czechoslovakian .22 long rifle, a Browning 16-gauge automatic, a Remington .30-'06, a 9-millimeter Mannlicher-Schoenauer, a Sauer 20-gauge shotgun, two .38 pistols, and a mammoth .45 American frontier-style revolver. Henry McKenzie had never allowed himself many personal luxuries, but he did not consider expensive guns as luxuries. None of his double rifles had a safety catch or an automatic ejector. Henry McKenzie did not believe in overcomplication of weapons, nor did he believe that any man fit to carry arms was milksop enough to need contrived protection against himself. The purpose of a gun, Henry McKenzie thought, was to shoot as fast and as accurately as possible, with a minority of potential mechanical breakdown. Holding two extra-heavy express bullets in his left hand, he was able to fork them into a double rifle, after shaking out the expended shells, so swiftly that he could fire four bullets out of his doubles more rapidly than most men could shoot half a magazine from a rifle with a bolt action. Each of these guns had been fired many times, and as many times cleaned, by Peter McKenzie, even when he was so small that the huge .500 left a purple-tan bruise on his skinny shoulder.

Critics I deem perceptive accuse Ruark of sentimentality. The longer he lived, the more a maudlin, self-pitying identification with his characters and heroes marred his work; his last novel, *The Honey Badger,* is almost unreadable. More enlightened sorts deplore his "racism." I'd count him more ambivalent than bigoted. He was, naturally perhaps, a creature of his upbringing, as are we all. Even—or especially—when he is trying to be fair, some of his opinions appear shockingly retrograde sixty years later. Ironically, some who shared his opinions of Jomo Kenyatta came to lament the former Mau-Mau's long semi-benevolent rule as the last stable period in Kenya. When he stops editorializing and just describes, his account of a clash of cultures embodied in two young Kenyans is more evocative of Kipling's "Ballad of East and West" than any kind of cheap politicking, and should not blind an open-minded contemporary reader to his ability to evoke another time and place. He has the skill; here's a little vignette of life on safari as taste of another kind of African life:

> *If you came back to camp for lunch, if you were hunting close by, you might have one pink gin or a bottle of beer before you ate. Or if you were going to be gone all day you found a bottle of beer apiece in the chop box, with the coarse-grained home-cooked bread and the flat-sliced cold meat and the rock-hard butter and the cold baked beans and clammy spaghetti and the pickles which made your lunch. You ate the lunch under an old baobob or a towering fig tree or a thorn tree, snoozed a bit, waiting for the heat to drop, and then hurried on until seven, when it got too black to shoot. Then it took you an hour, sometimes two hours, to get back to camp, bouncing along in the grass or on a disappearing track, the wind bitter, every joint with a separate ache, and birds and foxes and rabbits skittering ahead, with Peter swooping the jeep suicidally to avoid running them down . . . It seemed then, in the last half hour that you would surely die if you did not have a drink of uniced gin, a scotch with warm water with the wiggly things and dusty sediment in it.*

Nice drawings too.

ALSO READ:
Tennis and the Masai, by Nicholas Best, satirical but realistic novel about Kenya a generation later, with prep schools, aristocratic British holdovers, rich Masai—guess who is sillier—and a man-eating leopard. Life goes on. . .

CHAPTER 91

The Hunting Animal
by Franklin Russell
1983

The Hunting Animal by Franklin Russell is a strange dark hymn to predation that seems never to have received any attention in the sporting or nonsporting press, despite having a mainstream publisher and the damndest collection of blurbs I think I've ever seen—Wright Morris, Jim Harrison, Tom McGuane, anthropologist John Pfeiffer, William Kittredge, and Vance Bourjaily. Perhaps Russell is too fierce for the nonhunters, too complicated for the simple-minded hunter whose philosophy is defined by what products he owns, and far too unsentimental for either.

There seems to be two extreme views of killing to eat. One, held by some eastern sects and the late ornithologist-philosopher Alexander Skutch, says that death and predation are the ultimate evil. (Skutch, a Connecticut Yankee vegetarian with a plantation in the tropics, lived his beliefs by shooting "evil" snakes and hawks and bragging about it to his admirers.) The other, more tragic, says that the only sure things are that the universe is very beautiful and that everything in it is part of eating and being eaten.

The Hunting Animal is for fans of the second view only. It is a string of connected essays, first about human hunters—Russell himself, an ancient buffalo hunter he met as a boy, British officials in his tiger-haunted Indian childhood, deer-shooting professionals in New Zealand, kangaroo slaughterers in Australia—then on to nonhuman hunters from a leopard to penguins, and to prey like capelin and lemming that are hunted by everything that moves. He sees beauty and savagery and evokes it all with clear-eyed . . . not detachment exactly, but refusal to apologize. He is sad about the passing of the tiger and buffalo but knows how hopeless it is to weep, and how damned beautiful the whole dance of eating and being eaten is.

The caribou tracks, etched by the angle of the fresh light, were pounded into circling roadways, like the petals of many white flowers engraved

230

into the snow. I perceived that these flowers, which seemed to mark the
involuntary circling of the caribou, were actually the handwriting of
wolves accompanying the moving animals . . . The graceful flowers were
not geometry, then, but designs in a ballet of death.

When I embarked on this project, it was Guy de la Valdene who reminded
me to reread this fine book. Thanks, Guy. Strong stuff, and a must-read for
those who sense that there's more to hunting than all the platitudes served up
by the sporting press.

CHAPTER 92

Lives of the Hunted
by Ernest Thompson Seton
1901

Ernest Thompson Seton is as important a figure in our history as any designated "sporting writer"—a hunter, a pioneer in conservation and animal writing and wildlife art. He is an unacknowledged influence on many of the writers in this book, and one acknowledged by as odd a literary descendant as paleontologist and dinosaur popularizer Robert Bakker. Ironically he's more claimed today by anti-hunters than by hunters, because he sympathized with predators; the most explicitly hunting book with his name in it is by his wife, Grace, whose work follows.

I have no trouble admiring Seton while still being a hunter. My bigger problem was to pick a single Seton book. I could have cheated and recommended his magnificent five-volume *Lives of Game Animals*, a unique combination of art and science that is both hard to find and expensive. But why not recommend one of his still-popular books of animal biography, which are just as nice and still available cheap, even as first editions from the early 1900s?

Two of these each include one of his best "lives." *Wild Animals I Have Known* has "Lobo," his lightly fictionalized account of trapping one of the last great cattle-killing wolves in northern New Mexico, his best known and most controversial piece. *Lives of the Hunted* has the other iconic hunting portrait, "Krag, the Kootenay Ram," the account of a Dall sheep's life in British Columbia. Picking between them finally involves flipping coins. By the time he wrote *Lives of the Hunted*, he was embroiled in debates with Roosevelt and John Burroughs, who accused him of "faking." In his introduction to it, he defends the historical validity of both "Lobo" and "Krag" and comments ironically on his straightforward ambivalence. First he explains why he can't win:

I have been bitterly denounced, first, for killing Lobo; second, and cheaply, for telling of it to the distress of many tender hearts . . . In what frame of mind are my hearers left in regard to the animals? Are their sympathies quickened to the man who killed him, or to the noble creature who, superior to every trial, died as he had lived, dignified, fearless, and steadfast?

And lest you put him in the anti-hunting camp, he then continues:

. . . I do not say I champion any theory of diet. I do not intend primarily to denounce certain field sports, or even cruelty to animals. My chief motive, my most earnest underlying wish, has been to stop the extermination of harmless wild animals; not for their sakes, but for ours, firmly believing that each of our native wild creatures is in itself a precious heritage that we have no right to destroy or put beyond the reach of our children.

His cold-eyed account of the death of the big wolf's mate is as harrowing as anything in Cormac McCarthy's border trilogy. "We each threw a lasso over the neck of the doomed wolf, and strained our horses in opposite directions until the blood burst from her mouth, her eyes glazed, her limbs stiffened and then fell limp. Homeward then we rode, carrying the dead wolf, and exulting over this, the first death-blow we had been able to inflict on the Currumpaw pack." Bullets and powder cost money.*

As Seton says elsewhere, "There is only one way to make an animal's history un-tragic, and that is to stop before the last chapter." Most of us who love Seton started reading him in our grade-school years, and therefore learned something young readers do not learn today. Read him for that, and for his endless inventive illustrations that range from fantasy to biology and prefigure the works of everyone from T. H. White to Konrad Lorenz and Anglo African scientist and artist Jonathan Kingdon. Read him because he doesn't take easy sides, and because at his best he makes you think and feel.

ALSO READ:

Ernest Thompson Seton's *Lives of Game Animals, Monarch, The Big Bear,* and *Two Little Savages*

Raptor Red, by Robert Bakker

King Solomon's Ring, by Konrad Lorenz

A Field Guide to East African Mammals, by Jonathan Kingdon

---

* I doubt we would have the more famous Aldo Leopold essay on "a fierce green fire" without his fellow New Mexico wolf killer's earlier confession.

CHAPTER 93

A Woman Tenderfoot
by Grace Gallatin Seton-Thompson
1900

This is the real Seton hunting book.* Ernest Thompson Seton's work is pervaded by hunting and his past, but a superficial reader could be forgiven for getting the impression that he had turned against it, while his wife Grace's *A Woman Tenderfoot* is not just a memoir rich in its evocation of the "Old West" in its youthful days but can be read as an intentional how-to hunting manual. Grace Gallatin was a well-educated, sometimes controversial early feminist from a good eastern Establishment family who had a career in her own right, and who wanted others to be able to share her good fortune. This collaboration with her husband reads well today, and I think it may have reached its intended audience: My copy includes an inscription and date by Miss Mina Claudin, who received the book as a gift on Christmas in 1900.

In looks, it is a beautiful, typical Seton book, with an embossed cover of a howling coyote and black-and-white illustrations ranging from the whimsical to the beautiful on every other page. Its narrative framework is a diary-like account of several trips to Jackson Hole and the Wyoming backcountry soon after they became accessible to sophisticated urbanites like Mrs. Seton. Her motivation is straightforward. After an invocation, "THIS BOOK IS A TRIBUTE TO THE WEST," she continues, "I can only add that the events related really happened in the Rocky Mountains of the United States and Canada; and this is why, being a woman, I wanted to tell about them, in the hope that some going-to-Europe-in-the-summer-woman may be tempted to go West instead."

True to her word, her opening chapter is a detailed list of equipment from hat pins to aluminum plates, bedroll specifications, telescopes, rubber tubs, and gun cases, with advice on packing and the stern admonition to

---

* Ernest Thompson Seton was born Ernest Seton Thompson in Scotland, and changed his name to favor his more romantic matronym when he found that Setons were present on both sides of his family. He and Grace were married and divorced before the name change.

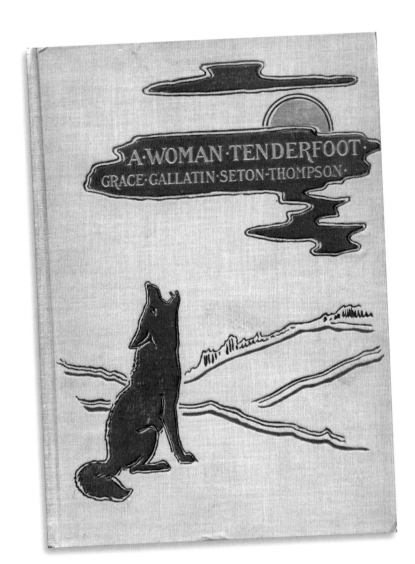

A·WOMAN·TENDERFOOT·
GRACE·GALLATIN·SETON·THOMPSON·

hire a *male* cook, and adds the only Ernest Thompson Seton dress patterns I suspect anyone will ever see.

The rest is a narrative of adventure and unabashed accounts of shooting deer, elk, and antelope. The attentive gun nut might also note that she shoots all these animals with the newfangled .30-.30 Winchester Model 94; like Karamojo Bell and the Helmerickses, theoretical ballistic inadequacy never troubled her, and many an elk fell to its puny loads.

About death she is neither sentimental nor nervous. Of her first bull elk she writes:

I sighted along the metal barrel and a terrible bang went booming through the dim secluded spot. The elk raised his proud, antlered head and looked in my direction. Another shot tore through the air. Without another move the animal dropped where he stood. He lay as still as the stones beside him, and all was quiet again in the twilight.

Death had been so sudden. I had no regret, I had no triumph—just a sort of wonder at what I had done—a surprise that the breath of life could have been taken away so easily.

It's hard not to think that thoughtful hunters of her time were less self-conscious about the hunter's life than ours, even in introspection. A writer included in this collection once said of a friend who shall remain unmentioned that he was a good hunter and writer; "I just wish he didn't cry so much." Grace Seton does not cry in print, and her brief moment of self-analysis reads better:

One elk with an eleven-point crown, and one antelope, of the finest ever brought down, is the tax I levied on the wild things. Of the many, many times I have watched them and left them unmolested, and of the lessons they have taught me, under Nimrod's guidance, I have not space to tell, for the real fascination of hunting is not in the killing but in the seeing the creature at home amid his glorious surroundings, and feeling the freely rushing blood, the health-giving air, the gleeful sense of joy and life in nature, both within and without.

CHAPTER 94

The Tender Carnivore and the Sacred Game
by Paul Shepard
1973

We've covered the conservative arguments in favor of hunting and conservation with Ortega y Gasset. Now let's look at the visionary, or possibly the barking mad: Paul Shepard's 1973 masterwork, *The Tender Carnivore and the Sacred Game*.

Paul Shepard was a learned professor and one of the patron saints of the present Deep Ecology movement. But far from being some sort of tofu-eating vegan, he was in his mind a resurrected hunter-gatherer from the Neolithic to the bloody bone, the man who single-handedly gave birth to the idea of the invention of agriculture as our species's Original Sin. "The collapse of an ecology that kept men scarce and attuned to the mystery and diversity of all life led as though by some devilish fall to the hunting and herding of man by man, to the hoarding of grain and the secular owning of all space." He adds, only slightly more temperately, "To denounce farming and rural life, so relatively serene at a time of urban crisis, seems to flaunt the last landscape of solace and respite. But in my view the urban crisis is a direct result of the food producing revolution."

The rest of *Tender Carnivore*, his first real book, is a magnificent polemic and revolutionary manifesto, dauntingly well documented to prove his case. It ends with an utterly utopian scenario of his ideal society, which may look attractive but is . . . well, look at his plans for North America. No one is allowed to live anywhere but in two ribbon megalopoli lining the east and west coasts, Brobdingnagian, mile-high arcologies built by some yet-undiscovered technology. The entire interior of the continent is a hunting preserve; permanent settlement is forbidden.

And there are *no domestic animals*. Says Shepard, "It is hard to speak of domestic animals as failures because we are so fond of them." Of course he

238

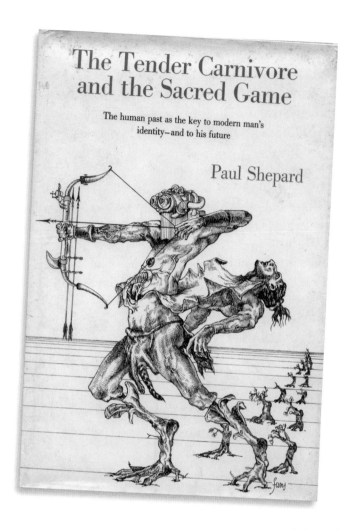

does consider them just that. But while he cites some good facts about the degeneration of some animals under domestication, his obvious lack of familiarity with them, his lumping of all domestic animals together as products of one process, and his lack of understanding of such pre-agricultural partnerships as the horse and especially the dog undermine his thesis.* The last line in his chapter on domestication is: "Since these changes have not taken place in man, man is not properly a domestic animal, although civilization has disrupted his epigenetic stability and loosed a horde of 'goofies' [his charming term for anything not "wild"]." He actually *says,* and apparently believes, that

* I wonder what he'd think of the current incipient domestication of the large falcons?

"Being a carnivore—and thus both scarce and in competition with man for food, the dog, I suspect, is relatively unimportant in civilization compared, say, to the goat or camel." Need I say that no study agrees or has supported this statement?

Shepard says that what he outlines here is not a Utopia. "A cynegetic world is not a vision of a lost paradise, it is inevitable, a necessity if we are to survive at all." I can celebrate the originality, passion, and poetic truth of his vision and utterly deny the necessity to apply it to society, better to use it to heal the soul. *Tender Carnivore* is perhaps *best* seen as a Utopia, like More's *Utopia* or Butler's *Erewhon* or Huxley's *Island;* an extended, brilliant metaphor. The social engineering needed to achieve it might be worse than anything the world has ever seen; see S. M. Stirling's *Draka* and its predecessors for an "alternative-world" variety, one that looks as attractive as Shepard's until you lift the hood and see the engine that powers it. Whether all Utopians, left or right, are fascists at heart is a question beyond the scope of this humble reviewer. I only know that on occasion I have had to fight an unholy alliance of animal-rightist vegans and bow-hunting Shepard acolytes, united and dedicated to banning the use of "goofies"—that is, my hounds, dogs of an ancient Asian land race that has been with us since the Neolithic—in hunting.

Be careful what you wish for. Meanwhile, read Shepard as a visionary, eat a side dish of home-grown vegetables with your wild meat, and wash it down with a glass of fermented domestic grain.

ALSO READ:
In addition to Stirling and his *Draka* books, try *Beasts* by John Crowley, a more modest future tale with genetically engineered beasts, a Shepardian arcology, a hacked peregrine, and an intelligent dog.

CHAPTER 95

The Old Way: A Story of the First People
by Elizabeth Marshall Thomas
2006

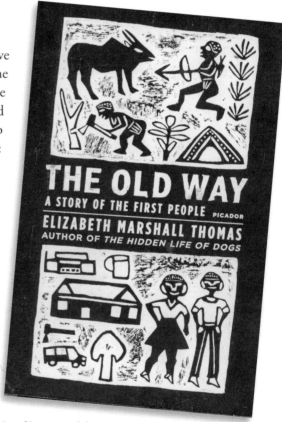

Elizabeth Thomas went to live among the Bushmen of the Kalahari in 1948 when she was still a young girl, and lived an enviable double life in two of the best human realms: that of the Neolithic hunter-gatherer, the Old Way, and that of a civilized western intellectual. She went on to write a remarkable number of good books, ranging from the cynological to the anthropological; from *Hidden Life of Dogs* to the Bushman text *The Harmless People* to the unique Paleolithic novel *Reindeer Moon,* which opens with the narrator, a ghost, hanging around the smoke hole of her people's tent to inhale the essence of hunted animals. (Sure beats *Clan of the Cave Bear!*)

She was nineteen when her father took her to study with the Bushmen; she returned thirty years later to see how they had fared, and this book is the remarkable result. She knew their culture had survived for millennia, as she describes in *The Old Way:* "To me, the experience of visiting this place and these people was profoundly important, as if I had voyaged into the deep past through a time machine. I feel that I saw the Old Way, the way of life that shaped us, a way of life that now is gone. I also feel that I saw the most successful culture our kind has ever known, if a lifestyle can be called a culture and if stability and longevity are measures, a culture governed by sun and rain, heat and cold, wind and wildfires, plant and animal populations." But could it endure the late twentieth century?

Incredibly, she was instantly recognized by an older man who had not seen her since she was a baby and called her by a name she had forgotten. "How can he remember me? How can he possibly recognize me, thirty years older, thirty years later, covered with dust, and at such a distance? . . . but that's the Ju/wasi, with their formidable powers of observation and memory."

Remarkably, her Old Way had survived. She combines her memories with present-day observations to cover the variables of the Bushman way of life and its universality in a series of chapters about hunting, gathering, dangerous animals (especially lions), the relations between men and women, the cycle through the year, and their attitudes about knowledge, religion, and conflict. A mildly technical chapter on arrow poisons is unique, and she thinks it was an important invention.

On a global scale, the discovery of this poison is often viewed as a side issue, important only to the Bushmen, without relevance to the rest of the world. Yet this marginalizing view may be quite wrong, as the discovery of poison may have played a significant role in the development of the bow and arrow. True, the people of Paleolithic Eurasia are usually credited with the bow and arrow. However, the weapon may have originated as two unrelated objects, the bow beginning as a musical instrument and the arrow beginning as a thorn or a porcupine quill.

At the end she muses on the "hunter-gatherer life of the savannah which began when our ancestors lost the shelter of the trees." She thinks, "Who knows the antiquity of these cultural features? Did they serve our ancestors in rain forest times? Were they developed on the savannah? Whenever they started, they served our species well and many of us still admire them, but mainly it's the Ju/wasi who continue to uphold them."

Let us hope. Maybe, with our civilization's new respect and the remoteness and "worthlessness" of their home, the forbearance of the South African governments will allow the Ju/wasi to continue in their and our Old Ways.

CHAPTER 96

The Tiger
by John Vaillant
2010

John Vaillant's *The Tiger: A True Story of Vengeance and Survival* is better than good—a contemporary classic in my uncommon favorite genre: stories about (to quote a book title) the edge of the wild, where humans and "nature" are not artificially separated but meet, acting on each other. Vaillant is a journalist and naturalist who already wrote one unusual nature and human book, *The Golden Spruce,* but nothing prepared me for this anachronistic, timeless combination of thriller, natural history, and subtle plea for conservation, a nonfiction book that reads like a novel.

Tiger is set in "Primorye," the Russian Far East—*not* Siberia, despite the common westerner's geographic confusion and its near-arctic winters, but rather a unique and almost unknown land, a thinly populated, huge block to the east and south of Siberia proper. Primorye is a rugged place of mixed deciduous forests, few roads, and a flora and fauna that mixes the northern (bears and elk) with the subtropical (leopards and tigers), inhabited by a never-prosperous populace of mixed Russian and native descent who now eke out their lives by such expedients as beekeeping and subsistence poaching.

Its protagonists are a single huge tiger, a ragged bunch of drunken poachers, and a patrol of anti-poaching rangers dedicated to protecting tigers over a huge area, with no money and inadequate tools. The beginning, as an unnamed hunter and his dog approach a dark cabin on a freezing evening, is a masterpiece of tension and quiet terror; the ending is utterly cinematic but real (the book is based on over two hundred interviews). In between, Vaillant skillfully cuts from one character to another, building an almost unbearable tension even as he dramatizes the serious issue of Asian poaching, an animal holocaust driven by the Chinese traditional medicine market.

He manages to evoke sympathy for a man-killing tiger that rivals James Corbett's (at one point the tiger drags a mattress out under the shelter of a spruce to await his next victim in comfort; he waits for another *in his bed;* toward the end, à la Kipling's "Letting In the Jungle," he appears to be contemplating the elimination of a village); but also for destitute subsistence poachers tempted by the Han Empire's eternal appetite for animal parts; above all for the underpaid, overworked, and threatened Russian rangers, who use SKSs in 7.62 X 39 (on brown bear, moose, and sadly tiger if they must) because they are the *best* rifles available! I have a certain poor man's (and Russophile's) love/hate for the rugged international redneck rifle and its humble cartridge, but I would never use it on animals bigger than deer if I didn't have to! On the other hand, see the chilling scene where a poacher pulls the trigger on an ancient Mosin in a more powerful caliber; instead of the firing pin falling, in the words of songwriter James McMurtry, it "didn't, quite. . . ." It doesn't end well; perhaps the rangers are doing the best they can.

In fact, my only quibble with the book is regarding firearms: If you know a bit, some of Vaillant's terminology can be momentarily confusing; if you don't, you may not even notice. The reader should understand that a poacher's badly hand-loaded 16-gauge single-shot shotgun is not a "rifle," and is even less powerful than the SKS, which is. Using an inherently inadequate tool to shoot an Amur tiger is a maddeningly typical example of fatalistic drunken Russian foolery, the kind that all too often brings on Nemesis on wheels.

But really, a very minor complaint—this is an amazing book, one to stand with Arseniev and Corbett, its worthy predecessors. A novelist who has won every American literary award sent me an early galley, asking that I return it as soon as I finished, and I was so impressed I asked—well, demanded!— another copy from the publisher to quote to my friends until the real thing came out months later. I have been making everybody read it ever since.

ALSO READ:
The Man-Eaters of Tsavo, by J. H. Patterson (the real "Ghost and Darkness")

CHAPTER 97

It's My Delight
by Brian Vesey-Fitzgerald
1947

IT'S MY
DELIGHT

BRIAN
VESEY-FITZGERALD

DRAWINGS BY
WATKINS-PITCHFORD

. . . is just that.

This 1947 work on English poachers and hare-hunting is one of my favorite books on the list, and one of the oddest. Written by a hunter and naturalist who was ubiquitous on the English sporting scene in the first half of the twentieth century and beautifully illustrated by B. B. under one of his other names (a curt "Watkins-Pitchford"), it is full of lore about hares and sighthounds and scent hounds and hawks, all of relevance to me; of things like preparing hares that have been killed by dogs for taxidermists (which may be of interest to you); and of things like the dog training culture of Gypsies, which you have probably never thought about.

"I have written in two previous books about the dogs owned by James Arigho, a Romani-Tinker friend of mine. These dogs—and I've seen them at work on several occasions—seem to know exactly what their master means by every word and every gesture."

I am sorely tempted to say that you either like this kind of thing or not, but that avoids the question of if you know this kind of thing exists at all. Books like Brian Plummer's touch on the question of English poaching, which is traditionally a class "thing," rather than a matter of stealing or in any way anti-conservation; its illegality had and has more to do with England's history than with modern concerns like endangered species. In England, poaching is celebrated in myth, legend, and song.

Ironically, with the exception of Brian Plummer (Plummer was an exception to everything), those that actually chronicle poaching are mostly, like Vesey-Fitzgerald, middle- or upper-class writers with a bit of the renegade in their souls. *It's My Delight* is a little odder even than that; if it didn't flow together so beautifully, it would seem like a random, free-associating catalog of Vesey-Fitzgerald's enthusiasms. For instance: He was never a falconer, but at the sport's nadir he predicted it would never die, and made original observations about it that I, a lifelong falconer, have never thought about: "You can today pay a very considerable sum for a pair of guns from a first-class maker, but you will be a fool indeed if you pay the price of a pair of good hawks in Stuart's times." Or how about this one? "A good goshawk regards his master's hand as its home."

It's My Delight is still my manual for the hare; many of his observations of the European version ring true for our local jackrabbits as well. He will educate the curious reader about them, and give that reader a context for more ferociously focused books like Brian Plummer's. That, and the illustrations, my favorites of all B. B.'s except for possibly those in *Manka,* are enough justification to write about, read, and own the book. But his defense of the eccentric might hide a serious message as well, one that has a real if not obvious importance in our time, when more and more laws are passed against everything from hunting with hounds to coursing to private breeding of dogs. That most of the harmless acts described in a book of delights are in danger of being criminalized in the United States surprises many people I talk to, but it might not surprise Vesey-Fitzgerald: "A law that cannot be enforced will not be respected."

ALSO LISTEN TO:
The CD *Best of Show of Hands,* particularly the song "Longdogs." The English folk group's fans are known as "Longdogs" from the chorus of the song: "I am a longdog, I am a poacher." There is a funny YouTube as well. The tradition lives.

CHAPTER 98

The Goshawk
by T. H. White
1951

The Goshawk is a book about excru-
ciatingly bad falconry, and might
be the best book about the experience of falconry ever written.

In 1936, Terence Hanbury
White (Tim to his friends) was
thirty years old. He had just left a
job as head of the English department at Stowe school to live in
a crumbling primitive keeper's
cottage and write books. He
had already produced seven seriocomic novels, all well
received and at least one very good, but he was dissatisfied. His last book
had been different; compiled from his field diaries—fishing, shooting, hunting, flying small planes—it abandoned irony for the immediacy of outdoor
experience. The critic James Agate paid it the perfect compliment, saying it
"is about subjects in which I am not even faintly interested. It is enchanting."

He was a quintessential newly emancipated freelance writer, not quite
broke, but with expensive tastes: a Bentley convertible that he had just
totaled, salmon fishing, shooting, drinking. He was flamboyant, adventurous, sometimes bombastic; also sensitive and, beneath the bluster, terrified.
His £500 advance would not last forever. He "could not make my friends
understand that I was working too." In a moment of despair he wrote to his
old mentor L. J. Potts, "Writing books is a heartbreaking job. When I write a
good one, it is too good for the public and I starve, when a bad one, you and
Mary are rude about it."

In such a mood he conceived of a strange idea. In his wide reading on
natural history, he had encountered a nineteenth-century falconry text. In it

he read, "a sentence which suddenly struck fire from my mind. The sentence was: 'She reverted to feral state.' A longing came to my mind that I should be able to do this myself. The word 'feral' has a kind of magical potency which allied itself to two other words, 'ferocious' and 'free.' To revert to a feral state! I took a farm-labourer's cottage and wrote to Germany for a goshawk."

Such a headlong start is typical White. Later he admitted, "I had never trained a serious hawk before, not met a living falconer . . ." Falconry is almost impossible to learn without a human mentor, but White didn't have one, and started alone.

Alone with Gos, that is, who is every bit as much a character (at one point White refers to him as "a person who is not human"). The plot, which begins in comedy, approaches tragedy, and is reconciled in knowledge, is the tale of a bungled love affair.

There is a reason that US falconry regulations require a master-apprentice relationship. Books are never quite enough. White made the same mistakes, over and over, throughout the whole affair. He misjudged the bird's moods and appetite. If Gos did well, he overfed, then overcorrected him and let him get too hungry. Once he hauled the still-leashed hawk down from a tree with a salmon rod, earning its righteous indignation.

Admissions like these drive smug old falconers to fury. They—*we*—all made similar mistakes when we trained our first birds. Reading *The Goshawk* is like reliving a hopeless youthful love affair. You feel each mistake, each stupidity, each irrevocable slip just as you perform it and cannot call it back. White and Gos proceed, from bumble to bungle to curse, weirdly interspersed with Zen-like moments of understanding and calm. "As I put Gos to bed in the darkness, a new thought emerged. This time it was a quotation: To scorn delights and live laborious days. But it presented itself the other way about, saying: To live laborious days for their delight."

The story ends in loss: White loses Gos with his leash attached and never sees him again. As his biographer puts it, he "felt that book and livelihood were gone too," although he recovered and succeeded with a second hawk, Cully, in part because he had learned what *not* to do.

He put the project aside. One reason was his embarrassment, another his recognition that Gos's death seemed insignificant with war on the horizon. It wasn't until well after that, in 1949, when his publisher removed an uncomfortable lump from under a couch cushion and discovered the lost manuscript. He brought a copy back to London and wrote to White that he wanted to publish it. White agreed with just a little embarrassed reluctance, saying, "I have become a much better falconer since then." He wrote a new coda with Cully's first successful hunt, and the book was published, to excellent reviews.

Since then, despite White's misgivings and the discomfort of unreflective falconers, it has rarely been out of print. Some of his readers are hawk trainers with the insight to see themselves in White, and to see the wisdom in his folly. White, not some falconry guru, realized the hard-earned irreducible core of falconry: "The thing about being associated with a hawk is that you cannot be slipshod about it." Others see that falconry is a discipline, a practice, a meta-phor for the difficulty and necessity of real relationships with nature, "because the faculties exercised were those that throve among trees rather than houses, and because the whole thing was inexpressibly difficult."

I reread *The Goshawk* every year, not because I am a falconer, but because it is one of the best books ever written about a human and an animal, as fresh and contemporary as though it had been written yesterday.

ALSO READ:
T. H. White's *England Have My Bones* and *The Godstone and the Blackymor.* The first is based on his hunting, fishing, and shooting diaries; the second, written about his years in Ireland, has chapters on wildfowling and grouse hawking.

Recently, poet-scholar-falconer Helen Macdonald of Cambridge University arranged for us to spend some days in the White papers at the Harry Ransom Center in Austin, Texas, one of the most remarkable literary archives existing. We found that books that we had practically memorized had often been cut more drastically than needed before publication, probably by White himself. A new edition of *The Goshawk* seems to be needed, not to mention fairly complete "new" ones like his never-published companion volume *The Merlins* and his sadly unfinished goose-shooting novel. Let us hope his readers can be both loyal and patient.

WATCH FOR:
Helen Macdonald's twenty-first-century female falconer's take on *The Goshawk,* forthcoming from Jonathan Cape.

CHAPTER 99

Gone to Ground
by T. H. White
1935

Long before he wrote *The Goshawk* and *The Once and Future King*, T. H. White was a young sporting school-master who wrote novels on the side and under a pseudonym. His critics seemed to think he emerged as him-self in the book of selections from his shooting, foxhunting, and flying dia-ries, *England Have My Bones*, a book about his passions. Perceptive diaries are fun, and White's are delightful; I have had the privilege of reading the actual notebooks in their present home at the astonishing Harry Ransom Cen-ter at the University of Texas in Austin, which I suspect holds more English writers' papers than the entire United Kingdom.

But I would argue that transmuting such raw material into literature is more interesting than transcribing a day's experience, and that the best fiction says more than any diary can. By this measure, young Tim White's first true "T. H. White" book was this collection of tales in the framework of a satirical novel, *Gone to Ground*, which he published under his own name in 1935. Its structure is older than that of the novel: Like the plague survivors in Boc-caccio's *Decameron*, a group of refugees from a vaguely described apocalypse gather in an underground bunker to eat and drink and while away their time telling tales.

In White's book, almost all the stories are of the chase, of salmon fishing and foxhunting, of dogs and shooting and the minds of animals and country people. The surrounding framework is often silly; every young comic writer of the time seemed to be channeling Evelyn Waugh's contemporary social satires, without his particular talent. It doesn't matter, because the stories themselves are full of delights, from beautiful descriptive paragraphs about such things as grass snakes tossed off in conversational asides, through semi-supernatural fantasies, all the way to the profound and chilling. All but one or two are worth not just reading, but *re*reading.

Among the best are the tall tale of a hound pack's long chase after a were-wolf (with a muttered side comment about a winged horse that belonged to Seigfried Sassoon), a poignant one about an earl who lived his life as a spaniel after seeing a greyhound cruelly killed when he was a child, and the story of a shape-changing troll who endangers a visiting naturalist in Lapland that reads like a combination of natural history and horror movie. His portrait of a salmon fisher who hooks a mermaid may however be a little *too* whimsical, despite its realistic river setting; it lost me when the mermaid mixed untranslated Greek quotes with Eliza Doolittle sound effects.

My two favorites are one about the life and downfall of a midget squire with a passion for shooting, and one that may be my favorite story about hunting and fishing in the English language. The first is interesting because it foreshadows White's fascination with the eighteenth century and its sporting stalwarts, far more eccentric than any in the nineteenth century, never mind the twentieth. "James Hirst Warcliffe used to hunt with the Badsworth on a bull, and had trained a black sow to stand game. She was excellent with partridge, pheasant, blackgame, snipe and rabbit, but never pointed a hare." (Incidentally, the bull and sow were real historical creatures!) His miniature squire shoots a .410; "a normal flint-lock would have been nearly beyond his powers to carry."

The best story, later anthologized as "The Black Rabbit," is an old man's memory of meeting a mysterious keeper when he was a sensitive child, torn between his love for sport and a tender heart.

I loathed killing things, and yet I wanted to kill them. I trembled with lust for those half-pound trout, when I was on the point of catching them, and when I had caught them I was dismayed. I shuddered at knocking them on the head, had to avert my consciousness, and invented a convenient theory that it was kinder to let them suffocate. I wonder what it was. It may have been the fear of death.

One day the boy follows a black rabbit and meets a Presence in the form of a keeper, a figure with a hammer gun and cracked boots who is not what he seems. This embodiment of nature first terrifies, then enlightens him with poetic—not justifications, more like Zen Buddhist koans—parables, portraits of the essence and terrible beauty of the chase in all its forms.

He talked to me about the world, not the human world, with its intellectual cross purposes, but the animal one. He talked about the strange toes of the crested grebe and the red teeth of the merganser, and grouse disease, and furunculosis, and scent, and charges of shot, and the old days of horse hair instead of gut, and the generation of the eel, and adders swallowing their young, and woodcock carrying them, and whether flies settle on the ceiling, and the spawning of salmon, and of what a fish can see.

The keeper talks the boy through all the traditional field sports of England. "Look at that covey on the right, going straight away from here, like chips from a sharpened pencil, and see his gun come up to throw out its fingers of smoke before the bang, and look at the two birds turning end over hip, in a flutter of exploded feathers." He counters each of the boy's objections, not with a justification, but with a description, which finally becomes explicit, for the keeper was "the god of the animals, to which we humans are a branch.

"I said, 'Poor fish!'

"'Yes,' said the Keeper, Pan, nodding his head. 'But in Scotland the line cuts the water, like a wire cutting cheese.'"

ALSO READ:
The death scene of the heroic hound in White's *The Once and Future King*, and the harrowing but hilarious ordeal of the boy Arthur, transformed into a merlin in the same book.

CHAPTER 100

The Gun-Punt Adventure
by Colin Willock
1958

In the matter of punt gunning: probably, if you are American, Everything You Know Is Wrong. You "know" that punt guns are massive, primitive, dangerous poacher's tools used by greedy commercial hunters. Or rather, they were, but they have been obsolete since at least World War I. The main place they were used was Chesapeake Bay.

Whereas in reality, you are right on one thing: They *are* massive. A 4-bore shooting a quarter-pound load is considered a "little" punt-and-shoulder gun. As for the rest: There are still muzzleloaders around, but breech-loading, steel-barreled specimens were made in the twentieth century by the best English makers, including Holland & Holland. The greatest danger in their use is that the biggest ones make the little, kayak-like stalking punts top-heavy, and may capsize one in freezing water. Although muzzleloaders were used by professional hunters who legally supplied markets in England, wildfowl cannons were too expensive, and the boom of a big gun too obvious, to appeal to poachers. The ones in use today, though legal, are part of a sport so rarified that probably fewer than thirty people pursue it, paddling tiny craft on the margins of the North Sea, hoping for one or two well-set-up shots in a season. It may be the most esoteric field sport left on earth.

I have had the privilege of corresponding with a few punt gunners; they range from romantic artists to passionate machinists who have painstakingly milled their own screw-breech artillery-style actions for their big guns. They have little in common; obsession rather than class or money is their only common denominator. "Modern" fowlers agree that the best contemporary account is this one by Colin Willock, a prolific sporting writer and sometime BBC character who decided to explore the world of punt gunning in the 1950s and wrote down his experiences, which range from the technical to the adventurous to the ridiculous.

Even in 1958 it was a sport appealing to intrepid do-it-yourselfers. No big guns had been made since before World War II, fine ones were rarely for sale, and what was left ranged from nineteenth-century muzzleloaders by good makers to professional fowlers' relics held together with wire. Willock and his fowling friends' first specifications were practical: a boat of some sort small enough for two people to carry and low enough in profile to stalk wildfowl, and what we in America would think of as a big gun, though they didn't. "Whatever armament we finally settled on was likely to be of *small calibre* [my emphasis] preferably a big shoulder gun." We will revisit this matter.

The search was on. They find a double 6-bore Riley muzzleloader for sale, a working shooter, but worry about its petite size. "It's not very big. A six-bore load is only two ounces." Little? The gun, which they buy for £18 (they worry about its disappearing before they can get it: "A picture of herds of wildfowlers fighting for a muzzleloading 6-bore appeared to me briefly . . . it barely occurs to me that we were probably the only gunners in England with the faintest interest in such an outlandish weapon") weighs *sixteen pounds.*

Unsatisfied with its power, they continue to look for other guns. They get a line on a 4-bore, and against their better instincts buy an ancient genuine muzzleloading punt gun they call the Wash Cannon. Meanwhile, they need to build a boat, and of course give in to endless agonies of decision about how they should do *that.*

They buy the 4, which is similar to the 6 but Nitro-proofed and choked. The pictures of their testing these little guns are pretty amusing. I defy any American to look at plate 29, which shows a fellow in a tweed jacket firing a gun as long as he is tall, its barrels 45 degrees above the horizon in recoil, and come up with the adjective "small." They buy a modern breech for the Wash Cannon despite some difficulties in machining it, which necessitates submitting it to proof. It blows up.

"I did not hear the report she made when the Proofmaster fired a further 6 ounce of powder to 6 of shot through her, though, on the basis—if one believes such things—that mothers sometimes have a premonition when their children, far away, are in mortal danger, I suppose I might have caught a faint echo . . . I heard afterwards from Bill Roper that the bang was quite impressive, as well it might have been, the explosion did not issue entirely from the muzzle of the gun in the accepted fashion." (Bill is not sympathetic. "You should think yourself lucky . . . lucky that you weren't behind it. That's what proof is for.")

The adventure continues. They get the boat built, put it in the water, and Jack, Willock's hunting partner, takes it out on the marsh with the double 4, hoping for a "very big shot—perhaps twenty birds." He gets two teal. They persist and finally deem the adventure a success when a shot bags two teal, ten wigeon, and a pintail. That's it—punt gunning in the modern world. It is a tribute to Willock's writing and this excellent book that I would love to try it.

ALSO READ:
The Art of Wildfowling, by Abel Chapman
The Wildfowler, by Roger Moran

MY HONOR ROLL: BEST . . .

Short story (tie)	"Last Day in the Field"	Caroline Gordon
	"The Black Rabbit"	T. H. White
Essay	"The Longest Silence"	Thomas McGuane
Memoir	*Blood Knots*	Luke Jennings
Novella	*The Last Running*	John Graves
Autobiography	*Tales of a Rat-Hunting Man*	D. Brian Plummer
Novel	*Ninety-Two in the Shade*	Thomas McGuane
Weird novel	*Dance of the Dwarfs*	Geoffrey Household
Poem (tie)	"The Pike"	Ted Hughes
	"The Heaven of Animals"	James Dickey
Travel book	*Pheasant Jungles*	William Beebe
Natural history	*Illumination in the Flatwoods*	Joe Hutto
"Beast Beyond the Fire"	*The Tiger*	John Vaillant
Upland shooting	*New England Grouse Shooting*	William Harnden Foster
Falconry	*The Goshawk*	T. H. White
Philosophical work	*A Sand County Almanac*	Aldo Leopold
History	*The Origins of Angling*	John McDonald